Themistius

On Aristotle
Metaphysics 12

Ancient Commentators on Aristotle

GENERAL EDITORS: Richard Sorabji, Honorary Fellow, Wolfson College, University of Oxford, and Emeritus Professor, King's College London, UK; and Michael Griffin, Assistant Professor, Departments of Philosophy and Classics, University of British Columbia, Canada.

This prestigious series translates the extant ancient Greek philosophical commentaries on Aristotle. Written mostly between 200 and 600 AD, the works represent the classroom teaching of the Aristotelian and Neoplatonic schools in a crucial period during which pagan and Christian thought were reacting to each other. The translation in each volume is accompanied by an introduction, comprehensive commentary notes, bibliography, glossary of translated terms and a subject index. Making these key philosophical works accessible to the modern scholar, this series fills an important gap in the history of European thought.

A webpage for the Ancient Commentators Project is maintained at ancientcommentators.org.uk and readers are encouraged to consult the site for details about the series as well as for addenda and corrigenda to published volumes.

Themistius

On Aristotle
Metaphysics 12

Translated by
Yoav Meyrav

BLOOMSBURY ACADEMIC
LONDON • NEW YORK • OXFORD • NEW DELHI • SYDNEY

BLOOMSBURY ACADEMIC
Bloomsbury Publishing Plc
50 Bedford Square, London, WC1B 3DP, UK
1385 Broadway, New York, NY 10018, USA
29 Earlsfort Terrace, Dublin 2, Ireland

BLOOMSBURY, BLOOMSBURY ACADEMIC and the Diana logo are trademarks of Bloomsbury Publishing Plc

First published in Great Britain 2020
This paperback edition published in 2022

A catalogue record for this book is available from the British Library.

Library of Congress Cataloging-in-Publication Data

Names: Themistius, author. | Meyrav, Yoav, translator.
Title: On Aristotle : metaphysics 12 / Themistius ; translated by Yoav Meyrav.
Other titles: Themistius' paraphrase of Aristotle's Metaphysics 12. English

Description: London ; New York : Bloomsbury Academic, 2020. | Series: Ancient commentators on Aristotle | Includes bibliographical references and index. | Summary: "This is the only commentary on Aristotle's theological work, Metaphysics, Book 12, to survive from the first six centuries CE - the heyday of ancient Greek commentary on Aristotle. Though the Greek text itself is lost, a full English translation is presented here for the first time, based on Arabic versions of the Greek and a Hebrew version of the Arabic. In his commentary Themistius offers an extensive re-working of Aristotle, confirming that the first principle of the universe is indeed Aristotle's God as intellect, not the intelligibles thought by God. The identity of intellect with intelligibles had been omitted by Aristotle in Metaphysics 12, but is suggested in his Physics 3.3 and On the Soul 3, and later by Plotinus. Laid out here in an accessible translation and accompanied by extensive commentary notes, introduction and indexes, the work will be of interest for students and scholars of Neoplatonist philosophy, ancient metaphysics, and textual transmission"– Provided by publisher.
Identifiers: LCCN 2020023403 (print) | LCCN 2020023404 (ebook) | ISBN 9781350127241 (hardback) | ISBN 9781350189294 (paperback) | ISBN 9781350127258 (ebook) | ISBN 9781350127265 (epub)
Subjects: LCSH: Aristotle. Metaphysics. Book 12. | Metaphysics–Early works to 1800. | Philosophy, Ancient–Early works to 1800.
Classification: LCC PA3893.M5 T4713 2020 (print) | LCC PA3893.M5 (ebook) | DDC 110˜dc23
LC record available at https://lccn.loc.gov/2020023403
LC ebook record available at https://lccn.loc.gov/2020023404

ISBN: HB: 978-1-3501-2724-1
PB: 978-1-3501-8929-4
EPUB: 978-1-3501-2726-5
ePDF: 978-1-3501-2725-8

Series: Ancient Commentators on Aristotle

Typeset by RefineCatch Limited, Bungay, Suffolk

To find out more about our authors and books visit www.bloomsbury.com and sign up for our newsletters.

Acknowledgements

The present translations have been made possible by generous and imaginative funding from the following sources: the National Endowment for the Humanities, Divison of Research Programs, an independent federal agency of the USA; the Leverhulme Trust; the British Academy; the Jowett Copyright Trustees; the Royal Society (UK); Centro Internazionale A. Beltrame di Storia dello Spazio e del Tempo (Padua); Mario Mignucci; Liverpool University; the Leventis Foundation; the Arts and Humanities Research Council; Gresham College; the Esmée Fairbairn Charitable Trust; the Henry Brown Trust; Mr and Mrs N. Egon; the Netherlands Organisation for Scientific Research (NOW/GW); the Ashdown Trust; the Lorne Thyssen Research Fund for Ancient World Topics at Wolfson College, Oxford; Dr Victoria Solomonides, the Cultural Attaché of the Greek Embassy in London; and the Social Sciences and Humanities Research Council of Canada. In particular, this volume was supported by a BA/Leverhulme Small Research Grant. The editors wish to thank Yehuda Halper for his comments; Dawn Sellars for preparing the volume for press; and Alice Wright, Publisher, along with Georgina Leighton at Bloomsbury Academic, for their diligence in seeing each volume of the series to press.

Contents

Translator's Acknowledgements

This translation was set in motion by Carlos Fraenkel, who initiated it and allocated funding for it a long time ago, overseeing its various stages ever since. It was originally intended to be a co-translation, but regretfully, constraints of time and circumstance have deemed this to be otherwise. Nevertheless, translating this work would not have been possible without Carlos, and I am highly indebted to his mentoring and friendship.

I owe many thanks to Yehuda Halper, who spent a lot of time and energy reading and commenting upon significant portions of this translation, offering priceless advice concerning content and readability and saving me from many errors. Special thanks are also due to Stephen Menn, for valuable insights on some of the more puzzling passages in this puzzling text, and to István Bodnár for his advice concerning the astronomical parts. I also thank my dear friends and colleagues Orna Harari, Michael Engel, and Daniel Davies for numerous helpful comments and suggestions, and Hanna Paulmann for her help during the proofing stage. I am sure that the present translation still contains many shortcomings; I am solely responsible for all of them.

Warm thanks are due to Richard Sorabji for his encouragement, advice, and patience as this translation slowly progressed, as well as for his comments and suggestions concerning the introduction. I would also like to thank Dawn Sellars and John Sellars for their professional and pleasant preparation of this book for press.

Since arriving at the Maimonides Centre for Advanced Studies (MCAS) in Universität Hamburg, I was able to test-drive parts of this translation in front of many members of the Centre. I would like to thank the staff and fellows there, and especially MCAS's director Giuseppe Veltri and its co-directors Racheli Haliva and Stephan Schmid. I cannot think of a better working environment.

This translation is dedicated with love, respect, and gratitude to my parents, Nurit and Shmuel Meyrav.

Conventions

[. . .] Square brackets enclose words or phrases that have been added to the translation for purposes of clarity.

Introduction

Book 12 of Aristotle's *Metaphysics* is one of the most important compositions in the history of philosophy, as it contains Aristotle's most comprehensive account of God. Despite the work's importance in Aristotle's corpus, as well as it being a key event in Ancient Philosophy, it is nearly absent from the rich tradition of philosophical commentaries in Late Antiquity. Apart from Alexander of Aphrodisias' systematic commentary – of which only partial evidence survives, in Arabic translation – the earliest surviving interpretative work about *Metaphysics* 12, though modestly called a 'paraphrase' (a genre much more sophisticated than may appear), is in fact an influential reinterpretation of Aristotle's text at greater length than the original, composed by Themistius (317-*c.* 390 CE).[1] Born in Paphlagonia (in the northern part of Asia Minor) and spending most of his adult years in Constantinople – where he also ran a successful school – Themistius occupied different political functions in the Eastern capital. Managing to remain a leading political figure under six different emperors, he was also one of the finest orators of his time. Sometimes dismissed – by ancient and modern authors – as a flatterer, a sophist, or a spin doctor, and being no stranger to subtle manipulation, white lies, and a tendency for self-aggrandizing disguised as humility, Themistius was nevertheless able to play an important role in shaping imperial policies on religious toleration and freedom of speech, and his core politico-philosophical views as expressed in his orations remained consistent throughout his career.

Apart from a few exceptions, Themistius' corpus falls into two groups: his orations (public and private),[2] which were delivered throughout his career, and his paraphrases of Aristotle's works, which are usually taken to belong to an early period.[3] Despite various efforts by scholars, it is difficult to place

Themistius within one of the traditional schools of thought in Antiquity. Themistius learnt philosophy from his father Eugenius – whose own philosophical orientation is an open question – but who himself had learnt from Themistius' grandfather. In other words, Themistius is a part of an idiosyncratic legacy that had no formal ties to any of the established schools.

Despite its unique position as the only ancient interpretative composition about Aristotle's *Metaphysics* 12 that has survived in its entirety, Themistius' paraphrase has received relatively little attention from scholars of Ancient philosophy.[4] This is not due to a failure to acknowledge the work's philosophical and historical significance, but because its source material is removed from its original context: Themistius' Greek text is lost, its Arabic translation survived only in part, and the earliest complete version of the paraphrase survives in Medieval Hebrew. This state of affairs and its bearings on the text and its translation are described in the last part of the present introduction.

The paraphrase's cultural and linguistic domains of influence are also somewhat unusual; whereas the work did not leave any identifiable mark on Late Antique philosophy,[5] its impact on Medieval Arabic (and subsequently Hebrew) philosophers was considerable. Themistius' paraphrase, being the only complete ancient interpretation of *Metaphysics* 12 available in Arabic, served as a guide for philosophers writing in these languages in their attempt to penetrate Aristotle's enigmatic text, and in many ways conditioned the manner in which they understood it.[6]

Themistius' paraphrase contains several novel philosophical elements that go well beyond what Aristotle writes explicitly, often leaving the reader to wonder whether the ideas it contains can indeed follow from his words. I address some of these ideas below, but first let me offer some remarks about Themistius' distinctive paraphrastic method of interpreting Aristotle and the challenges it poses.

Themistius' Paraphrases

Paraphrasis, an exercise in rhetorical training, is frequently mentioned in ancient manuals of rhetoric.[7] Mastering it was considered essential for the successful composition of different kinds of speeches and for the sake of acquiring proficiency and the ability to express oneself in the style of various poets, historians, and other authors. The basic principle of the *paraphrasis* was 'changing the formulation while retaining the same thoughts', and this was accomplished by a set of methods applied on a target text, either in a simple manner or by way of combination of methods. The exercises were considered beneficial in helping students understand the meaning of the object paraphrased. They were useful for memorizing texts, allowed students to express themselves in the manner of the ancients, and rendered texts clearer and more expressive.

According to Zucker, the *paraphrasis* transformed from an exercise into a literary genre in light of the need to mediate texts that 'ceased to be readily accessible to the readers of an epoch'. In Aristotle's case, the problem was not only to understand the ideas that the text communicates – for which a traditional commentary would suffice – but also to understand it on a more literal level. The paraphrase, Zucker argues, offers an 'intellectual adaptation', a 're-actualization' that enables its author to make a work available to a larger audience.[8] The mediation aspect of this acclimatization of the text shows how – contrary to Themistius' 'mock-modest' testimony[9] – the paraphrases are not only composed for the sake of their author, but also for the sake of a certain audience. In Themistius' case it is a tool for teaching Aristotle's works, objectively difficult in their own right, and – centuries after having been composed – requiring mediation.[10] Whether or not Themistius is the actual *inventor* of the genre is an open question; at the very least, he presents himself as such.[11]

Themistius introduces the need to mediate Aristotle's text and the considerations behind it on various occasions. Depending on the context, the narrative changes – ranging from poetical statements about initiation and prophecy to matter-of-fact statements that Aristotle's text is badly written and badly organized – but the end-result is the same, echoing the benefits of the *paraphrasis*: understanding, clarity, accessibility, and ease of memory.[12]

Recent years have seen many advances in the study of Themistius' paraphrase as a genre in itself, as well as of its expression in his individual paraphrases. Scholars have fleshed out Themistius' connection to the ancient rhetorical tradition, the pedagogical function of his paraphrases, paraphrasing techniques, and the paraphrase as an arena for philosophical engagement and innovation. The analysis of Themistius' paraphrases is different from the analysis of more traditional commentaries, which preface portions of interpretation and discussion with quotation, in part or whole, of passages taken from Aristotle's text (lemmata). Themistius' paraphrases operate directly upon Aristotle's text, without first quoting passages of it, and most of the time adopt Aristotle's voice.[13] Themistius' engagement with the text ranges from simply repeating it to rewriting it altogether, depending on a set of considerations that is not always easy to uncover. Sometimes he omits from Aristotle's text (anything between single words and complete chapters); sometimes he replaces it (anything between simple terms to complete arguments); sometimes he adds to the text (anything between glossing and lengthy independent digressions); and sometimes he changes its structure (anything between moving words from place to place and changing the text's argumentative sequence).[14] The aggregated result is a text that is different from Aristotle's original, and perhaps the main challenge it poses is to isolate Themistius' voice from Aristotle's. A corollary challenge is to distinguish between instances in which Themistius' independent voice expresses his interpretation of Aristotle and instances in which he consciously departs from Aristotle's view. In other words, the paraphrases render it inherently difficult to determine where Aristotle ends and Themistius begins.

As various studies have shown, Themistius' procedure is not uniform throughout his corpus of paraphrases and differs concerning length, tone, digressions, and liberties he takes with Aristotle's text. Whereas in general the paraphrases of the *Posterior Analytics* and the *Physics* are more in line with the *paraphrasis* principle of 'changing the formulation while retaining the same thoughts',[15] Themistius' paraphrase of *On the Soul* is broader in intention and perhaps reflects a development in his paraphrasing technique.[16] Somewhat ironically, its scope approaches that of the commentaries that Themistius originally tried to avoid;[17] it is full not only of independent philosophical discussions, but also of polemics against various other philosophers and commentators.

Themistius' Paraphrase of *Metaphysics* 12: Overview and Selected Themes

The paraphrase of *Metaphysics* 12 is about three times longer than Aristotle's text,[18] far beyond the relative minimalism of the paraphrase of the *Posterior*

Analytics and the uneven but slightly longer paraphrase of the *Physics*.[19] It is more akin to the paraphrase of *On the Soul*, except that it does not engage in direct polemics against contemporary or recent authors and only mentions figures to whom Aristotle alludes in the course of his discussion. If some of Themistius' discussions and digressions are aimed as responses to some of his contemporaries or his predecessors, they are not presented as such in the text.

Although only paraphrasing Book 12, it seems to be a self-subsisting unit rather than a part of a paraphrase of the whole of the *Metaphysics* (although this cannot be ruled out). There are numerous forward and backward references, but all within the confines of *Metaphysics* 12, and Themistius sometimes incorporates material from other parts of Aristotle's *Metaphysics* (without reference) to thicken the discussion. The paraphrase also seems to contain a few references to the paraphrase of the *Physics*.[20]

Themistius' paraphrase of *Metaphysics* 12 is known (or notorious) and studied mainly for its interpretation of Aristotle's description of God's self-intellegizing as entailing the intellegizing of all the existents, an idea that had significant impact on subsequent medieval authors in the Arabic and Hebrew worlds.[21] Themistius' influential discussion of spontaneous generation as a counter-example to Aristotle's critique of the Platonic Ideas (7,20-8,27) has also received quite a bit of scholarly attention.[22] These seemingly distinct discussions are in fact components within Themistius' overarching theme in the paraphrase: an attempt to find in Aristotle a rigorous set of ontological explanations that show how everything must trace back to the first principle, as – true to its name – it is the only unqualified beginning. In what follows I survey some ideas in Themistius' paraphrase that I find interesting as interpretations of and/or departures from Aristotle's text. This is part of an attempt to uncover Themistius' overall approach to the text he is paraphrasing.

Themistius considers Aristotle's *Metaphysics* 12 as a coherent unit that enquires into the principles of existents. This is clear from the outset, where he writes:

> Aristotle said: 'existent' is said in many ways. But we, when we set out to enquire into the principles of the existing thing, we only set out to enquire into the principles of substance, because substance is the most fitting existent in this respect (1,3-5).

In his opening remarks, Themistius situates Aristotle's text ('The subject of our enquiry is substance; for the principles and the causes we are seeking are those of substances') within Aristotle's dictum 'existence is said in many ways' (a frequent statement in the *Metaphysics* that does not in fact occur in Book 12).[23] Themistius argues that since substance is the most worthy of the name 'existent', an enquiry into the principles of substance will result in an account of the principles of all the existents.[24]

This approach is consistent throughout the paraphrase, which presents a gradual movement from different kinds of substances to different kinds of principles, and from these to the first principle. In this respect, Themistius' paraphrase is theological throughout and he certainly does not regard Aristotle's discussion of the perishable substance in Book 12 as a part of physics; the natural substances are not discussed in so far as they are natural, but in so far as they are substances whose principles we are seeking. Examination of the paraphrase of Chapters 2–5 of the text – which are generally referred to as the physical part of Aristotle's discussion (Themistius, of course, is unaware of this later division into chapters) – reveals that Themistius inserts various passing remarks, modifications, and separate discussions that connect the world of coming-to-be and perishing to higher principles. By the time he arrives at the more traditionally considered 'theological' part of *Metaphysics* 12, Themistius has already ontologically linked every aspect of the natural world to God (the 'first' principle), well beyond what Aristotle's text offers, at least explicitly.

To this end, Themistius works on Aristotle's text comprehensively, and often pushes the limits of what can plausibly follow from Aristotle's account. A moderate example of this is Themistius' attempt to bypass the problem that modern scholarship refers to as 'topical matter' in Chapter 2. In this Chapter Aristotle argues that while the matter of natural perishable substances can receive all four kinds of change (in substance, quantity, quality, and place), celestial substances have a different kind of matter, which only enables change in place. Themistius, instead, introduces the notion of 'body' (or occasionally 'substrate') and systematically avoids the term 'matter' until deep into his paraphrase of Chapter 3, where he restricts the term to the world of coming-to-be and perishing, defining matter as 'the body that receives the form' (6,13-14) in the process of coming-to-be. Celestial bodies, then, do not have 'matter' because they never underwent a change in form. This is part of Themistius' overall attempt to create ontological distance between perishable substances and eternal substances. It is noteworthy that when describing God in later parts of the paraphrase, Themistius time and again insists that God is both immaterial *and* incorporeal (e.g. 23,5; 25,18), a distinction not present in Aristotle's discussion at *Metaphysics* 12.

Another example of this approach is found in Themistius' restatement of Aristotle's critique of the Platonic Ideas (at the end of Chapter 3) and the subsequent discussion in which he employs the counter-example of spontaneous generation as a defence of sorts. Since this part of Themistius' text has received a fair share of scholarly attention, there is no need to revisit it thoroughly.[25] It should be noted, however, that a philological analysis of this part has shown that Themistius' reply to Aristotle is *not* done with the intention of reinstating Platonic Ideas. By noting that some creatures do not share a form with their 'parent' (e.g. bees and dead cattle), Themistius' main point is to furnish a metaphysical setting that prevents the parent in biological reproduction from being the formal cause of its offspring. This sits well within the context of the paraphrase's attempt to more firmly ground divine causality in nature. In this case, the objection to Aristotle is expressed in Themistius' insistence that an organism's form is not attained from its parent, but from latent principles (*logoi*) in matter that are actualized by a certain 'soul that is in the earth', of divine origin, when matter is blended properly.[26] A complementary discussion to this appears in Themistius' rearrangement of Aristotle's distinction between proximate and remote causes, where he stresses that the causal relations between natural substances are ultimately subordinate to their remote efficient causes, which are 'the principles of the proximate causes' (11,4). In other words, in natural coming-to-be, the parent is not the formal cause, and it is an efficient cause only locally but not without qualification. The whole discussion can find its orientation in Themistius' revision of the question that Aristotle sets out to answer at the beginning of Chapter 4. Aristotle asks how principles and causes of things can be thought to be the same; Themistius, instead, asks how the first principle can be the principle of all things (8,30). By the end of the Chapter, when Aristotle briefly mentions the existence of a first mover, Themistius stresses that the whole point of the discussion was to move from proximate movers to the first principle, which is the first mover, whose relationship to the natural substances is not one of proximity (10,8-10).

Regarding Themistius' paraphrase of Aristotle's discussion of the celestial realm and God, before addressing the novel aspects one should note that Themistius expresses a need to reinforce some of Aristotle's argumentation regarding the existence of an eternally moving substance and an eternal unmoved mover. The existence of an eternal substance that is in constant motion is proved in *Metaphysics* 12 on the basis of the argument for the eternity of time, assuming that since time is a modification of movement, if time is eternal than so is movement, and consequently there is a substance that is eternally in motion. Themistius, in his paraphrase of Chapter 6, mentions this argument and elaborates upon it (12,4-21), but seems somewhat discontent and expresses the need to arrive at the same conclusion through the analysis of motion taken by itself. To achieve this he adds to the discussion three completely new arguments for the eternity of motion, each of which is founded upon analysis of a different component of it – namely the mover, the concept of motion, and the moved object (12,22-13,10).[27] A similar sense of discontent arises with reference to Aristotle's proof for the existence of an eternal unmoved mover. Aristotle's argument is based upon the idea that a moved mover is an intermediate between two extremes. Themistius, in his paraphrase of Chapter 7, prefers to replace this argument with one that he had already introduced in his paraphrase of the *Physics*: if something is composed of two things, both of them can exist separately; since there exists something that both moves and is moved, then there must exist something that only moves, without being moved (17,10-15).[28]

Themistius' elaborate discussion of the idea that Aristotle's God's self-intelligizing is in fact an intelligizing of all the existents – an idea that can be interpreted in many ways, and also involves problems of textual transmission – has received considerable scholarly attention, most notably in the studies of Shlomo Pines and Carlos Fraenkel.[29] Here I would like to suggest a conceptual connection between this idea and the idea that Themistius understands Aristotle's God as the efficient cause of the world, and as such not only in the sense of a mover, but also in the sense of a maker who makes according to what is contained in its intellect. There are a few rather straightforward utterances in this vein, as well as indications that can be gathered from different places within the paraphrase. For instance, when paraphrasing Chapter 3, Themistius seems to introduce a distinction of sorts between coming-to-be and creation, as if the former is a type of the latter (5,26-32), but he does not elaborate on this. Also, in Themistius' elaboration upon, and digression from, Aristotle's critique of Anaxagoras' *Nous* at the end of Chapter 2, Themistius seems to be advocating a demiurgic cosmogony in which 'the Creator' *and* matter (or 'the body') are respective principles of plurality, in different ways: 'The plurality of things that come-to-be comes from two things: the Creator, in the plurality of forms He gave the body, and the body, for the body has been set as a recipient' (5,20-1). Finally, when describing the ontological descent of the chain of existents at the paraphrase of Chapter 10, Themistius uses the language of design and suggests that in putting earth in the middle for the sake of the circular motion of the celestial bodies, God's work was 'finished' (33,27-9).

The last feature of the paraphrase to which I would like to draw attention is a set of digressions in which Themistius uses political language to describe God's authority over the cosmos (besides passing remarks, the main discussions appear at 17,18-18,1; 25,21-26,16; and 31,10-27).[30] This feature does not occur in Aristotle's text, with the exception, perhaps, of the example of the general and the simile of the freeman at Chapter 10. This is interesting for a number of reasons: first, it adds a political dimension to Themistius' understanding of the ancient ideal of likeness to God. Second, it provides a rare occasion to find a common element between Themistius' paraphrases and orations through the employment of the notion of law; whereas God in Themistius' paraphrase of *Metaphysics* 12 is the law, the emperor in the orations is often described as 'living law'.[31] And finally, it can serve as a starting point to explore some ideas about the relationship between politics and metaphysics in medieval Arabic and Hebrew philosophy.[32]

Text and Translation

The textual history of Themistius' paraphrase of *Metaphysics* 12 is complex and frustrating. While a detailed account is beyond the scope of this introduction, an overview of the process of transmission in time and space should reinforce the caution with which the present translation should be met.

The sad beginning is that Themistius' original Greek is lost, nor was I able to detect any allusions to it in subsequent literature in Greek. The paraphrase was translated into Arabic, most likely by Isḥāq ibn Ḥunayn (*c.* 830-910/11) in Baghdad, but not all reports agree on this.[33] Unfortunately, only parts of this translation survive. The beginning of the translation – covering Themistius' paraphrase of Chapter 1 and the first lines of the paraphrase of Chapter 2 – survives in a single manuscript whose other pages are lost.[34] There also exists an abridgement (whose author is unknown) that shortens Themistius' paraphrase of Chapters 6–9.[35] Despite different opinions presented on this matter, the dependence of the abridgement upon the complete translation can be established beyond doubt once both are compared to the complete Hebrew translation discussed below, and most of the discrepancies can be explained by the abridger's technique. Both versions of the Arabic were edited and published by Badawī in 1947. His edition is of great importance, but contains noticeable errors, many of which have already been detected by Richard Frank, whose meticulous set of notes on the text, published in the late 1950s, remains indispensable.[36]

The other main sources for the Arabic text are Averroes' (1126-1198) generous quotations from Themistius' paraphrase (in Chapters 1, 3, and 7) in his long commentary on Aristotle's *Metaphysics* (*Tafsīr Mā Ba'd al-Ṭabī'a*);[37] the theologian Ibn Taymiyya's (d. 1328) lengthy quotation from the paraphrase of Chapters 4 and 5 in his *The Way of Prophetic Sunna* (*Minhāj al-Sunna al-Nabawiyya*);[38] and the relatively heavy use (sometimes quotations, mostly paraphrases with glossing) the philosopher and polymath 'Abd al-Laṭīf al-Baghdādī (1162-1231) makes of Themistius' paraphrase of Chapters 6–9 in his *Book on the Science of Metaphysics* (*Kitāb fī 'ilm Mā ba'd al-Ṭabī'a*).[39] Other, less pertinent sources, are not instrumental to the present translation.[40]

The earliest *complete* surviving version of Themistius' paraphrase is in the form of a Hebrew translation, made from the Arabic, dated to 1255. It is the work of Moses ibn Tibbon, a third generation of the celebrated Provencal family of translators. (The Hebrew translation, in turn, was translated into Latin during the sixteenth century by Moses Finzi and published in 1558 in Venice. This translation is so far removed from the original that it will not concern us here.[41]) In 1903, as part of the *Commentaria in Aristotelem Graeca* series, Samuel Landauer published a semi-critical edition of the Hebrew text, accompanied by his revision of the Latin translation.[42] Landauer's edition is a remarkable achievement given the dearth of material at his disposal; he had none of the Arabic sources that we possess today, and some of the surviving Hebrew manuscripts were not available to him. The only fair complaint about Landauer's edition is that his critical apparatus is too selective, occasionally not recording important variants. Still, his aim was expressly modest: to provide a usable text based on what he took to be the best readings. Nevertheless, since he did not conduct a thorough analysis of the Hebrew manuscripts, his general remarks on their mutual relationships are inaccurate and his editorial choices sometimes seem random.

Examination of the ten surviving Hebrew manuscripts reveals three different versions of the Hebrew translation.[43] These versions (labelled, respectively, I, II, and III) express the translation and revision process of the Hebrew text. Version II, according to our analysis, is a thorough revision of Version I, whereas Version III is a light edit of Version II with some traces of Version I.[44] Which of these should be ascribed most properly to Moses ibn Tibbon and dated to 1255 is an open question that does not have bearings on the present translation.[45] It is important to note, however, that in places where only Hebrew text survives, revision processes among the different Hebrew versions are instrumental in determining the underlying Arabic, especially since the revisions were for the most part consistent.[46] Readers will find several examples of this in the notes.

The present volume is the first translation of Themistius' paraphrase into English and the second translation of the work into a modern language, following Rémi Brague's French translation, published in 1999.[47] Brague's translation is based on Landauer's edition of the Hebrew, Badawī's edition of what survives of the Arabic text, and additional printed fragments in Arabic and Hebrew. It also consults Frank's critical remarks on the text throughout. Despite the merits of his translation, Brague could not always avoid reproducing the shortcomings of the material upon which he relied. Still, his edition is of high value for its historical notes and skill in tackling several difficult passages, and the work on the present translation derived much benefit from an engagement with Brague's choices, as is evident in the notes.

In the early stages of work it became clear that the printed editions of Themistius' paraphrase are no longer sufficient (as can be gathered from some of the comments above) and that the textual tradition should be examined afresh. This is not only because the available printed material does not rely on in-depth analysis of the manuscript traditions, but also because much new material has surfaced in the meantime. The translation was therefore postponed until the conclusion of the philological analysis, which resulted in a new critical edition of the Arabic fragments and the Hebrew complete translation, recently published.[48] The new edition is the basis for the present translation, and the reader can refer to it for detailed discussions of all the source materials, their relationship, and the manner in which they were used, beyond the basic information provided here. Numbers in parentheses follow the pagination and line numbering of the Hebrew text as printed in Landauer's CAG edition, which the new edition reflects in the margins. The Arabic portions of the new edition face the Hebrew exactly and reflect the pagination of other printed Arabic sources in its own margins, so all references are standardized.

To say that translating a translation of a translation of a lost text is tricky is an understatement. Whereas the Arabic and Hebrew translations can teach us many things about Isḥāq ibn Ḥunayn's and Moses ibn Tibbon's respective terminology, technique, and procedures and should be studied for their own sake (as they indeed are), they sometimes mask the original which they are translating. Hence, translating them for their own sake would not do much service to the scholar of late antique philosophy who is more interested in what Themistius said than in how he was translated. The desirable situation, of course, would be to offer translations of both the original and its Arabic translation (and others, if applicable), which would give the reader the sense of a complete tradition. This has been done, for example, in Dimitri Gutas' landmark edition and translation of Theophrastus' *On First Principles*, which includes not only a translation of Theophrastus from the Greek, but also a translation of Isḥāq's Arabic version.[49] However, in the present case, with the Greek lost, the (modern) translator is faced with a difficult choice: whether to translate from the Hebrew and Arabic, which would be safer but would also preserve their modifications of meaning, or whether to translate from a 'theoretical space' which may be arrived at by attempting, when possible, to retrace the path from Hebrew to Arabic, and from Arabic to Greek.

Despite this being the more difficult course, the present translation indeed occupies a 'theoretical space' somewhere between the Greek, Arabic, and Hebrew. I believe that in the present text this can, to some extent at least, be achieved, for the following reasons: (i) Themistius is working directly upon

Aristotle's Greek text, which we have, and whose textual tradition has been richly studied. This, combined with a better understanding of Themistius' paraphrasing techniques, supplies something to fall back on in those places where he is closely following Aristotle. (ii) Isḥāq ibn Ḥunayn and Moses ibn Tibbon are both well-known and relatively well-researched medieval translators much of whose output has been published and vocabulary made available. (iii) There is the precedent of Isḥāq translating Themistius in the form of the paraphrase of *On the Soul*, of which we have the original Greek and most of the Arabic, published alongside valuable philological studies.[50] (iv) We have other cases of Moses ibn Tibbon translating Isḥāq ibn Ḥunayn. (v) Several online lexicons and databases render cross-language research considerably more accessible. In this respect, the immense *Glossarium Græco-Arabicum* (Bochum) and the rapidly growing *PESHAT in Context* database (here in Hamburg) are invaluable for Arabic and Hebrew, respectively.

However, lest the reader should become too optimistic, it should be stressed that the extent to which translation choices are defensible varies greatly, especially when I chose to deviate from the literal meaning in Arabic or Hebrew in favour of hypotheses concerning the underlying Greek. All instances of this sort are explained in the notes, as well as instances when I am unsure about the text or still in the dark. Finally, while for the most part I maintain consistent terminology, in matters of syntax and style I have tended to prefer readability over literalness (or so I would like to think).

Since available evidence concerning different parts of the text varies in quantity as well as in quality, I cannot avoid this translation sometimes being imbalanced and only hope that subsequent scholarship will help to clarify what is yet unclear and revise that which warrants revision. Here, unfortunately, von Stolberg's famous appeal to study Greek and cast the translation into the fire cannot be upheld.

Notes

1 For Themistius' life and career see J. Vanderspoel, *Themistius and the Imperial Court: Oratory, Civic Duty, and Paideia from Constantius to Theodosius* (Ann Arbor: University of Michigan Press, 1995). The best survey of Themistius' works is found in R. B. Todd, 'Themistius', *Catalogus Translationum et Commentariorum*

8 (2003), 57–102. Additional information about the Arabic and Hebrew tradition is found in Y. Meyrav, 'Themistius' Paraphrase of Aristotle's *Metaphysics* 12', PhD diss., Tel Aviv University, 2017, pp. 10–17.

2 For an overview of Themistius' Orations and their division into 'public' and 'private' see R. J. Penella, *The Private Orations of Themistius* (Berkeley: University of California Press, 2000), pp. 1–9. The 'private' orations are roughly divided into: '(1) apologetics and polemics, (2) cultural [...] programmatics; (3) material of autobiographical interest; and (4) philosophical discourses' (ibid., p. 9). They are discussed systematically ibid., pp. 10–48.

3 This is the opinion of most scholars, e.g. Vanderspoel, *Themistius*, p. 37, and Penella, *Private*, p. 4, mostly based on Themistius' own account in his twenty-third Oration. For a different view see Y. Meyrav, *Themistius' Paraphrase of Aristotle's* Metaphysics *12* (Leiden, Boston: Brill, 2019), p. 118, n. 21.

4 Aside for the scholarship mentioned in the present introduction, see a recent overview in Meyrav, *Themistius*, pp. 9–13.

5 The only account of *Metaphysics* 12 written in Greek after Themistius is Pseudo-Alexander's commentary, which is assumed to be written by Michael of Ephesus (mid-eleventh century) on the basis of an anonymous commentary composed after the first half of the fifth century, which Golitsis suggests to be by Asclepius (sixth century). For this complex state of affairs see Concetta Luna, *Trois études sur la tradition des commentaires anciens à la* Métaphysique *d'Aristote* (Leiden: Brill, 2001), pp. 1–32, and P. Golitsis, 'Who Were the Real Authors of the *Metaphysics* Commentary Ascribed to Alexander and Ps. Alexander?', in R. Sorabji, ed., *Aristotle Re-Interpreted* (London: Bloomsbury, 2016), pp. 565–88. This warrants a separate study, but judging by Sharples' analysis of this commentary, at least, it has nothing in common with Themistius' understanding of Aristotle's text. See R.W. Sharples, 'Pseudo-Alexander on Aristotle, *Metaphysics* Λ', in G. Movia, ed., *Alessandro di Afrodisia e la 'Metafisica' di Aristotele* (Milan: Vita e pensiero, 2003), pp. 187–218.

6 See a very general overview with further references in Meyrav, *Themistius*, pp. 13–20. But this is just scratching the surface.

7 See A. S. Kakavelaki, 'On the Origin of Paraphrasis as a Philosophical Exegetical Method' [in Greek], *Philosophia* 45 (2015), 269; A. Zucker, 'Qu'est-ce qu'une *paraphrasis*? L'enfance grecque de la paraphrase', *Rursus* 6 (February 2011); and recently Meyrav, *Themistius*, pp. 111–15. Although this method is mentioned frequently in various rhetorical works, the only known systematic exposition of it is included in Aelius Theon's *Progumnasmata*, published in M. Patillon, *Aelius Théon: Progymnasmata* (Paris: Les Belles Lettres, 1997). For an overview of Theon's account see ibid., pp. CIV-CVII. See also Zucker, 'Qu'est-ce qu'une *paraphrasis*', §§4, 6, 16; Kakavelaki, 'Origin', 270. Aelius Theon is usually considered to belong

to the mid-/end of the first century CE, but this has been challenged by Malcolm Heath, who suggests pushing the author forward to the fifth century CE. See M. Heath, 'Theon and the History of the Progymnasmata', *Greek, Roman, and Byzantine Studies* 43 (2002), 129–60.

8 Zucker, 'Qu'est-ce qu'une *paraphrasis*', §74.

9 See H. J. Blumenthal, 'Photius on Themistius (cod. 74): Did Themistius Write Commentaries on Aristotle?', *Hermes* 107, no. 2 (1979), 177.

10 Todd lists many indications for classroom use of the paraphrase of the *Physics*, such as dialogues, references to earlier discussions, second person address, rhetorical ridicule, and rhetorical questions. See R. B. Todd, *Themistius: On Aristotle's* Physics *5–8* (London: Bloomsbury, 2008), p. 5, n. 11. Similar features are found in the present text, for example, references to earlier discussions (11,19; 16,20), second person addresses (6,12; 15,9), debates with imaginary interlocutors (9,4-13), and rhetorical questions (8,5-7; 32,26-27).

11 Themistius was either the inventor of the philosophical paraphrase, or the earliest surviving representative of it. (For this problem and further references, see Meyrav, *Themistius*, pp. 113–14, especially n. 12 for 'predating' candidates.) At the very least, he *presents* himself as the innovator of this style of commentating (see ibid., p. 121). Zucker ('Qu'est-ce qu'une *paraphrasis*', §41) suggests that even if Themistius did not 'invent' the paraphrase, he should be regarded as an innovator because of the systematic character of his paraphrases, which secured their place as an independent genre within philosophical exegesis.

12 The dominance of memory within the various explanations warrants further study.

13 Todd summarizes this elegantly, noting that the paraphrases 'were designed to clarify the texts of some central works of Aristotle, and thereby make them accessible to relatively advanced students. The voice of the paraphrasist is often that of Aristotle, sometimes identical, but normally operating in a more expansive, yet sometimes more summary, mode, occasionally altering the expository order of a text, and, in rare cases, speaking independently through digressions, queries, or excursuses that clarify texts considered poorly organised or obscure.' R. B. Todd, *Themistius: On Aristotle's* Physics *4* (London: Bloomsbury, 2003), p. 1.

14 Of these, the more minimalistic changes pose challenges in the sphere of textual criticism, because it is not always possible to determine if slight variations between Themistius and Aristotle reflect conscious changes or problems of textual transmission (either concerning the text of Aristotle in front of Themistius, or the manuscript tradition of the paraphrase itself).

15 Despite the semblance of simplicity, M. Achard ('Themistius' Paraphrase of Posterior Analytics 71a17-b8: An Example of Rearrangement of an Aristotelian

Text', *Laval théologique et philosophique* 64, no. 1 (2008), 19–21) uncovers Themistius' complex paraphrastic procedures to reveal that Meno's paradox in Aristotle deals with two distinct problems, namely the impossibility of knowledge and 'the problem of validity of universal premises with regard to unknown instances', which is known as the sophistic 'veiled' argument (ibid., 32–3). For a similar type of analysis, on a different part of the text, see Achard, 'La paraphrase de Thémistius sur les lignes 71a1-11 des *Seconds Analytiques*', *Dionysius* 23 (2005), 105–16. See also P. Volpe Cacciatore, 'La parafrasi di Temistio al secondo libro degli Analitici Posteriori di Aristotele', in C. Moreschini, ed., *Esegesi, parafrasi e compilazione in età tardoantica, Atti del Terzo Convegno dell'Associazione di Studi Tardoantichi* (Naples: D'Auria, 1995), pp. 389–95, who analyses 'the specific modalities' of Themistius' presentation of Chapters 1, 2, 4, 7, 11, and 12 in the first book of the *Posterior Analytics*.

16 The introductory remarks in his paraphrase of Aristotle's *On the Soul* introduce methods that are difficult to demarcate. According to Todd, these methods 'are unfortunately described in generic terms that cannot be easily attached to the content of the paraphrase, and may well refer to overlapping procedures.' See R. B. Todd, *Themistius: On Aristotle's* On the Soul (Ithaca: Cornell University Press, 1996), p. 4. Capone Ciollaro identifies four methodological devices in Themistius' paraphrase of *On the Soul*, which incorporate meta-procedures: (i) broader redactions, with transpositions of terms, as well as morphological and lexical changes; (ii) original additions to Aristotle's text, for explanatory purposes; (iii) extensive digressions with references to earlier interpreters; and (iv) omissions, from single words to complete passages. See M. Capone Ciollaro, 'Osservazioni sulla Parafrasi di Temistio al *De Anima* aristotelico', in Claudio Moreschini, ed., *Esegesi, parafrasi e compilazione in Età Tardoantica, Atti del Terzo Convegno dell'Associazione di Studi Tardoantichi* (Naples: D'Auria, 1995), pp. 81–90.

17 Todd presents a calculation of the ratio by word count of Themistius' paraphrases against Aristotle's text: in the eight books of the *Physics*, the ratios are 2.18, 1.84, 2.27, 1.99, 1.10, 1.12, 0.38, and 0.88; in the two books of the *Posterior Analytics*, the ratios are 0.99 and 1.06. For the three books of *On the Soul* the ratios are 2.63, 2.21, and 2.91—but the ratio for *On the Soul* 3.5 is a staggering 27.18 (See Todd, *Physics 4*, p. 4, n. 4).

18 A rough calculation based on the present English translation of Themistius' paraphrase against Ross' English translation of *Metaphysics* 12 shows that the paraphrase is three times longer than Aristotle's text, according to the following distribution: 5.2 (Chapter 1); 2.5 (Chapter 2); 4.0 (Chapter 3); 1.7 (Chapter 4); 1.3 (Chapter 5); 3.9 (Chapter 6); 4.6 (Chapter 7); 1.6 (Chapter 8); 5.1 (Chapter 9); and 3.3 (Chapter 10).

19 See above, n. 17.

20 The relationship between the works might explain the relative brevity of the paraphrase of *Physics* 8. Todd (*Physics 5–8*, p. 7, n. 24) suggests that the paraphrase on *Metaphysics* 12 might have assumed the audience's knowledge of the paraphrase of the *Physics*, and indeed there are some allusions to it (e.g. 16,10 ff.).

21 The most notable discussions of this are S. Pines, 'Some Distinctive Metaphysical Conceptions in Themistius' Commentary on Book Lambda and their Place in the History of Philosophy', in J. Weisner, ed., *Aristoteles: Werk und Wirkung*, vol. 2: *Kommentierung, Überlieferung, Nachleben* (Berlin & New York: De Gruyter, 1987), pp. 177–204; C. Fraenkel, 'Maimonides' God and Spinoza's *Deus sive Natura*', *Journal of the History of Philosophy* 44, no. 2 (2006), 169-215, esp. 185-7 and 203; I. Kupreeva, 'Themistius', in Lloyd L. Gerson, ed., *The Cambridge History of Philosophy in Late Antiquity*, 2 vols (Cambridge: Cambridge University Press, 2010), vol. 1, pp. 414–16. For an account on the identity of thinking with its object in Aristotle, see R. Sorabji, *Time, Creation and the Continuum* (London: Duckworth, 1983), pp. 144–5.

22 R. Sorabji's volume *Aristotle Re-Interpreted* contains the most recent findings on the issue in three contributions: D. Henry, 'Themistius and the Problem of Spontaneous Generation', pp. 179–94; Y. Meyrav, 'Spontaneous Generation and its Metaphysics in Themistius' Paraphrase of Aristotle's *Metaphysics* 12', pp. 195–210; and J. Wilberding, 'The Neoplatonic Commentators on 'Spontaneous' Generation', esp. pp. 226–7. See also Sorabji's introduction, pp. 17–18.

23 This expression appears in Aristotle nine (or ten) times in the *Metaphysics*: 4.2, 1003a33; 4.2, 1004a22; 5.10, 1018a35; 6.2, 1026b2; 6.4, 1028a5 (excised by some editors); 7.1, 1028a10; 10.1, 1052a15; 11.3, 1060b32; 13.2, 1077b17; and 14.2, 1089a7. It is also discussed in the *Eudemian Ethics* (1217b25-35). The most famous example is the opening sentence of 4.2, but Themistius seems to draw from 7.1, 1028a10, as he expands upon Aristotle's argument here according to the argumentation in the first part of 7.1. For a systematic discussion see G. E. L. Owen, 'Logic and Metaphysics in Some Early Works of Aristotle', in I. Düring and G. E. L. Owen, eds, *Aristotle and Plato in the mid-Fourth Century* (Gothenburg: Eilanders, 1960), pp. 163–90.

24 It is also notable that Themistius focuses on 'principles' where Aristotle mentions both 'principles' and 'causes'. This is not the only occurrence in the paraphrase where Themistius focuses Aristotle's terminology about principles for the sake of precision. See Meyrav, *Themistius*, pp. 139–40.

25 See above, n. 22.

26 Analogous to this is Themistius' refusal to allow the celestial bodies to be their own source of eternal motion at the end of Chapter 7. See the analysis of this

passage in D. Twetten, 'Aristotelian Cosmology and Causality in Classical Arabic Philosophy and Its Greek Background', in D. Janos, ed., *Ideas in Motion in Baghdad and Beyond* (Leiden & Boston: Brill, 2016), pp. 330–1.

27 For an analysis of the argument for eternal motion see P. Adamson, 'The Last Philosophers of Late Antiquity in the Arabic Tradition', in R. Sorabji (ed), *Aristotle Re-interpreted*, pp. 467–8, as well as pp. 472–4 for its reverberations in Arabic thought. Adamson understands this argument as an example of a metaphysical argument in a physical setting, where 'it is the nature of the *cause* that determines the eternity of its effect' (ibid., p. 468).

28 See Themistius, *in Phys.* 223,1–3: 'In all cases of things being combined from two [constituents] it could be learnt that if one of the things in the mixture can exist per se, then the other can exist per se too' (translated in Todd, *Themistius:* Physics *5-8*, p. 83).

29 See above, n. 21.

30 As Twetten ('Aristotelian Cosmology', p. 330) and G. Guldentops ('La science suprême selon Thémistius', *Revue de philosophie ancienne* 19, no. 1 (2001), 113-14) have already noticed, Themistius' politicization of the cosmos is a theme that connects the present paraphrase to his orations. For the political metaphor in ancient metaphysics and its inherent difficulties see P. Adamson, 'State of Nature: Human and Cosmic Rulership in Ancient Philosophy', in A. Höfele & B. Kellner, eds, *Menschennatur und politische Ordnung* (Paderborn: Wilhelm Fink, 2015), pp. 79–94.

31 See, e.g. *Oration* 34 (216,13-14): '[T]he God who guides this whole cosmos and those [divinities] who make the rounds with him are devotees of a practical and political philosophy, who keep the whole of nature steady and unharmed through the course of time' (tr. Penella, *Private*, p. 213); The emperor expresses the 'law animate' (*Oration* 5 64b4-8)—just like God in the paraphrase. Schramm argues that 'the rule of the emperor should be the image of the cosmic order of God.' See M. Schramm, 'Platonic Ethics and Politics in Themistius and Julian', in R. C. Fowler, ed., *Plato in the Third Sophistic* (Boston & Berlin: De Gruyter, 2014), p. 135. In general, see ibid, pp. 132–5.

32 Watt noticed this with regard to al-Fārābī but suggests a route through rhetoric. See J. W. Watt, 'From Themistius to al-Farabi: Platonic Political Philosophy and Aristotle's *Rhetoric* in the East', *Rhetorica* 13, no. 1 (1995), 17–41.

33 Other candidates in the Arabic bio-bibliographical tradition are Abū Bishr Mattā (*c.* 870-940) and Shamlī (ninth century), but it would be difficult to make a case for them based on the available evidence. Some Hebrew manuscripts testify that the celebrated polymath Thābit ibn Qurra (d. 901) revised Isḥāq's translation, which is plausible. All these issues are discussed in detail in Meyrav, *Themistius,*

pp. 27–31. For the Arabic translation movement in general, the best reference is D. Gutas, *Greek Thought, Arabic Culture* (London: Routledge, 1998).

34 The beginning of the original complete Arabic translation, which contains the paraphrase of Chapter 1 and the beginning of Chapter 2 (corresponding to 1,1-4,13 in the text), is preserved in MS Ẓāhiriyya (Damascus) 4871, which dates *c.* 1155-1163. The text appears at ff. 38*r*-38*v*, under the title *Maqālat al-Lām Sharḥ Thamasṭayūs Tarjamahu Isḥāq ibn Ḥunayn*. It was originally edited in 'A-R. Badawī, *Arisṭū 'inda al-'Arab* (Cairo: Maktabat al-Nahḍa al-Miṣriyya, 1947), pp. 329–33, and recently edited afresh in Meyrav, *Themistius*. For a detailed philological discussion see ibid., pp. 32–3.

35 The abridgement is found under the title *Min Sharḥ Thamasṭayūs li-ḥarf al-Lām* in MS Ḥikma 6 of the Dār al-Kutub Library in Cairo, 206*v*16-210*r*7. It was originally edited in Badawī, *Arisṭū 'inda al-'Arab*, pp. 12–21, and recently edited afresh in Meyrav, *Themistius*. For a detailed exploration of the abridgement, its technique, and its authorship see ibid., pp. 48–62. In general, the author of the abridgement is only interested in core theological issues and disregards Themistius' other discussions (for a summary of his agenda see ibid., p. 54).

36 R. M. Frank, 'Some Textual Notes on the Oriental Versions of Themistius' Paraphrase of Book l of the *Metaphysics*', *Cahiers de Byrsa* 8 (1958/9), 215-30.

37 Averroes, *Tafsīr Mā ba'd al-Ṭabī'a*, ed., M. Bouyges (Beirut: Dar el-Machreq, 1948), 1410,4-15 (= Badawī, *Arisṭū*, 329,6-13; 1,5-13 in our text); 1492,3-1494,14 (=7,26-8,27 in our text); 1635,4-1636,13 (22,11-29 in our text; 1635,6-9 overlaps Badawī, *Arisṭū*, 18,15-17). English translation in C. Genequand, *Ibn Rushd's Metaphysics: A Translation with Introduction of Ibn Rushd's Commentary on Aristotle's* Metaphysics, *Book Lām* (Leiden: Brill, 1986). French translation in A. Martin, *Averroès: Grand commentaire de la* Métaphysique *d'Aristote, livre Lambda* (Paris: Les Belles Lettres, 1984). See discussion in Meyrav, Themistius, p. 39, and pp. 514–26 for the Hebrew tradition of Averroes.

38 This was first reported by Marc Geoffroy, who ascribes this finding to M. Taïeb Farhat. See M. Geoffroy, 'Remarques sur la traduction Usṭāṯ du livre Lambda de la *Métaphysique*, Chapitre 6', *Recherches de théologie et philosophie médiévales* 50, no. 2 (2003), 420. Ibn Taymiyya's lengthy quotation is attributed to Aristotle and does not mention Themistius' name. See Ibn Taymiyya, *Minhāj al-Sunna al-Nabawiyya*, ed. M.R. Sālim (Al-Riyāḍ, 1986), vol. 1, 170,19-173,7 (=9,24-11,4 in our version). See the discussion in Meyrav, *Themistius*, p. 48.

39 The text is printed in A. Neuwirth, *'Abd al-Laṭīf al-Baġdādī's Bearbeitung von Buch Lambda der Aristotelischen Metaphysik* (Weisbaden: Steiner, 1976) and should be used in consultation with the textual variants in D. Gutas, 'Editing Arabic Philosophical Texts', *Orientalistische Literaturzeitung* 75, no. 3 (1980), 213-22. For

'Abd al-Laṭīf al-Baghdādī in general see C. Martini Bonadeo, *'Abd al-Laṭīf al-Baġdādī's Philosophical Journey: From Aristotle's* Metaphysics *to the 'Metaphysical Science'* (Leiden: Brill, 2013). Since 'Abd al-Laṭīf al-Baghdādī uses Themistius in various ways in his texts, using it for control purposes should be done with caution. See the discussion and methodology in Meyrav, *Themistius*, pp. 39–48.

40 There are also lesser fragments of different kinds in an anonymous eleventh-century philosophy reader (MS Marsh 539, Oxford), Pseudo-al-'Āmirī, Avicenna (*c.* 980-1037), and al-Shahrastānī (1086-1153), which are occasionally helpful but are not discussed here. See the analysis and further references in Meyrav, *Themistius*, pp. 33–9; pp. 62–4.

41 M. Finzi, *Themistius: In Metaphysicorum Librum Duodecimum* (Venice: Hyeronimum Scotum, 1558).

42 S. Landauer, ed., *Themistii in Aristotelis Metaphysicorum librum Λ paraphrasis hebraice et latine*, Commentaria in Aristotelem Graeca 5.5 (Berlin: Reimer, 1903). It is important to note that the Latin text in Landauer's edition is a revision of Finzi's translation, whose original can only be found in the Venice edition (see previous note). As Frank comments ('Notes', p. 216, n. 4), the Latin version 'is poor, even as revised by Landauer, and affords virtually no control over the Arabic version.'

43 For a detailed analysis, see Meyrav, *Themistius*, pp. 65–98. The manuscripts are described on pp. 66–74.

44 This version only survives in one manuscript (Torino—Biblioteca Nazionale Universitaria Cod. AI 14) that was not available to Landauer.

45 A preliminary discussion of this highly complex issue is taken up in Y. Meyrav, 'Arabic-into-Hebrew Translation Strategies and Procedures in the Hebrew Manuscript Tradition of Themistius' Paraphrase of Aristotle's *Metaphysics* XII', in R. Leicht and G. Veltri, eds, *Studies in the Formation of Medieval Hebrew Philosophical Terminology* (Leiden: Brill, 2020), pp. 195–8.

46 Besides the manuscripts of the work itself, a few other Hebrew sources contain useful data for the establishment of the text. These are discussed in Meyrav, *Themistius*, pp. 95–105; pp. 514–26.

47 R. Brague, *Thémistius: Paraphrase de la* Métaphysique *d'Aristote (livre Lambda)* (Paris: Vrin, 1999).

48 Meyrav, *Themistius*.

49 D. Gutas, *Theophrastus:* On First Principles *(known as his* Metaphysics*)* (Leiden: Brill, 2010).

50 M. C. Lyons, *An Arabic Translation of Themistius' Commentary on Aristoteles De Anima* (London: Cassirer, 1973).

Textual Emendations

The following list notes departures from the Hebrew text printed in Yoav Meyrav, *Themistius' Paraphrase of Aristotle's* Metaphysics *12: A Critical Hebrew-Arabic Edition of the Surviving Textual Evidence, with an Introduction, Preliminary Studies, and a Commentary* (Leiden: Brill, 2019). The emendations are discussed in their respective endnotes. There are no emendations for the Arabic text.

5,4	Insert another *hu'* after *hu'*
7,21	Read *ha-mityalledet* in place of *ha-meyalledet*
12,5	Insert *kevar* after *hena*
22,10	Read *hanaḥatam* in place of *hana'atam*
35,12	Read *nimshakh elav* in place of *nimtza'*

Themistius

On Aristotle
Metaphysics 12

Translation

Chapter 1[1]

1,3 Aristotle said: 'existent' is said in many ways.[2] (**1069a18-19**) But we, when we set out[3] to enquire into the principles of the existing thing, we only set out to enquire into the principles of substance, because substance is the most fitting[4] existent in this respect.[5]

1,5[6] **(1069a19-20)** For the All is [either] united, like the union of the organs of the human body or the parts in the body of a plant; or composed of things that touch each other, like the composition of a house or a ship; or combined of dispersed things, like the combination of an army or a city. In each case,[7] its first part is substance, and its place in the All [is like] the place of the heart in an animal's entire body.

1,8 (1069a20-1) If [the All] is not organized in one of these ways, but rather is like what exists in numbers – first one, then two, and then three – or like what exists in straight-lined shapes – first triangle, then quadrangle – then, in a similar way, substance [still] exists first, and then quality, quantity, and the like.[8] For the existence of substance is prior to the existence of anything that follows it, just as one is prior to the other numbers and the triangle is prior to the other shapes.

1,13 (1069a21-2) For all genera[9] are not described as existing in the same manner, but substance is more fitting [to be described as existing]. Other things are described as existing by virtue of their existence in substance, since they are either its quantities, qualities, motions, or the like. Their share[10] in existence is through their relationship[11] to substance. And we, if we describe the other genera with words that indicate existence – there is nothing puzzling [about it], because we actually apply these words to substance.[12]

1,18 For example, when we say 'this board is white', our 'is'[13] is among the words that indicate existence. We do not apply this word to the board's whiteness, but to the board itself. Likewise, we apply similar words to what we deny of the accidents and more so to what we affirm [of them]. **(1069a22-4)** For we apply them, for example, to what is not white, when we say 'this is not white', and to what is not straight, when we say 'this is not straight'.[14] Similarly, when we say 'this board is not straight', we apply our 'is not' to the board itself. Likewise, when we say 'this board is straight', we apply this word, i.e. 'is', to the board.

1,25 (1069a24) For it is impossible for us to separate an accident from substance in thought – let alone by seeing[15] – in the way that it is possible for us to separate substance from all **[2]** other genera. This is not [to say] that it is possible for a sensible substance to be naked of accidents in any way. However, while one and the same substance exists stably, the accidents that exist in it are not stably the same. Rather, they alternate and succeed one another; some occur and some wither, e.g. quantities, qualities, actions, affections, places, times, and other genera like them. The principle of all these genera, their element, and their foundation is substance.

2,6 (1069a25-6) The ancients testify to the truth of what we are saying; for when they set out to enquire into the principles, elements, and causes of existing things, they set out to enquire into the principles and beginnings[16] of substance – not the principles of qualities, quantities, or the like. The difference between the two investigations – i.e. the investigation into the number of the genera of existing things and the investigation into the number of the principles of existing things – has been explained here.[17] For the principles are of substance alone, and every substance's principle is enquired into in so far as it [i.e. the substance] is numerically one. But the genera stand in thought[18] as the result of obtaining what has been collected from particulars each of which is similar to the other.

2,13 (1069a26-8) But people today, since they are preoccupied with logical exercise,[19] posit general things as more fitting than particulars to be substances, so that they even posit general things as the principles[20] of particular things. For they posit universal man as the principle of Socrates or Plato, and the horse in general[21] as the principle of *this* horse or *that* horse. **(1069a28-31)** But the ancients followed the senses, because at their time philosophy had just been recently [founded], and they posited particular things as more fitting to be principles of substance. And since they posited fire, earth,[22] water, and air as the principles of substance, they did not posit earth in general, fire in general, or the two other [elements] in general as the elements of the existing things – nor did they posit body in general as that element, but rather *this* fire,[23] *this* earth, *this* water, and *this* air.

2,21 We have already sometimes theorized about the issue, namely which of these two groups is more correct in its statements – those who posit general things as prior in existence, or those who posit particular things [as prior in existence]. When we continue[24] what we set out to do, nothing will hinder our investigation of this. For now, it is sufficient to recall that anyone enquiring into the principles of existing things should necessarily enquire into the principles of substance.

2,27 (1069a30-3) There are altogether three substances. Everyone agrees about two of them, because they are both sensible, falling under the sense of vision: one of them is perduring in the same state, and the other is changing. That which is perduring[25] is the substance of the celestial bodies, while the perishable one is the substance of whatever goes about on[26] the earth, such as[27] plants and animals. This substance alone[28] is the substance whose elements and foundations have been enquired into in earlier discussions.[29] It has become clear that it is[30] either composed of many things – namely of earth, fire, and the rest of the four [elements] – or[31] of other things, simpler[32] and fewer in number; or [composed] of at least one thing, which sometimes expands and becomes rarefied, and sometimes contracts **[3]** and becomes dense.[33]

3,1 These are two of the three substances besides which there are no other substances. **(1069a33)** The third substance is unmoved, eternal, everlasting, and does not admit of any type of change;[34] neither [change] which bodies going about on the earth such as plants and animals undergo until they are brought out of their natures altogether and perish, nor change in place, which is the only [type of change] that these bodies share with the aforementioned celestial bodies. For it was posited as impossible for the celestial bodies' substance to be in different states at different times. However, it is not impossible for it to be in different places at different times. Its nature is founded on this.[35]

3,7 (1069a33-4) The unmoved and incorporeal substance is excluded[36] from any change. Therefore, we say that this substance is distinct from sensible substance; but we do not claim that it is distinct from it in place. For it would be false [to say that] a substance which has no place at all – and which is not contained by the boundaries of body[37] that contain all things[38] that have a place – is distinct in place.

3,11 But when we say that this substance is distinct from sensible substance, we indicate a certain difference between the two substances. For since we consider one of these two substances to be completely unmoved and unchanging, not receptive of alteration in any respect – neither by another, nor by itself – and[39] since we find that all sensible substances[40] are sometimes in one state, sometimes in another, we would be correct to consider the former intelligible substance to be so distinct from the latter sensible substance[41] that there is nothing in common between them at all[42] – neither by nature, nor by any accident. Our aim in the present discussion is to speak about this first, unmoved substance and to relate accurately everything that our predecessors thought about it.

3,19 (1069a34-6) Regarding what these people thought, some of them divided this[43] substance into two, and some of them posited it as a single nature. Those who divided it into two[44] are the ones who said that Ideas and mathematical extensions[45] are intelligible[46] substances that are prior to and principles of sensible substances. Those who posited that there is one [kind of] intelligible substance are those who presumed that the mathematical extensions are the substances and gave up on Ideas.[47]

3,23 (1069a36-b2) Sensible substance needs natural science, since that substance in general cannot avoid motion. The former substance [i.e. the intelligible substance], as it were, needs a science more venerable than natural science, because the two substances have nothing in common at all; not in accident, not in place, not in time, not in any kind of change,[48] not in growth, and not in decline. Nor do the two have one principle from which they were created; the first [substance] does not have a principle at all, and the second [substance]'s principle is the first substance. They are also[49] not known by a single science, because one of them is sensible and the other is intellectual. That substance which is unchanging and unmoved is prior by nature to changing substance, which flows like a liquid.

3,29 Since most of what is in us is fashioned by sensible substance, let us discuss it first, given its affinity and resemblance to us. **(1069b3-5)** We already discussed it sufficiently in the *Physics* and explained that no sensible substance can avoid being changing, and that its change is from contraries to contraries. Change does not come **[4]** from all [types of] contraries, but only from proper proximate contraries.[50] Hence white comes from what is not white, but not from whatever is not white (for it does not come from sound, sound being not white) but from black, red, or other colours like these.

Chapter 2[51]

4,3 (1069b7-9) We have explained that under these two contraries must necessarily be another, third substratum. For one of the contraries does not carry the other, but that which carries both is that nature which sheds[52] one contrary and receives the other. **(1069b9-13)** There, when discussing kinds of change, we stated that their number in this substance [i.e. the corruptible sensible substance] is four:[53] (i) change in a thing's definition (which makes what it is known[54]). For example, a human comes-to-be from [something] other than human, or water [comes-to-be] from [something that is] not water, but from air. This change is sometimes called[55] 'coming-to-be' and sometimes [called] 'perishing'. (ii) The second [type of] change is in quality and is called 'alteration'. (iii) The third [type] is in quantity, and is sometimes called 'increase' and sometimes 'decrease'. (iv) The fourth [type] is in place, and is the transition from place to place.

4,10 We do not consider this last,[56] fourth type of change we mentioned as impossible for celestial bodies, because they are also[57] moved from place to place and, in a certain respect, from contraries to contraries (for a type of contrariety – according to opposition[58] – exists also in places, like forward or backward motion). No motion in place can avoid these directions.[59] What is more, a pair of contraries is insufficient in this [type of] change; **(1069b13-15)** but just like the other [types of] changes, it needs a body that underlies the pair of contraries to be moved from one to the other.

4,16 However, this celestial body is different from the body that underlies things that come-to-be and perish. For the body that underlies things that come-to-be and perish changes completely,[60] while a celestial body changes only in position.[61] All things upon which its or any of its parts' nature are constituted are unchanging and unmoving. But it has, however slightly, a semblance of being in potentiality or actuality, for its parts will first be potentially in a certain place, and afterwards be there in actuality.

4,21 (1069b15-18) This thing – i.e. going out from potentiality to actuality – is common to all sensible substances: e.g. going out from potentially white to actually white, going out from potentially two cubits [long] to actually two cubits [long], and going out from being potentially Socrates to being actually Socrates (for the semen from which Socrates came-to-be was already potentially Socrates).[62]

4,25 (1069b26-7) The well-known problem[63] raised by all natural [scientists], namely how can an existing thing come-to-be from that which is non-existent, is herein removed. **(1069b18-20)** For a thing that comes-to-be does not come-to-be from what is non-existing absolutely, but from a [thing] that is non-existing in one respect and existing in another respect. For a thing from which what comes-to-be comes-to-be is potentially the same thing that comes-to-be, but actually, it is not.

4,29 (1069b24-6)[64] In all changing things, that which changes cannot avoid being a certain body. Even everlasting substances – which do not receive coming-to-be or perishing – cannot avoid [having] a body because they change in place.

4,32 (1069b27-8) But the non-existing is threefold: one is that which does not exist at all; another is the privation that is placed opposite to the thing that comes-to-be; and the third [is] that which is in potentiality.[65] Now that which comes-to-be cannot come-to-be **[5]** according to the first two senses; for it[66] cannot come-to-be from that which does not exist at all or from privation, as it persists.[67] However, it[68] can come-to-be from a body that receives change when it [i.e. the body] is potentially that thing that comes-to-be, but actually it is not it.[69]

5,4 Yet that this is so in a certain case does not mean that any thing can randomly come-to-be from any body.[70] For a boat cannot be built out of stones and a human cannot be begotten from anything. Rather, a boat can be built of wood; a house – of stones; and a human – out of human semen. But not every human is [born] from just any human semen, but each individual human comes-to-be from [specific] semen. A horse also [comes-to-be] from horse's semen [and so forth].

5,8 (1069b29-32) If the body from which things that come-to-be come-to-be were one and the same in all its states,[71] and did not have fundamentally [and] by nature a varying *logos*,[72] then plurality – which we see that was already created – could not have been created from it. For when a thing is truly one, it cannot receive plurality; it needs to have fundamental potentiality that will enable it to be [both] one *and* receive plurality. It would be incorrect to say that the Creator [first] rendered something to be incapable of receiving a possibility for plurality, and then, coercively, brought plurality out of it, for that is unfitting of the wise.[73]

5,14 (1069b20-1)[74] Anaxagoras thinks that the Creator is one, and that He is wise.[75] But when he was asked how come there is a plurality of things that come-to-be, given that the Creator is one and the body from which coming-to-be occurs does not receive plurality, he replied: 'the thought of the Creator; like a mason, a carpenter, or a craftsman, He takes a certain body, separates it off as needed, connects it, conjoins it, and compounds it in different forms, according to what He needs.'[76] We do not find the thing to be as Anaxagoras said, for we find that the body has already completely changed: first into the four elements, and then into the plants and the animals. The plurality of things that come-to-be comes from two things: the Creator, in the plurality of forms He gave the body, and the body, for the body has been set as a recipient. This is like if you imagine a person take a piece of wax and make many forms of animals, plants, and inanimate things from it. For the plurality in these forms comes-to-be due to two things: one is the craftsman[77] who crafts them, and the other is the wax upon which his craft works. The craftsman[, because] he crafts many forms, and the wax, because it can receive a plurality of forms.[78]

Chapter 3[79]

5,26 (1069b35-1070a4) In addition to the other things we mentioned in the *Physics*, we also explained that forms[80] cannot come-to-be (i.e. are not created in the manner of coming-to-be) by themselves,[81] and neither can that which receives them.[82] For round, which comes-to-be in a gold [ring], cannot come-to-be as it is in its substance by itself through a craftsman.[83] Nor can the [ring's] gold come-to-be as it is in its substance through a craftsman. Rather, the gold [in the ring] comes from a mineral [i.e. the mineral gold], and comes-to-be round through a craftsman. Whoever maintains that each of the two [viz. round and gold] comes-to-be separately says something that can be extended ad infinitum. For if a recipient body is created in the manner of coming-to-be, then clearly its coming-to-be would be from one recipient body, and its perishing, when it perishes, would be into another [recipient] body [and so forth].

6,1 (1070a4-9) We have already explained that every individual natural thing comes-to-be from something like it, to which solely its name applies.[84] This is so not only for things that come-to-be by nature (e.g. human comes-to-be from human), but also, at times, for things that come-to-be by art. For a house is, indeed, created from a house, i.e. an embodied house [comes-to-be] from a non-embodied house.[85] Art is a principle of one [thing] in another [thing], while nature is a principle in the thing itself. Everything that is created in natural things through altering its natural shape, and [every artificial thing that is created through] impairments, come-to-be when the body from which what comes-to-be comes-to-be is impeded from proceeding along its [regular] course.[86] It is more fitting to ascribe this cause to the privation of a principle, rather than to call it a principle. Thus, e.g. there would seem to be an impairment occurring to a ship because of its pilot's[87] weakness in piloting it when he is impeded by a certain impediment.

6,10 Accordingly, all substances that exist are three:[88] the first is completely unchanging and unmoved. This substance is not apprehended by the senses, but is rather apprehended by the intellect. The other two substances are subject to the senses: one of them is perduring, and the other is perishable. **(1070a9-13)** You should divide perishable sensible substance into three substances: one as matter,[89] i.e. the body that receives form; the second as form; and the third is that which is composed of both. These three substances, as it were, transform so as to exist as a this-something in itself.[90] Among all of substance's properties, this [i.e. being a this-something in itself] is the most proprietary to substance. For you, when you refer to any other attributes [of a thing], [know that] it is not a 'this-something' due to them.[91]

6,16 Among [perishable sensible] substances, the farthest away from being a this-something in itself is matter;[92] for matter is formless in its nature. However, it is also a thing that desires to seem as a this-something in itself and to be counted as a substance. It is as if it refuses to be seen so long as its nakedness of form perdures, ashamed of exhibiting its meagreness and poverty. Sense does not apprehend it unless[93] it assumes a form, but intellect apprehends the privation of form from it by analogy,[94] and knows that it is 'bastard',[95] i.e. it pretends to have what it does not [have],[96] because it does not have a [specific] form to rely upon. But once all forms are removed from it, it retreats[97] to it[self]. When it retreats to the first[98] matter, sometimes it exists in a matter that is close to everything else with respect to the power of apprehension. For *this* matter [viz. that which can be apprehended by the senses] is a this-something in itself, since it has a form, like the copper of sculptures or the boards of a ship. This is more so for matter in things that are distinguished rather than united [in their manner of composition], e.g. bricks or stones in a house. Accordingly, from concealment, weakness, and remoteness matter transforms so that it may seem as a this-something in itself, though simultaneously escaping from being seen, not maintaining stability even for a short time so as to be apprehended by the eye.

6,29 The form that covers matter, and by which [matter] assumes a form, is more fittingly a this-something in itself. But of all substances, that which holds priority in being a this-something in itself is the particular composite substance, such as so-and-so and so-and-so among people, or other particulars among other [kinds of] things.

6,32 (1070a13-17) Now, we should start to enquire[99] whether it is possible for a certain form that is naked of body to exist; or [rather] whether every form is in body, so that every form is of a composite substance; or perhaps it is [7] possible for [each form] to exist in thought,[100] but it is impossible for it to exist separately. We say that artificial forms are like this [i.e. the latter option], as is clear in their case; for the form of a bed, e.g. cannot avoid existing either in the wood or in the carpenter's thought; and the form of health cannot avoid existing either in the body or in the doctor's thought. These things neither come-to-be nor perish, but they exist or do not exist in a different respect,[101] as we have said many times.

7,6 (1070a17-20) But we cannot escape [from saying] that some forms in nature are abstracted[102] from a body, like soul or intellect. This is why he who spoke of Ideas[103] posited Ideas of natural things and kept away from positing Ideas of artificial things. But we see that most of the forms of things in nature are involved with body,[104] like the form of fire and the form of flesh. On the whole, it is impossible for any form of a particular substance found in nature to subsist without a body. **(1070a21-4)** Any form that is an efficient mover undoubtedly exists before what is created from it, even if it is in a body. Thus, Socrates' father was before Socrates and Terah[105] was before the sculptures he made. Forms of composite substances necessarily exist together with them, not before them; e.g. Socrates' health is together with Socrates, not before him, and the shape of *this* globe is together with it, not before it.

7,14 (1070a24-7) We ought to theorize whether or not any form eventually remains after the composition perishes. It seems that among some of them there is nothing to prevent them from remaining. Soul, for example, is perhaps so; but if not all of it is so, then its intellect alone. It would seem impossible for [soul] to remain in its entirety.

7,17 (1070a27-30)[106] But if the form that existed before [its successor] is the agent for the formation of that [i.e. the succeeding] form – so that a human is indeed created from a human, and a horse is indeed created from a horse, and in every case the particular from a particular (for the universal does not beget and is not begotten, but what begets and is begotten is indeed a 'this' and a 'that') – what need do we have, then, concerning coming-to-be, for the Idea Plato spoke about? And what need does a begetting[107] form have for another form [viz. the Platonic Idea] as a model for it, given that it is itself a model for that which is created from it? For the name and definition will be common to both, and their form is one, and it is of the nature of the begetting form to beget another form like it. And we find that art does not need an Idea to set as a model for anything it makes, so that, for example, when it sets out to make a chair, it is incapable of making it unless it has a model. For art in itself is the model for the chair, because the form of the chair subsists in the thought of the carpenter who makes it, just as the medical art is the form of health, and carpentry is the form of a house.

7,27[108] This argument is persuasive[109] for discarding the [Platonic] Ideas, but its author neglected[110] the great number of animals that are created by [things] different from their like [i.e. their co-species], in spite of their great number. For we see a species of hornets that is begotten from bodies of dead horses; and we see bees begotten from bodies of dead cattle; and we see frogs begotten from putrescence; and we see mosquitoes – which are a kind **[8]** of a small-bodied fly – begotten from wine after it is spoiled. And we do not find that nature originates these things from things like them in form.

8,2 And we know that in the semen or seed of every single animal or plant there are *logoi*[111] proper to each, through which only those animals and plants which are begotten from it are begotten and no others. As a result, a horse cannot come-to-be from a man's semen, nor a man from a horse's semen, nor one plant from the seed of another. Where are the counterparts[112] of these *logoi* in that from which this [spontaneously generated] animal is begotten? Unless a suitable *logos*, ready to create whichever animal species is possible for it once it found proper matter out of which it could create that animal, was already set in nature, [the spontaneously generated animal] would not be brought into actuality.[113]

8,7 Do not be deceived by contempt[114] for these animals, but keep in mind that they fill us with admiration for the artisan; his skill in working upon clay is greater than his skill in his work upon gold and ivory. If you theorize meticulously about animals bigger than that [i.e. than spontaneously generated animals], you will find that nature proceeds according to the same course there too. It is necessary that there be *logoi* and forms[115] already set in nature, upon which it [i.e. nature] does its work. For if a man is indeed begotten by man, the father exerts no artistry[116] in this composition of his [i.e. the combination of matter and form], which cannot be in a different or better state than his own. He arrives at this state because certain *logoi* and forms were set in nature in each of the substances; not by the father's artistry, but from the *logoi*. A body can only work on the periphery of [another] body, but nature works on the body's magnitude as a whole.

8,16 There is nothing puzzling about nature not understanding the directing of its work towards the end aimed at, since it us unaware and does not think about its activity. This indicates to you that these *logoi* have been inspired[117] by a cause nobler, more venerable, and higher in rank than it [i.e. than nature],[118] namely the soul that is in the earth[119] which Plato thought had been created by the secondary gods, and Aristotle thought had been created by the sun and the inclined sphere. Therefore, it [i.e. nature] performs its activities and is directed[120] towards the aim without understanding it, just as we see inspired people talk and foretell the future without understanding what they are saying.

8,23 In sum, *logoi* and forms must necessarily exist in nature, since [otherwise] a thing would need something like it in order to be begotten, and not everything that is begotten has something like it from which it is begotten. But when we enquire into[121] a certain [individual] form, from which a certain actuality arises, we know that it [i.e. the actuality] is not created only by it [i.e. the individual form].[122] This form [i.e. the actualized form], then, is created as if it had been latent in something else, and it is truly latent in the begetting nature.

Chapter 4[123]

8,28 Since we set out to enquire into the first principle of existing things, it is appropriate for this enquiry that we first address preliminary questions in the manner I shall mention.

8,30 (1070a33-5)[124] The first thing [i.e. problem] that I should address preliminarily is the discussion [of the question] whether all existing things can have one and the same principle – so that that [same] principle is the principle of substance, the principle of relation, the principle of quantity, the principle of quality [and so forth] – or every genus has a different principle. **[9]** Now if 'principle' is said in many respects – such as a thing from which motion starts; a thing for the sake of which what comes-to-be comes-to-be; and an element – this question should first aim at the elements: is the element of all existing things one, or does every genus have different elements?[125]

9,4 (1070a35-6) But it would be incorrect to say that all their elements are one and the same, so that substance, relation, quantity, and quality [and so forth] have the same elements. **(1070a36-b4)** Should someone think that this is so, we would ask them:[126] what is this element (if there is one), or what are these elements (if there are many)? And is it external to the ten genera, or within some of them? If it is external to them, it would need to be another genus besides the ten [genera]. It [i.e. the 'eleventh' genus] would have to be prior to the ten, for an element is prior to things of which it is an element. But no genus whatsoever is prior to substance (we have already explained this earlier in another place in our discussion).[127] **(1070b4-7)** If [the adversary] keeps away from this [i.e. from the opinion that the element is external to the ten genera], and posits the element under substance, it would follow for him that the element of substance is [also] the element of relation, quality, quantity, action, affection, and having [and so forth]. It would also follow for him – and reason rejects this – that the element of substance falls under the [category of] substance; but elements are prior to and simpler than things that are composed of them, just as letters are prior to a word [composed of them].

9,14 (1070b7-8) Let us suppose that the elements are not under a certain genus and ask the author of this statement [i.e. that all things have the same elements] if they are among things whose description includes all existing things, like 'one'. If he says that the elements of all things are like that, we say that simple things are more fitting than composite things to have descriptions like these. From his statement,[128] it follows that simple [things] would not be elements of composite [things], because composite things would [also] be thus described; but [that would also mean] that composite [things] are elements of simple [things].

9,18 Further, if 'existing' or 'one' were a principle of the ten genera, and if principles are different from things that come-to-be from them (e.g. a point is different from a line, 'one' is different from a number, and creating is different from created things), then 'existing' or 'one' would not be the essence of substance, not the essence of quantity, and not the essence of quality [and so forth], otherwise one existent [would actually be] two existents.[129] **(1070b9-10)** Accordingly, it is impossible for the elements of all things to be one and the same,[130] except in an analogous sense.

9,24 (1070b11-13) If we continue what we have already supposed, it is appropriate to explain that all existing things have [altogether] three principles: form, matter, and privation. For example, in sensible substance hot is as form, cold as privation, and matter is that which has both of these potentially. **(1070b20-1)** In the realm of quality: among colours, whiteness is as form, blackness as privation, and surface (as analogous to matter) is the thing that underlies them both; [another example:] light as form, darkness as privation, and the body that receives light is what underlies them both.

9,30 (1070b16-19) It is impossible for the elements to be absolutely the same for all things; but in an analogous sense[131] it is appropriate for them [i.e. the same elements for all] to exist. **(1070b22-5)** But now we do not seek the element of existing things, but rather intend to enquire into their principle.[132] Both are their [i.e. the existing things'] causes; but **[10]** while a principle can exist outside a thing [of which it is a principle] – e.g. the moving cause[133] – elements can only inhere[134] in things that are [made] of them. Nothing prevents an element to be called a principle, but a principle is not undoubtedly an element[135] (for it is possible for a moving principle to be outside the [thing that is] moved[136]).

10,4 (1070b28-32) But in natural things, the proximate mover[137] has the same form [of its effect] (for indeed man is begotten by man). In things that are made according to thought,[138] it [i.e. the mover] is the form or the privation, e.g. medicine or ignorance of it, and carpentry or ignorance of it.[139] **(1070b33-5)** In many things the moving cause is the form, just as medicine is in a certain respect health, because it is its mover,[140] and the form of a house is in a certain respect carpentry. And indeed, man is begotten by man. Our intention [here] is not to enquire into the proximate mover, but to enquire into the first mover, from which all things are moved.

Chapter 5[141]

10,11 (1070b36-1071a3) Clearly, it [i.e. the first principle] is a substance, for it is the principle of substance, and the principle of substance can only be a substance. It is the principle of substance and the principle of all existing things. The apprehensiveness in asserting this in the past was mistaken,[142] for the rest of the things are modifications[143] or motions of substance. We should investigate what this substance, which moves the entire body, is: should we suppose that it is a soul, an intellect, or [something] else? [This,] after being careful and cautious not to ascribe[144] to the first principle any accident that happens[145] to other existing things.

10,17 (1071a5-7) But in other existents one can find potentiality, being in different states at different times, and not persisting in one state. Things that come-to-be and perish exist in this way; for in them you find the same thing sometimes in potentiality and sometimes in actuality. For example, wine sometimes exists in actuality – after it is fermented and becomes intoxicating

– and sometimes exists in potentiality, when the moisture from which it is begotten is in the grapevine itself.[146] [Similarly,] flesh is sometimes in actuality and sometimes in potentiality, in the elements from which it is begotten.

10,23 (1071a7-11) When we say 'potentially' and 'actuality', we mean nothing but 'matter' and 'form'. By 'form' we mean the form that can exist separately, or[147] that which is composed of form and matter.[148] 'Separate' is, e.g. light or darkness if they could be separated from air; that which is composed of the two [i.e. form and matter] is, e.g. a healthy body and a sick body. By 'matter' I mean the thing to which both states can be predicated, just like a body is sometimes healthy and sometimes sick. **(1071a11-14)** And this thing, which is [sometimes] in actuality and [sometimes] in potentiality, may vary not only in the elements[149] that exist in the things which are composed of them – i.e. form and matter – but also in external things that move them,[150] whose matter is not the [same] matter of the things that come-to-be from them, and whose form is not [the same as] their form, but different from it.

10,30 When you set out to investigate the first cause, you should keep in mind that some moving causes have the same form[151] as the moved thing [and are] close to it, while some are farther[152] from it. **(1071a14-17)** A proximate cause **[11]** is, e.g. the father [to the son]; the sun is a farther cause; and the inclined sphere is [a cause that is] farther than the sun.[153] These things are not causes of a created thing in the sense of matter, form, or privation; rather, they are movers. And they are movers not by being of the same form [and] close like the father; rather, they are farther and stronger with respect to actuality, because they are also the principles of the proximate causes.[154]

11,5 (1071a17-22) In investigating the first cause, you should also keep in mind that some principles are universal and some are particular [and] individual,[155] and that the principles in truth are not the universal [principles] but the particular [and] individual [principles]; just like 'this' is the principle of 'this', and a specific person is the cause of a specific person – not the universal, because the universal does not exist, but this [man] is this [man's] father, and, e.g. this B is the cause of this BA.[156] **(1071a27-9)** But if a universal is posited as a cause, it would be a cause of a universal, e.g. substance to substance and quantity to quantity. But we should seek the true principles in particular things. For matter is not a person's matter in an absolute manner, but your matter is your matter and my matter is my matter; similarly, your form is your form, and my form is my form – not the universal form, but the particular [form]. Also, the mover [is like this].[157]

11,12 (1071b1-2) We have just explained how the principles of all things can be one and the same, and how they can be not the same.[158] **(1071a33-5)** The principles of all things can be one and the same in three ways: universally; analogously;[159] and from the [fact] that the principles of substance are the principles of all things. (In other things, [the predicate] 'existent' comes from substance. And if they 'are' from substance, it has already been explained that they 'are' from the principles of substance).[160]

11,17 We should first remember and keep all these things [that we said], and then set out towards the principle that we are seeking. Let us return to what was already mentioned a little bit so that it is assured.

Chapter 6[161]

11,19 (1071b3-5) We have already said that all substances are [of] three [kinds] and that two of them are natural substances and the third substance is unmoved. The two natural substances were already explained above, and we enquired into them sufficiently in our previous remarks. At present, we seek the substance that is unmoved and also unceasing. From now on, we shall enquire[162] whether it is possible for there to be a substance unworn by time, and which is not subject to change and alteration,[163] but remains in the same state eternally.

11,23 We already said many times that it is impossible to constitute this principle upon a demonstration, because demonstration comes only from causes and principles, and it is impossible for the first cause – which is[164] the first principle – to have a prior cause or principle. But perhaps we can achieve our intention in the following manner: since we think that the first principle of all existing things should have two attributes[165] – one is to be eternal and the other is to be unmoved – we ought to enquire into each of the two attributes separately. First, we shall enquire[166] whether it is possible for there to be some eternal substance, and then we shall enquire if it is possible for there to be an unmoved substance.[167] When we proceed in this manner, we will achieve our intention easily, for our enquiry will be in the manner of someone who sets out to carry something heavier than he is able to lift, and so divides it and then has the strength to carry it. The weight of the enquiry will be easier for us if we proceed in this manner.[168]

11,33 (1071b5-6) We say: if all substances were perishable, and if all substances were prior among all existing things, then it would follow that all existing things are perishable. And if the issue is as we said earlier, namely that the All is [either] united **[12]** or constituted upon succession and order,[169] then substance is its root, its foundation, and the beginning of its parts. So if every substance were to perish, it would have to follow that none of the things that are dependent upon substance would remain. Whoever reflected[170] about this matter even a little bit would find that substances and other existents must necessarily have a substance that persists in its existence and from which they have their [own] existence.

12,4 It is not puzzling that among existents there should be an eternal substance, for we already find here[171] [i.e. in the natural world] things of an accidental nature that are eternal and do not perish. **(1071b6-9)** For motion is not an abstract, self-subsisting nature,[172] but undoubtedly [belongs] to body or to substance. And time is even less[173] so [viz. an abstract, self-subsisting nature], since time is closely related to motion and cannot avoid being either its quantity or its modification.[174] It is impossible to predicate either coming-to-be or perishing to time or motion – not [even] if one has extreme love of dispute and dialectic.[175] For if we suppose that time comes-to-be, it would follow that time be before it came-to-be; and if we suppose that it perishes, it would then remain[176] after it perished. We already said this in the past in the natural treatises, and we mention it [i.e. this argument] now because we specifically and necessarily need it for what we are about to enquire into regarding things on which knowledge of the first principle relies.

12,13 Motion and time do not come-to-be or perish; nor can we make any argument that assumes this.[177] Concerning the notion of time, this is very clear, for the statements 'there was a moment before which there was no time' and 'there will be a moment after which there will be no time' are utterances whose elements contradict their proposition.[178] For everything that is similar to these utterances[179] – i.e. 'when', 'was', 'will be', 'before', and 'after' – which the author of this proposition cannot find a way to avoid making use of, are, indeed, parts of time, limits of time, or significations linked to time. It is impossible for anyone who employs one of these terms in order to affirm that time is created not to posit [the existence of] time before its creation. And anyone who employs some of [these] utterances as something through which he intends to affirm that time perishes, it would follow for him – just like in the first example – that time persists after its perishing.

12,20 (1071b9-10) Now if time is eternal, then motion is undoubtedly eternal (for indeed time is its quantity or modification).[180] We should then enquire into motion itself.[181] We say that motion cannot avoid being either unceasing or created. If it is created, its mover already existed before it. But how is it possible for us to imagine that its mover is eternal and that motion did not come from it eternally? There is nothing to hinder [motion] from coming from [the mover], nor did an accident occur in one of its [i.e. the mover's] states after which it [*sc.* the mover] created it [i.e. the motion], because everything that is created is indeed created from it [i.e. the mover], and there is nothing besides it to impede it or impel it.

12,26 It is impossible for us to say[182] that [at first] it was not within its power to have [something] come-to-be from it,[183] and then, later, it was within its power, because that would necessitate an alteration in it, and would necessitate there being something other than it that had altered it. If someone said[184] that it [i.e. the mover] is hindered by something, then he would add a further absurdity – in addition to the absurdity of affirming the existence of something other than it – because it would follow that the hindering cause is stronger than it. But how would it be possible for this cause [i.e. the hindering cause] to hinder it [from causing motion] for an infinite duration and then finally let it go? It is impossible for this to be so unless [the hindering cause] was altered or changed. It is also impossible for that hinderer to persist in the same state while the mover sometimes abstains from [causing] motion, and sometimes causes motion.

12,33 Now motion can only be created **[13]** by motion; one who says this [i.e. that motion came-to-be] necessitates that motion already existed before motion came-to-be, because alteration, change, and resting are species of motion and succeed it.

13,3 It is impossible for that which is moved[185] to be anything but a body. If we say that that body[186] was not created, but was moved from [a state of] rest, we need to make known the cause for which it was moved and changed from rest to motion. If we say that this body is created, then its motion would have been created before its body,[187] and this would be nothing but [saying that] there was motion before motion. And it is impossible for us to posit that motion was created from rest. Were we to suppose that the body could be created from something that does not exist at all, then these two propositions would be combined, and the starting point[188] of the creation of the body would be the starting point of the creation of its motion. Since this is impossible, nothing can be created out of something that does not exist at all, and indeed it is impossible for motion to be brought from rest.

13,10 Now that it has been explained that motion is eternal and that time belongs to motion, what follows from this, as well as the specific discussion of these notions, will be easier for us. Now if motion is eternal, then the moved body is [also] eternal, for if this is the case with an accident, then it is all the more so the case with a substance. **(1071b10-11)** The first motion is motion in place, while the second and third motions have other properties.[189] We already explained that some motions in place are rectilinear and others are circular. Only the latter can be continuous,[190] since other [i.e. rectilinear] motions are all halted by a stop (if you remember what was said by the demonstrative necessity in the *Physics*).[191] Continuity is a necessary attribute of eternal things, since no one can say that something that changes and stops[192] is eternal. Let us say this also in another way: time is continuous, since it is impossible for us to think of a segment cut out of it. Accordingly, we must also say that motion is continuous, for time is created from motion. If of all [kinds of] motion, only circular motion is continuous, we ought to posit circular motion as eternal. It follows that the mover of this motion is eternal, since it is impossible for something that is not eternal to be a cause of eternal motion. It is never the case that an inferior thing is a cause of something superior.[193]

13,25 We have now explained sufficiently that the first mover is eternal. Since it is so, it follows necessarily that it is an active cause of everlasting motion.[194] **(1071b12-14)** For if it were a mover, but if it would not move[195] everlastingly, then clearly its moving would also not be eternal.[196] **(1071b14-16)** We already explained that this is impossible, since there would be no benefit in eternal substances if we were to posit them like those who said that Ideas subsist apart as stationary models.[197] **(1071b16-17)** But if they are eternal natures [that are] prior to the sensible [natures], we ought not suppose this nature to be inactive [and] idle,[198] but rather as capable of moving and altering [i.e. capable of causing motion and alteration].

13,31 (1071b17-19) When I say 'capable', I do not mean to say that it [i.e. the eternal nature] goes out of potentiality to actuality; for we should keep it away from potentiality altogether. This substance should not be counted among substances that have both potentiality and actuality, for it is impossible for the first principle to be an existent of the [same] nature as that which has potentiality.[199] For it would follow from this **[14]** that this principle needs a different principle, which is in actuality, so that it [i.e. the latter] will be that which brings it [i.e. the former] from potentiality to actuality. It is impossible for something potential to bring itself into actuality, since a potential thing is a weak nature and essentially imperfect. Indeed, perfection occurs to it when it becomes actual, but in some cases it is possible that it will not become actual. For that which is in potentiality inclines towards one of two opposing sides, and [even] if it has a greater inclination towards one of the two sides, it [still] cannot avoid having a relation to the other [side]. **(1071b19-22)** Therefore, among existents there ought to exist a principle whose actuality is substance.[200] And since it is eternal, it is immaterial, because anything that has matter has some potentiality in its nature.

14,9 (1071b22-6; 1072a3-4) However, someone could proceed according to language[201] and say that something that is potential in its nature is in no way inferior to something in actuality, for the relation between potential and actual things is like the relation between early and late. When something of its nature [i.e. of the nature of potentiality] is in actuality, it undoubtedly has a potentiality that existed before it [i.e. actuality]. But it is *not* undoubtedly necessary for something that exists potentially to be brought into actuality. But this is apparent only in sensible things, for they are [things] in which both things – i.e. what is in potentiality and what is in actuality – exist together, for in these things potentiality always precedes actuality. However, if you compare potentiality and actuality in an absolute sense, you will find that actuality is prior by nature, since actuality is the activator and the mover of that which is in potentiality.

14,17 (1071b26-8) Indeed, the statement that the potential is prior to the actual is the stated view of people who hold the opinions of the ancient theologians, who took the birth of the world to be out of darkness and the abyss,[202] as Hesiod did. It is [also] the stated view of those who hold the opinions of ancient natural scientists, viz. those who posited matter as the most prior thing. For the proposition that all things exist together is like the proposition about infinite indivisible particles and other [views] that all these people stated. **(1071b28-31)** Indeed, the general error in all this is that they posited matter as the superior and prior principle. But how is it possible for matter to be moved without having some prior cause that moves it? For you will not find any matter that is moved by itself to a form. Rather, just as wood is not moved by itself towards the form of the chair, but [rather] by the artistry of a carpenter, the blood of the menses [does not move itself either]. What is more, it is not possible for earth to grow any plant by itself, nor [can] any seed [grow by itself], but the sun moves earth, the other elements, and the seeds for the coming-to-be of plants.[203]

14,28 Accordingly, we find that, as the power of truth will have it, what results [from the previous discussion] is that all who posit matter as the most prior existent are compelled to acknowledge a cause that is in actuality, even if they do not mean to. **(1071b31-3)** Thus Leucippus mingles everlasting motion into indivisible particles; Plato places confused[204] motion prior to the god's command;[205] **(1072a5-7)** Empedocles prescribes love and strife; and Anaxagoras discusses the intellect.

15,1 (1071b33-4) The cause of this eternal motion and the meaning of their term 'eternal' should have rather been made known.[206] For we do not find any [type of] motion which could be eternal except for circular motion in place. The reason for this is that it alone – unlike other motions – is continuous. **(1071b34-6)** We find no one who makes known whether the first motion of moved bodies is natural or besides nature. For we do not find anything that just happens[207] to move; rather, [things are moved] by nature, by intellect, or by coercion (when [one thing's] state is contrary to the other's state). **(1071b36-7)** We also do not find them say which of these motions is first – that which is by nature, that which is from the intellect, or that which is coerced – for all this makes an enormous difference.[208]

15,9 (1071b37-1072a3) But you, when you examine their account, [you will realize that] they posit the confused and disorderly motion[209] as the first motion. Then, after that, they put the ordered motion alongside the soul, the sphere, and the order of existing things. We find no argument to affirm that something disorderly is prior to something ordered. Rather we find that an ordered body is prior to that which is disorderly and that the sphere and all the celestial bodies revolve in everlasting cycles – some are lengthy, and some take a short time – which return with the utmost accurateness and precision to the point from which their cycle started.

15,15 (1072a9-10) The cause of that whose motion is everlasting and [always] in the same state ought to be posited as a cause whose state with respect to the movable bodies remains the same. **(1072a10-12)** As for that whose motion varies at various times, the state of the cause which moves it when it [i.e. the motion] varies is like the state of that which is itself moved. But we do not find that any body that comes-to-be and perishes persists in the same state at a single time. Therefore, these bodies need a cause that varies as they vary. Now since [the process of] coming-to-be and perishing is everlasting and uninterrupted, the cause which acts upon it should not only vary, but [also] be everlasting. **(1072a12-15)** It necessarily follows, then, that the variation of this cause is from itself [i.e. intrinsic],[210] and its [ever]lastingness is from a different cause, which comes either from the first cause or from another, different cause; but indeed, it should necessarily come from the first cause, for this cause is the cause of [both] its own everlastingness and the everlastingness of the second cause.[211] **(1072a15-17)** This is why this cause is better and more dignified. For you do not find any [other] cause to be perduring and remaining in the same state forever, as we find with the first cause. The special property of the second cause is variation, and the special property of the first cause is everlastingness – so that both[212] are necessarily the causes of everlastingness and variation.

15,27 (1072a17-18) Do you think that this account is merely hypothetical? The senses testify to the contrary; for not one [person] can be found to be affected by the blindness of his sense and intellect to the point that he does not see or understand that the first sphere, which contains all [other] spheres, has the same motion forever, and that the spheres of the planets **[16]** have varying motion forever, where some pass before others and others opposite[213] to each other. All things that come-to-be and perish receive [their motion] from them, i.e. from the everlasting motion and the varying motion. **(1072a18-21)**[214] Since this is so, what need do we have to enquire into other principles, give up these principles, and depend upon what the poets say and upon the creation of the existing things from darkness and the absurd mixture,[215] and in general – things that are naturally potential rather than actual?

Chapter 7[216]

16,5 We should rather rid it of all this and say that **(1072a21-2)** there exists a body that is moved without rest, and this motion is circular. This was explained not only in argument, but also in fact. **(1072a23)** If the motion is without rest, then that which is moved in it is eternal, and this is the first sphere. **(1072a23-4)** And if the motion of that which is moved is without rest, then clearly its mover's moving is [also] without rest and uninterrupted. Now the fact that it [i.e. the mover] is eternal and everlasting is explained, but we should [also] explain [the fact] that it is unmoved, according to what we said earlier.[217]

16,10 (1072a24-6) We say: we have already explained that if something is composed of two things, and one of them can exist self-subsisting apart, then the other thing can also exist self-subsisting apart.[218] Now if a thing that both moves and is moved exists, and a thing that is only moved – without moving – exists [as well], it necessarily follows that an unmoved mover exists. For it is that which is by nature completely immaterial[219] and whose essence is actuality.[220]

16,15 (1072a26-7) One should not be puzzled that there is an unmoved mover, for every object of desire moves in this respect [i.e. as unmoved], and every object of intelligizing that moves us to perform certain actions is [also] a mover in this respect [i.e. unmoved]. But since there are numerous things that are our (and other animals') objects of desire or intellect, they are not unified in us.[221] For an object of desire immovably moves the desirer without having the same nature as things that are objects of intellect. But in first principles,[222] which are completely immaterial, an object of desire and an object of intellect are one and the same thing. It is an object of desire because it is an object of intellect,[223] not the other way around; namely, [it is not the case that] it is an object of intellect because it is an object of desire. We find this to be the same with desired things that are close to us, which we see, and these are [things] that we fancy or choose.[224] [Things] that we fancy are pleasant things, while [things] that we choose are things that are truly good. For we fancy things that we choose because we perceive them as good. We do not perceive them so because we set out to seek after them, but rather, we set out to seek after them because we perceive them so. But often we happen to perceive things like this differently from how they really are.[225] But what we perceive of the first desire (and[226] the first object of desire) is not different from how it truly is. It is truly as it seems to be, and whatever is intelligized of it is its [true] state. Therefore, [whatever] is intelligized of its state as good is truly good. This passion starts from what is intelligized[227] of the first cause, just as our appetite starts from thought and imagination. Every intellect's motion comes from the thing that it intelligizes, just as **[17]** thought's motion comes from the thing that is thought of, and imagination's motion comes from what is imagined.

17,2 (1072a31-4) There are many kinds of intelligized things, but the first intelligized thing is substance, and of substances, the [first is the] simplest [one], which is in actuality. This [substance] is unmixed with potentiality, and nothing is predicated of it or underlies it. For it is truly a one and simple nature. No material thing is simple or one per se;[228] but if potentiality exists in something, it includes plurality and compositeness. If you say that it [i.e. a material thing] is one, this is not so according to the true reference of 'one'. Although we often say that it [i.e. a material thing] is 'one' and that it is 'simple' – for we say 'one man' or 'one nation', and 'a simple premise' or 'a simple element' – when you understand [the issue] truly, you will find that what is said of them [i.e. that they are 'one'] is false, except for the first substance. For it [i.e. the first substance] is [the thing] about which 'one' [and] 'simple' are said truly. When you say that it is 'one', you are not referring to a quantity, like in the statements 'one nation' or 'one finger'. Nor is it the case when we say 'one man' or 'one horse', for in these things the existent [i.e. the subject] is one thing, and 'one' is another thing. But in this nature [i.e. the first substance], 'existence' and 'one' are one and the same.[229] The same holds for 'simple'. It [i.e. the first substance] is not said to be simple because something is composed of it, and not in comparison to something. Rather, it is simple by nature and no composition or multiplicity is apparent in it.[230]

17,15 (1072b1-3) This nature exists not only as the first mover of [all] things, but [also] as their perfection and their thing for the sake of which [i.e. the final cause]. **(1072a34-b1)** For a thing that is chosen for its own sake, whose beauty is in itself, and that is of ultimate excellence in itself, is indeed a principle and a perfection in itself.

17,18[231] The same holds for law, because law moves administration in the same way, and it [i.e. administration] comes-to-be from it [i.e. law]. For law is chosen and beautiful because of itself, and it is said to be of utmost excellence. Administrators are guided towards correct governance by theorizing about the law's order, and this is how they perfect and preserve administration. But law is not a substance. Rather, it is an activity of substance, [and as such it] withers and [only] subsists for a while. [On the other hand,] the first object of desire and the first mover is an immaterial substance, continuously lasting, simple, [and] whose nature is in actuality. This is like if we imagine the law through which administration subsists as living and self-intelligizing; through this [self-] intelligizing[232] it moves administration, and it truly moves as an object of desire.

17,24 Now God, may He be exalted, is ability, law, the cause of this world's order, intellect, truth, and the ultimate first. Every activity that comes from intellect is knowledge and thought.[233] And since we say that intellect's activity is [its] substance, it follows that the first cause's substance is knowledge and thought, the order of existing things comes from it, and it is that which everything that is posterior to it desires – some closer, some farther, like what is found in political administration.[234] For some people in the city are close to perfection and some fall short of it. We ought to consider this passion here[235] as similar to that which is found in a man who pursues the activity of law as a result of his appetite for it and for living according to it. For every adherence and servitude is by volition, and the choice [in this case] results from love and passion for this principle, whose **[18]** activity he pursues.

18,1 (1072b3-4) Someone who understands that all love for the first cause [comprises of] things' [desire] to be close to it and be like it has already surpassed the understanding of someone who says that it is like an animal's appetite for food. But this is not the case, for there are many kinds of desire, and there also are many kinds of things that are desired [and] loved. For appetite for food is contrary to appetite for the object of desire, and love of health is contrary to love of excellence [and] rectitude. For appetite for food is so as to be satiated by it; and appetite for an object of desire is so as to see it and be close to it; and appetite for health is so as to acquire it; and by saying that we have appetite for rectitude we mean [that it is so as] to live rightly. Likewise, the army has appetite for the commander, and the city [has appetite] for the king so as to follow them and pay attention to their commands.

18,9 Since we established what we have explained about the first cause – namely, that it is unmoved – there is nothing puzzling, then, if it is a first cause, that it is [also] substance and actuality.[236] All other things,[237] when they intelligize its essence,[238] have an appetite for it so as to pursue the activity of this intellect,[239] i.e. the order of existing things. This is like a law adhering person's appetite to live according to it, and the love that a person who is occupied by administration has to the path that administration prescribes.

18,14 Now[240] the first cause moves like an object of desire moves. The first [thing] that is moved by it, is close to it, desires it, and strives to resemble it is the first heaven and[241] the sphere of the fixed stars. Since it is close to it, it has already acquired – as much as possible – [its share] of its [i.e. the first cause's][242] rectitude, which it desires, just as a leader acquires his share of a king's rank if he is close to him – not in place, but in nature. After the heaven and its motion (i.e. the first motion) comes the next motion, which is the motion of the spheres of the planets,[243] and [then] all[244] the rest. These [latter] things receive coming-to-be and perishing and the nature which has multiple motions;[245] their motion is not only in place – as [is the case] in divine [substances] – but is [rather] in all its natures.[246] It follows, therefore, that the variation among moved things is very large, and 'possibility' in each of them is different.[247] If motion includes everything that is moved (for possibility is of the essence of motion), and some [moved things'] motion is only in place, while some are moved [also] in quality,[248] in substance, and in similar varying motions, [then] likewise we do not find 'possibility' to be one for all.[249]

18,25 But when we say that celestial bodies, which only change in place, can vary, we only mean that they can be in different places – not that it is possible for them to [vary] in another way.[250] **(1072b4-7)** But [in this context,] our saying 'it is possible' does not refer to the true reference of this term, nor is it analogous to that which inclines towards two sides.[251] Rather, it [refers] to [the fact] that they are not in a place in which they must necessarily be. For the true reference of our saying 'possible' applies to this weak and confused nature for which the possible is within the realm of **[19]** contradiction.[252] Since talking about 'possibility' in celestial bodies does not have [this] meaning,[253] they undergo only the first change, which occurs in place, and this change does not touch their nature from within.

19,3 (1072b7-10) Since the mover of the celestial bodies' motion (about which we said many times that it is the first motion[254] and the first change)[255] is unmoved in every respect, unaltered, and non-transposable, it cannot admit variation in substance or in any other respect.[256] For coming-to-be and perishing are very far from it, as are motion that comprises of increase and decrease (since this [too] leads to perishing) or motion in place (for it is also a slight change of a body). It [i.e. the first mover] moves without being moved, and if something is not susceptible of the first motion [i.e. motion in place], even less so is it susceptible of the other motions.[257] Possibility, then, is very far from it. **(1072b10-13)** Therefore it exists necessarily, and a principle that exists necessarily is a principle in the following manner (for that which cannot not be – whether changing or unchanging – is [both] necessary in this way [that we will now explain], and existing).[258] For 'necessity' is said in three ways: first, something that undergoes coercion, since it deviates from its end;[259] second, something without which a thing cannot achieve its best state; and third, something for which it is absolutely impossible to be otherwise.[260] **(1072b13-14)** On necessity like this [i.e. the third kind], then, the heavens and the nature of all are dependent.

19,15 (1072b14-17) Remaining in the utmost best [state], which we can accomplish for [only] a limited time,[261] exists for this substance eternally. For since we are constituted by different capacities, we find the path towards knowledge [only] with certain difficulty.[262] This is because most of the time[263] our intellect is preoccupied [and] has no leisure. However, although it is preoccupied by other things (since it is mixed with body), it sometimes – even if briefly – casts away things that hinder it from understanding and intelligizes itself unhindered. Through this it can have joy and everlasting delight, beyond measure.

19,21[264] Something that has a nature which cannot avoid knowledge – [even] for an instant – is [something for which] pleasure is not gained. Rather, it *is* pleasure and the best thing. **(1072b17-18)** If, for us, wakefulness is more pleasant than sleep (because activity is more pleasant than idleness), sensing [is more pleasant] than its privation, and intelligizing [is more pleasant] than ignorance, then *that* intellect is infinitely elevated with respect to nobility and excellence of thought. For a thing that is in actuality is always[265] more pleasant than a thing that is in potentiality, and nature rushes towards it [i.e. actuality]. Hence, hope is very pleasant, since it expects something that is in potentiality to come to actuality. Likewise, memory is not of potentiality, but of that which was in actuality. In something that has [both] potentiality and actuality, the pleasantness [derived] from actuality is greater; but how could this be compared[266] to the joy experienced[267] by something whose nature is only actuality – with no potentiality whatsoever – when it performs its activities and intelligizes itself? Vision, too, is delighted and strongly enjoys when it sees the best and beautiful sight without any impediment; [the same holds for] the palate, when it **[20]** tastes the best and most excellent flavours; and hearing, when it hears the best and most pleasant sound. **(1072b18-19)** [But] clearly, intellect has much more delight and joy[268] when it intelligizes the best object of intelligizing.

20,3 The best object of intelligizing is that which intelligizes its essence and its existence without being hindered[269] by anything else, impeded by something, or interrupted due to sense perception, like what is found in intelligized things that are conceived in thought as emptied of sensory objects.[270] But something that is by nature an object of intelligizing is unmixed with matter and is unchanging. Its constitution consists of intelligizing and being intelligized. The first [thing that] it intelligizes is itself, [and only] then something else, for otherwise it could not be an object of intelligizing by nature, but owing to the nature of that which intelligizes it.

20,8 (1072b20-3) This is the state of the divine intellect, which is the utmost best; it is not divided into one of these two, but both are of its nature together, i.e. that it intelligizes and that it is intelligized. Hence it is not said to be an object of intelligizing with respect to us, but with respect to itself (just like our [own] intellect is not said to be an object of intelligizing with respect to us, but with respect to itself). Just like it is the best intelligizing thing, so is it the best thing that is intelligized. Just as it is most truly an intellect, so is it also most truly an object of intelligizing. In so far as it intelligizes as an intellect, it intelligizes its activity, and in so far as it is in the state in which it intelligizes, it is simultaneously an intellect and an object of intelligizing. Everything in it is in contact[271] with everything; not like bodies that touch each other only on the exterior surface, but like what is said specifically about things that are intermixed, for everything in them touches everything. In the same way, everything in the intellect is interwoven, so that it is an intellect and an object of intellect simultaneously.

20,17 Sense is not the same as its object and remains outside it when its form is imprinted upon it.[272] But this is different in the case of intellect with respect to its substantial objects of intelligizing. Rather, it holds all forms, and no material substance remains outside; for there is no matter there, only an immaterial, bare form. [This form is] attached to that which intelligizes or thinks it, without being divided or having some of it[s parts] drawn away from each other (like [in the case of] of a sensory object with respect to sense), for it is implanted in the intellect.

20,22 In sum, as we have said many times, it is an intellect and an object of intelligizing simultaneously. It is not like our [human] intellect, which is repeatedly transposed from object to object,[273] and intelligizes now something that it did not intelligize before, due to the large amount of potentiality mixed in it.[274] The first divine intellect is not like this, for it intelligizes the objects of intelligizing that are existents in it [and] assumes their forms. In general – *they* are *it*, and *it* is its objects of intelligizing. It does not intelligize them like our intellect intelligizes, namely, by transposition and passing through them [one by one]; rather, it intelligizes all of them in a single instant.

20,28 Clearly, it intelligizes all existing things as they [truly] exist and as it put them as existents. All things exist in it together. It follows, therefore, that it intelligizes all of them together. If there is nothing puzzling about our intellect being the thing that we intelligize, all the more so should we consider this to be the case with the first intellect [i.e. that it intelligizes itself].[275] **(1072b23-4)** Indeed, our [human] intellect is divine because it resembles *that* divine intellect. If the thing that is of the utmost pleasantness and **[21]** the utmost best [is achieved] in us through knowledge, then all the more so concerning the first cause. For it perceives itself in the utmost best way, and it intelligizes itself[276] without needing an external nature in order to do so. Rather, the nature that it seeks is inside it. And the utmost pleasantness in its activity is not something that is sometimes missing or like someone who does [something] in order to achieve his end [i.e. pleasure] from a thing that he does not have; for all these things are modifications[277] that occur in our intellect. Rather, it [i.e. the first cause] is, substantially, the thing that is of the utmost pleasantness, just as it is, substantially, the thing that is of the utmost excellence.

21,8 (1072b24-6) If what God has always is similar to what we have sometimes, then it is wonderful; but if it is more than that, it is the most wonderful wonder

– and [indeed,] He has more.[278] His superiority[279] is clear, since He alone is in Himself simple, and He is not confronted by senses or any accident. He intelligizes all existents not as external to His nature or as foreign activities, but it is He who begets them,[280] and *what* they are is *Him*.[281] For God is law, reason,[282] and the cause of the order of all existing things. He is not like the law that is laid down in books. Rather, He is living law, as if we could imagine law as ensouled and essentially knowing and intelligizing.[283] This is like imagining Lycurgus[284] the lawgiver administrating the law that he ordered, continuously knowing the administration that he authored, essentially intelligizing the kings, ministers, and armed men, and tying this knowledge – by himself – into one unmoved and unceasing rope. But Lycurgus is physically dead, as is the government that he had invented. However, in a place where law exists and its giver lives an everlasting life, the administration is also everlasting.

21,19 (1072b26-30) The life of *this* lawgiver is not only everlasting – without beginning or ending – but [also] the utmost best. For intellect is the best life, and the most venerable of living things. His life [does] not [consist] in different states moment by moment,[285] like our life [does], but He is life itself. For He is actuality, and actuality is life. And just as He has the best actuality, He is the best living thing,[286] and just as He is eternal, continuous activity, He is also everlasting, eternal life. We say, then, that God, may He be exalted, is the utmost best everlasting, eternal life. It follows, therefore, that God has life, everlastingness, and is constant and eternal throughout all eternity. [But] we ought not say 'has', as we have occasionally said earlier; rather, God, may He be exalted, *is* life and *is* continuous everlastingness.

21,28 (1072b30-1073a3) It has been previously supposed (by the Pythagoreans, Speusippus,[287] and the like) that something of the utmost beauty and best was not like this from the outset. For[, they argue,] while the beginnings of animals or plants are causes for their coming-to-be, their utmost beauty or perfection is not in the seed, but in the end. Their assumption is untrue, for it [i.e. their beauty or perfection] already benefits from the roots. When something has both **[22]** potentiality and actuality, potentiality is [indeed] prior in time, but in an absolute sense, actuality is prior to potentiality, and man is prior to seed because seed comes from man.

22,3 (1073a3-5) It has already been explained sufficiently that there exists an eternal, unmoved substance that is distinguished from sensible [substances] not only in place, but by nature [as well]. It does not undergo change or alteration like they do;[288] [in fact,] it is completely unaffected.[289]

22,5 (1073a5-7) It has also been explained that it is not a body, does not have quantity, does not die, and is indivisible. **(1073a7-11)** For it moves for an unlimited time, and a limited magnitude that has power to move unlimitedly does not exist. We have already explained in our treatise about natural science that every magnitude is either limited or unlimited. The statement that it is unlimited has already been invalidated [and therefore every magnitude is limited]. But no one agrees or admits that a limited [magnitude] can have unlimited powers, especially if they would be ascribed[290] to it as an ensouled body. For it[291] would be incorrect to say that the sun and the other stars are limited while their powers are unlimited, because the power in the stars, which is unlimited, is not in them by nature, and not on account of their being bodies. Rather, either it depends on the first cause, or their soul is a power of the sort that does not belong to a body. For the first cause is that which rotates them[292] for an unlimited time. For if their power was of the sort that exists in body or magnitude, they would not persist in actuality, but would undoubtedly become tired and need rest. For the powers of the stars' bodies are limited because they [i.e. the stars' bodies] have potentiality. In every moment, they are in a different place than they were before. Sometimes they are in one place, and sometimes in another. And these places are, as it were, the boundaries of the motions.[293] If something that has potentiality is followed by an actuality at which it aims, it must have a limit and an extreme point. How can a cause that is always in actuality, that does not have potentiality at all, and that does not become different moment by moment, be thought to have magnitude or corporeality like things whose potentiality is always apparent, [regardless of] whether or not they are perishable?

22,24 In sum, an actuality that is essentially separate [from corporeality] can perdure unlimitedly along with the perdurance of time. An actuality that comes out of potentiality is the completion of a potential thing. An actuality like this cannot perdure for an unlimited time, for potentiality had already preceded before it. It follows, therefore, that the moving power in stars is unlimited [and hence does not belong to them in so far as they are bodies]. The stars do not acquire this power in the same way a thing that has potentiality does. But stars' motion in place is limited, and in this respect they have potentiality.

Chapter 8[294]

22,30 (1073a14-15) Do you think that these substances ought to be said to be one or many?[295] (I mean [substances] that are without magnitude and immaterial.) **(1073a15-17)** We should explore this, because when our predecessors discussed immaterial substances, they did not speak clearly about their plurality [i.e. whether there is more than one]. **(1073a17-21)** What is more, they did not discuss specifically the [exact] number of [these] substances. Some of them, who spoke of Ideas, argued that Ideas are immaterial and unmoved substances, but **[23]** they did not speak at all about their number, leaving the issue unresolved[296] (just like numbers, whose amount is unknown[297]). For they also say that Ideas are numbers; sometimes they extend them infinitely, and sometimes they limit them to ten.

23,4 (1073a22-5) But we, according to what we prescribed and defined, should posit that the first principle is one, immaterial, incorporeal, and that it moves the first everlasting and eternal motion, [itself being] beyond any motion or change. But [the fact] that there are other substances like this beyond the first principle is necessitated[298] by reason and testified by sense.

23,8 Every moved thing's motion comes from a mover. The first cause must necessarily be one and unmoved – neither essentially nor accidentally. **(1073a34-b3)** But the substances after it, which move the [celestial] bodies, must necessarily be as many as the moved bodies, and also unmoved essentially. However, they are moved accidentally, as is necessitated by the account concerning soul.[299] We should posit them not only as unmoved, but also as everlasting. For the stars' nature is a substance, and their mover is eternal, since a mover is prior to the thing it moves,[300] and a thing that is prior to a [certain] substance is undoubtedly [also] a substance.

23,14 (1073b3-5) As to determining the number of powers, we should set out to know it via a science that is peculiar to philosophy, I mean astronomy, because this is the science that strives to explain the number of each planet's motions[301] and the number of spheres that move it. We find that the number of spheres that carry the stars and the number of spheres that direct[302] them differ between Callippus and Eudoxus. But we [also] ought to demonstrate[303] that the number of moving powers and the number of moved bodies is the same; and [we also ought to demonstrate] that among the powers [there is] a first and a second [and so forth], which corresponds exactly to the order of spheres. The difference between them is not only in rank, but also in existence, in substance, in their descent in rank, and in their disadvantage. Their ranks are first and second [and so forth] because difference in substance should follow from this [i.e. from disadvantage].

23,22 (1073b5-8) I have said that astronomy is very peculiar in philosophy, for it alone enquires into eternal sensible substance. Other mathematical [sciences] investigate accidents that happen to bodies:[304] geometry investigates continuous quantity, and arithmetic investigates discrete quantity.

23,25 (1073b8-10) It is clear to anyone who has a bit of understanding of astronomy that each star has a plurality of motions and that each moved body is visible.[305] **(1073b10-17)** But concerning the number [of motions] each of them [i.e. the planets] has and the [total] number of planetary motions, we ought to report here what some geometricians say, and understand it so that our intellect can conceive their number definitively. Afterwards, we ought to enquire into this partly by ourselves and partly by learning from whoever investigates it. If we find in it [i.e. in the enquiry] something better than what whoever has already explored and investigated it has found until now, we shall mention them all [i.e. all the findings], and draw from whomever best investigated.

23,32 (1073b17-32) I say: Eudoxus held that the sun and the moon's respective motions [result] from **[24]** three spheres. The first is the sphere of fixed stars; the second – the zodiac; and the third – the sphere that is inclined across the breadth of the zodiac. The inclination of the sphere in which the moon revolves is broader than the inclination of the sphere in which the sun revolves. He holds that each planet's motion involves four spheres.[306] Of these four, the first two are the same as the first two spheres of the sun and the moon,[307] for the [combined] motion of the sphere of fixed stars (which is the mover of all spheres) and that which is beneath it – i.e. the zodiac – is common to all spheres. The third sphere [of a planet's motion] is the only[308] sphere whose poles are at the middle of the zodiac. The fourth sphere's motion is in the circle that is inclined at the middle of this [i.e. the third] sphere. In each star, the poles of the third sphere are peculiar, except for Venus and Mercury (the latter two have the same in common). This, then, is what Eudoxus supposed.

24,10 (1073b32-8) Callippus positioned the spheres in the same way Eudoxus had concerning the order of their intervals. He also agreed with him about the number of spheres in Jupiter and Saturn. However, he thought that two spheres should be added to the sun and two to the moon, in order to accord with their observations. He [also] thought that one sphere should be added to each planet besides them [i.e. Mercury, Venus, and Mars].

24,15 (1073b38-1074a4) If all of them – when they are combined – are to accommodate observation, each planet must have additional spheres to turn it (one sphere less [than has already been assigned] to each) and to turn the star below [it] so that it always returns to the place from which the first sphere [i.e. the outermost sphere] started. **(1074a4-14)** For only in this manner is it possible for all of them to rotate according to the rotation of the sphere of fixed stars.[309] Since, then, the [total number of] spheres by which they [i.e. the planets] are moved is eight for some [planets] and twenty-five for others – and indeed, only the spheres in which the lowest star is moved should not be turned – the spheres that turn the first two are six, and those that turn the remaining four are sixteen. The total number of spheres – the movers [of the planets], and those that turn these spheres – is fifty-five. If you do not add these aforementioned motions to the sun and the moon [like Callippus had], then the number of spheres is forty-seven.

24,25 (1074a14-16) Let this be [also] the number of motions.[310] Accordingly, we should [also] say that this is the number of substances and principles which move them without being moved,[311] as well as the number of sensible substances.[312] For the number of motions must be the same as the number of moved spheres, and the number of moving causes must be the same as the number of motions. **(1074a16-17)** We should say decisively that this procession is according to what we mentioned, but we should not judge whether this is indeed the [exact] number of motions; let us leave the necessary judgement about this to those whose art this is and who are stronger in this.

24,30 (1074a17-22) If there cannot be a motion that is not directed towards a certain star's motion, and [if] it is impossible for there to be a substance and divine nature which is idle, without [a peculiar] activity (for each of these substances is good, and does not withhold its peculiar activity, **[25]** which is included in its definition in the utmost excellence, having [already] completely attained everlasting life) – if so, then besides these bodies [we just demarcated] there can be no additional body without a moved [object].[313] Hence, *this* should be the number of substances.

25,3 (1074a22-4) For if there were other motions in the world, there would also be other moved bodies in it. But there are no substances in the world beyond those that are seen. Hence, there are [also] no additional motions or moving causes. **(1074a25-8)** For a moving cause can only be for the sake of a [certain] moving thing, and every motion indeed comes-to-be from a mover. A motion cannot exist for its own sake or for the sake of another motion, but [only] for the sake of the stars. **(1074a28-31)** I said that 'a motion cannot exist for its own sake or for the sake of another motion' because nature has already avoided and kept away from that which proceeds in vain and aimlessly, or infinite regress.[314] [For] a motion that comes-to-be for its own sake results in aimlessness; and a motion that comes-to-be for the sake of [another] motion [results] in infinite regress.

25,11 (1074a31-3) This being so, let us enquire into what follows from this discussion[315] and say that if there were more than one world, then it would undoubtedly follow that there is more than one first cause; all the more so, if all of them [i.e. the 'first' causes] belong to one species (like humans do). For the principles would also belong to one species, and all of them would be included in the number one. **(1074a33-5)** But things that are one in form and many in number are many because of matter;[316] for all human beings have one and the same definition, while the difference between Socrates and Plato is by way of matter. The first form and[317] first mover is immaterial and incorporeal. **(1074a35-8)** Hence it follows that the first mover is one in definition as well as in number. Likewise, since the motion of the moved body [i.e. the world taken as a whole] is continuous, it has to be one [as well].

25,20 It is not only the world that is only one, as we have explained in the natural treatises; the moving cause is also one, as we have explained in other books. From our explanations about natural things it follows that no body – heavy or light – can exist besides it [i.e. the world]. The true demonstration given in preceding physical statements – namely that it is impossible for motions to have multiple principles – necessitates that it would be most fitting[318] [to say] that the first nature, which is one, extends[319] throughout all spheres, and this is desire. [This is] like in administration of cities; the law is one, as is in the case of the king (namely, one),[320] but the entire community is moved by its passion to follow this law. For as we have said many times, this [i.e. the explanation of the motion of celestial bodies] is like their [i.e. the subjects'] passion when they love the administration that comes to them by the king's commands and leadership. For in administration we also find that the first object of desire for all is one, and this is law, or the king. We find that the community's near completion of the king's commands[321] is not the result[322] of a **[26]** uniform activity. Rather, some of them [act] as leaders, some as slaves, and some in both ways together; some of them [act] as military units, some as workers, and some as sailors. Further, some of the military units [act] as infantry, some as cavaliers, and some as archers.[323] We find that in life, several activities vary, as does governance; we also find that motions vary considerably – sometimes [even] contrasting each other. However, all of them aim at completing the same thing, and all of them fancy one thing as their object of desire, which is to be in accordance to the king's commands and arrangements.[324]

26,6 This thing [i.e. that which everything aims at] is one, unmoved, and without magnitude. But compared to other things it is manifold, for the motions that it induces are many, as are the activities and the substances which achieve them. Still, it contains all of them. For none of them could fancy it unless the peculiar forms in each of them and their [respective] peculiar activities are dependent upon it. They are collectively dependent on it because they follow it.

26,11 An indication that we were correct in saying that first substances, which are movers for the world and for the celestial bodies, exist, and that they are like an aristocracy,[325] is [found in] **(1074a38-b10)** what we took over from the ancients. For they also testified [to this] by saying to those who came after them – by way of allusion – that these bodies are divine and that the divine body encompasses[326] nature in its entirety. The other things [that they said] after that were articulated metaphorically in order to persuade the people and for the sake of laws and utility. They shaped these divine things according to the shapes of animal species – like lamb, fish, and lion – and gave them their names according to powers that they thought they had, or because of their activities, or because of their resemblance to these animal species. We primarily accept this first thing, namely that the ancients thought that the first moving substances are divine. We have inherited this from them and we regard them as true.[327] I find this statement to be divine.[328]

Chapter 9[329]

26,21[330] **(1074b15-17)** Since we have said that the first cause is an intellect – for one cannot ascribe to it a nobler or more precious life than the life we have described – we should investigate and theorize: in what respect is it such? **(1074b17-18)** First, before other questions,[331] we start by theorizing about this cause: in so far as it is an intellect, does it act and intelligize, or is it inactive and does not intelligize (like a sage who sleeps without exercising his knowledge)? Is the first intellect like this, i.e. having this nature without intelligizing or acting? But saying this would be virtually absurd! For if the first principle were an intellect that does not intelligize or perform any other activity,[332] what share would it have in veneration or nobility by moving everything while sound asleep, [all] things inclining to it, as in bodies, where we see an object of desire move[333] the desirers while asleep? To say that the first cause – which moves all existents [and] on which all thing are dependent – is idle, not performing any activity, and empty of its appropriate activity, is [tantamount to] killing the principle and fountainhead of life. Clearly, then, it undoubtedly intelligizes, because it is an intellect [27] and it acts.

27,1 We should investigate this activity and theorize about what it is. **(1074b21-3)** Inevitably, this activity is either intelligizing itself or intelligizing something else. If it intelligizes something else, it would be either always the same thing, or several things. But generally, if it were to intelligize something that is different from it and external to it – as sight sees visible objects that are outside its nature, and hearing hears [external] sounds – and if it [itself] were not the thing that it intelligizes, then that thing [i.e. the object of intelligizing] would control the intellect's intelligizing,[334] just as a visible thing is a mover for sight's seeing, and a heard [thing is the mover] of hearing's hearing. But in that case, the intellect's substance would not be intellect itself, nor would it be the intellect that controls[335] [intelligizing] in the manner we explained earlier.[336] It would only have potentiality that deems it fit to intelligize an intelligible other than itself. It would follow, then, that it is not a substance of the utmost excellence, for this substance [i.e. the divine intellect] was [taken to be] of the utmost excellence because it was an intellect and an intelligizer.[337] Its excellence and eminence were due to this.[338]

27,10 (1074b29-30) Moreover, if the intelligized thing were external, of a different nature than that of the intellect, it would clearly be superior and more venerable, since it would have been a certain cause[339] for the intellect's intelligizing. Just as vision is considered to be due[340] to objects of sight, so that it can perceive them, and [just as] hearing is due to sounds, so would the intellect be considered as due to intelligibles, and anything that comes-to-be due to another [thing] is inferior to that thing, which is considered to be its cause.

27,15 (1074b28-9) If this were so, then the intellect would be in potentiality; its continuity and constancy would necessarily tire and fatigue it, just like continuity of visible [things] tires and fatigues vision, and constancy and continuity of sounds tire hearing. For tiredness and weariness from activity are found in all the modifications[341] of a thing that goes out from potentiality to actuality. This is why sleep is necessary for animals.

27,18 (1074b23-6) Moreover, if the intellect intelligizes something else [besides it], it intelligizes it either as a thing that is naturally superior, like fine things or the good, or as lesser things [do].[342] Clearly, the case of individuals is inferior,[343] all the more so if it [i.e. the intelligizer] possesses an intellect before receiving[344] the form of an intelligized thing, so that it and the intelligized thing [would be] one and the same thing (for the most part)[345], as we have said and accepted.

27,22 Clearly, then, all inferior activities should be removed from it.[346] We say that it intelligizes things in a manner that is appropriate to what is of the utmost eminence, and that it does not change or alter in it [i.e. during intelligizing]. **(1074b26-7)** For [had it been otherwise,] its change or transition would be into something inferior, and consequently it would be akin to some motions.[347] **(1074b31-3)** Generally, if its excellence and eminence were [attained] from [the mere fact] that it intelligizes, and it would [be able to] acquire the intellect [even] through inferior things (and in that case, the intellect that it would intelligize would count among inferior things), then its excellence, which would result from its activity, would result from an inferior thing. If we were to escape all this (for [e.g.] to not acquire sight of [certain] things is better than to see [them]), then the substance that is of the utmost excellence, eminence, and nobility should not be considered as an intellect *simpliciter*, but rather as an intellect that intelligizes the best thing. **(1074b33-5)** For if we consider it thus [i.e. in the latter sense], then it intelligizes things of the utmost excellence and of the utmost divinity, and it does not intelligize other things that are external to it and to its nature.

27,32 The claim that gives up[348] the substance [i.e. grants that the first intellect is not the best existent] and assumes something else before it, which is more venerable and superior, is utterly reprehensible and absurd. Now, were we to [nevertheless] accept this, which of the [following] two statements ought we to maintain? Would we say that the [thing] which it intelligizes – [i.e.] the thing which is of the utmost excellence – is always one and **[28]** the same thing, or would we say that it is many things? And if it were many things, would it intelligize them all together, or by going over them one by one, leaving one and turning to another?

28,2 But absurdity follows from all these propositions.[349] For were it to intelligize always one and the same thing, then unescapably it would either perfect its intellect by this, or it would not. Now if it would perfect it by this, then it would be lacking. Were it not to perfect it[s intellect] by this, then it would have neither a [perfected] intellect nor self-sufficiency.[350] [On the other hand,] were the things that it intelligizes many, and it intelligized them by going over one by one, it would have needed memory and to acquire something that it does not have. [Alternatively,] were it to intelligize things in a single immeasurable instant, then the same question we have already asked about the one intelligible [i.e. the first option] necessarily follows: would it perfect its intellect by this, or would it not perfect it and remain imperfect? Further, it is by nature impossible for it to intelligize all things together. [Even] if it could intelligize some things together, it is impossible [to intelligize] them all.[351]

28,10 From all these absurdities follows the dispensing of the claim that the first intellect always acquires all things or many things. Rather, it intelligizes only one thing. This thing is of the utmost excellence and eminence, and since it [i.e. the first intellect] itself is the thing that is of the utmost excellence, it intelligizes its own essence. Hence there is no effort involved, for its aim and end are directed towards none other than its [own] essence, and it does not go out from potentiality to actuality (and *this* [i.e. going out from potentiality to actuality] is what effort and tiredness follow). But just as a person's love for oneself is not surfeited, its [i.e. the intellect's] intelligizing of itself does not tire it and it is not surfeited by it; and just as a person's love for oneself always exists, in every person, the same holds for a thing that intelligizes its essence, whenever it intelligizes it. And just like someone who desires oneself is the one who loves one's self and desires it, a thing that is intelligized and that intelligizes its essence is itself that which it intelligizes.[352]

28,19 The first intellect is the principle of all existing things, which are known in it. **(1075a5-10)** It does not intelligize them by going over them one by one or by leaving one and turning to another; rather, it apprehends them together[353] instantly. For our intellect, because of its weakness, cannot easily intelligize many things together, and its attention cannot be drawn[354] to many things together. This is like a weak body, which cannot carry many things [at once] (when it divides them it is easier for it to carry them), and like weak vision, that cannot apprehend many colours [at the same time]. However, for strong vision it *is* possible to apprehend many things together. But the divine intellect, since it is of the utmost completeness and perfection, does not need time for intelligizing; it intelligizes all things together instantly. Just like an eye with sharp vision sees many things together, similarly – and even more so – the first intellect intelligizes all the intelligibles together when it intelligizes its essence. These things proceed by way of perfection:[355] its correctness and universal knowledge are not in time (because it is beyond all quantities, and time is indeed the quantity of motion, while it [i.e. the first intellect] is unmoved) and it is not ignorant of anything.

28,31 [For example,] when you play the lyre, you cannot play all the notes [at the same time]; but if the lyre were ensouled, it could evoke both the highest and the lowest pitch sounds together. Similarly, God can easily contain many things together **[29]** and intelligize many things together.[356] Indeed, a dancer's soul can move many bodily organs together – like the hands, the feet, and the head – and to move all these organs collectively together, rather than moving some organs in part of it and some in another part. [If a dancer can do this,] how could it be correct [to say] that the intellect, which no place in the world evades, cannot move the entire world together, or that it could not intelligize all things together? Yet[357] his moving of many things together is a bigger marvel [than his intelligizing many things together].[358]

29,6 We should not deny the multi-fold extension and richness of God's power, nor should we compare it to our weak intellect. For in knowing things, He does not need to go over them one by one, nor does He need composition; He is not brought out from ignorance to knowledge, and has no need for concluding conclusions that are [yet] unaffirmed for it[359] from clear premises. For the divine intellect is like sharp vision, which does not need time to apprehend visible objects, but sees them all as soon as it encounters them, without delay – and much more so: when it directs itself towards the intelligibles, it comprehends the intelligible world in no time and without toil. If you want to differentiate[360] between sharpness of vision and divine intelligizing,[361] imagine the [relation between] the human intellect and its body: the intellect better understands and knows than this body [does], and is also quicker in its motions and actions. Accordingly, imagine that the divine intellect apprehends intelligibles quicker [than the human intellect] and attains them with greater ease. If you translate this difference in excellence, and the divine intellect's ease of apprehension, to [its] ease of rotating the world, you will not be far from the proper[362] analogy. Likewise, if you use the analogy of shape – as geometricians do – and say: 'just as *that* body is more transparent[363] than *this* body, so is *that* intellect more transparent than *this* intellect', there is no wonder that it can understand and intelligize many things together.

29,18 Also, nothing is puzzling about the first principle's essential intelligizing. For if you admit that the divine intellect is completely immaterial, and that it is the cause of the motion of the sphere, then just as you do not see its [i.e. the sphere's] motion [ever] come to rest, you could not say that God rests from His activity. And since we stated that in the world,[364] a body is a substrate and intellect is always in it, what could hinder the intellect, which is essentially active and produces motion?[365]

29,23 It has already been explained from all these considerations[366] that God is the first principle; that He knows His essence – and all things of which He is a principle – together; and that if he is a ruler in His essence, He is [also] a ruler of all things who are constituted upon Him.[367] Further, the statement that He knows[368] and that He intelligizes His essence is true, for by this He is the most venerable and lofty thing.

29,28 (1074b35-6) But we find that knowledge is of a different thing – i.e. the known thing – and that sense is of something different, namely, the sensed object; the same [holds] for thought and intellect.[369] Things that are intelligible in themselves are apprehended[370] because [e.g.] when a man becomes aware[371] of whiteness, he becomes immediately aware, in his soul, that he had become aware of whiteness. And when he becomes aware that the angles of a triangle are equal to two right angles, he has already become aware and intelligized that he has become aware.[372]

29,32 (1074b38-1075a5) We also say that, for some things, the known and the knowledge – and the intelligible and the intellect – are one and the same. For immaterial sciences are indeed account[373] and intellect.[374] They are no different from what is intelligized of them. They are distinguished from one another neither **[30]** because of matter, nor quantity, nor time period; rather, the intelligible's form and the intellect proceed together. The intellect is one and returns[375] upon itself, and both [things] are said of it together; namely, that it is an intellect and that it is an intelligible.[376] For intellect is one; it does not pass from one intelligized thing to another [intelligized] thing of a different nature. Rather, it returns upon itself. The thing that exists in both of them is one [and] immaterial, just like productive arts – when matter is removed from an art, we find nothing but a form of an artisan and his work (just as a chair is nothing but a carpenter's art, and just as the form of health, without a body, is also nothing but the art of medicine). Just like it is possible to attain knowledge of material things – since art and its form are one and the same – in immaterial things (namely, things whose essence has neither parts nor sections) there is nothing to prevent the intellect, the intelligible, and the thinking to be one and the same.[377]

30,10 This statement explains to someone who sets out to understand that the first intellect intelligizes the intellectual world. For He, if He intelligizes that He is what He is when He intelligizes Himself,[378] He already intelligizes of Himself that He is the cause and principle of all things.[379] Now 'principle' is said of form, of that for the sake of which, and of the beginning of motion. Similarly, the human intellect is said to be its [i.e. the human's] principle in three ways (for it is frequent, in some natural things, that the three meanings in which 'principle' is said apply to one and the same thing, like the case of the human soul). If God intelligizes Himself in so far as He is a form of all things, He is also the principle of all things' order. Undoubtedly, He apprehends simultaneously the things of which he is the principle as well as their order.

Chapter 10[380]

30,19 (1075a11-13) We should theorize whether there is a difference between the good and the utmost best,[381] whether each of the two is distinguished[382] from the other, or[383] whether the difference between them is one of rank. **(1075a13-15)** Now God is the order of all[384] [things] like in an army, for in an army, too, the good is order. Each military unit is also good, and more so – *this* man [i.e. the general], for he does not come-to-be because of order, but rather he is the cause of order. Therefore, the good is not a [certain] rank with respect to the intellect,[385] but it is in both together – i.e. in the order and in the order's cause – not adjacent[386] to the intellect.

30,25 God moves the existing things like prescriptions of political administration move the noblemen and the king's commands move the community. But the order that God is said to cause is as I shall describe: I say that **(1075a16-23)** all things are ordered together in a certain manner, but not in one and the same way, like swimmers or flyers (among animals), or like plants.[387] [Despite their differences,] all these things' states are *not* such that none of them relate to each other; rather, there is a relation between them. For the order of all of them, [taken] together, is directed towards one end, like in household governance, where freemen are not permitted to perform any action improperly. The activities of slaves and some animals are, to a small extent, included in what the whole[388] comprises, though most of it (i.e. the nature of each **[31]** and its principle) is accidental.[389]

31,1 The state of this world is also like this, because the stars' regulation[390] and perduring accord to one order, as do all celestial bodies – nothing in them is undetermined or unordered. As for animals on the face of the earth and plants, their general utility is small, for each of them acts and is acted upon mostly accidentally. **(1075a23-5)** But when they perish, it is so that another thing besides it can come-to-be – like a nourishing thing's need for food; things' growth, maturation,[391] and subsequent decline; and other general utilities like them. But a donkey's kick, a snake's bite, a pig's spilling of a water bag, and some deadly plants[392] [and similar examples] are not included in the general order at all. Saying this is more correct and better than to mix God with matter and consider these things to have something common with Him. What is more, for us, things that we think have no order should be considered to be different [from God] – absurd and scornful.[393]

31,10 We can, inasmuch as the nature of things allows us, determine that the world's being and governance are like a city's governance, where the king's command is carried out in the best manner. If the people of the city are sometimes commanded to do something, the king's command does not pass to all its parts in the same manner, and not everyone participates in this specific command – for he appoints some people as chiefs, others as chiefs' guardians, and others as their subordinates.[394] He charges some of them with the most inferior activity, at which point administration is completed. [Accordingly,] some share the king's royal rank to a large degree, and others less so. Likewise, the world and its governance resemble a kingdom which is ruled by one king, [and] all its parts (i.e. animals and plants) are ordered with respect to each another.

31,18 An indication of this is that all of them are created for one cause.[395] For all of them, since they desire to be in the state in which they exist,[396] fancy and desire the thing that exists truly.[397] They yearn for this one, seek it specifically, and strive for it.[398] No existent wants to be divided into a plurality[399] or to be brought out of its present state to its contrary. Something that is made out of many things also seeks and strives to be one thing. This, too, is like a city: although[400] it is a plurality, it aims at one thing. The army is one [because] its aim is what the general sees fit. An association of people aims at [what] its leader [wants]. This is also the case for activities or arts vis-à-vis things that are composed of many things, like a ship or a house; for both are constituted, when they are created, by their [respective] oneness. If someone has a desire for the many, like a rising king who seeks dominance,[401] he has this desire so that he can put them under one [rule].

31,28 (1075a25-7) We find that none of the ancients' statements about the first principle, which is truly first,[402] [indeed] exist in it or should be ascribed to it. Rather, they were content with[403] a principle that involves matter.[404] **(1075a28-32)** All of them agreed that all things are made of and come-to-be from contraries. But they erred in both things together. For not all things come-to-be (the best things in the world do not come-to-be), and the coming-to-be of all things that come-to-be is **[32]** undoubtedly *not* [only] from contraries (for they are mutually unaffected),[405] but a third thing, i.e. matter is needed besides them, as we have said many times.

32,2 (1075a32-4) But the ancients posited matter as one of the two contraries, like the people who posited the unequal as underlying the equal, or those who posited plurality as underlying one thing. This opinion is refuted in the same way, for matter does not exist as a contrary to anything that is created from it. The form[406] is created from privation that is in it [i.e. in matter] and[407] from that which is without form.

32,6 (1075a34-7) Some ancients divided the principles into good and evil; they posited evil as matter, and good as form. They put matter under all things but one, that is free,[408] and this is the first form. This, because all people know that the good is the form of the first principle. **(1075a38-b1)** Some people have already excelled in finding a conception of the first principle as the good, but neglected to say how it is a principle: as a perfection, as a mover, or as a form?

32,11 (1075b1-7) Absurd and repugnant as well is Empedocles' conception of love as the good. It is a principle as a mover (for it brings together) [. . .][409] from his statement that it is [a principle] as matter, because it is part of the mixture. We are not entitled to maintain this, [i.e.] to think that a principle with matter is in itself a principle that is a mover. For a principle that has matter and a moving principle do not have the same definition and essence.[410] One would have to enquire to determine which of the two is love.[411] It is also absurd for strife to completely perish,[412] as this nature is the nature of coercion.

32,17 (1075b8-10) Anaxagoras thought that the principle is the good that is a mover, for his 'intellect' moves. But he still has to explain the cause for the sake of which it moves. For the thing that moves, in itself, is the first thing, and it is different from the mover.[413] For its moving[414] cannot be for the sake of a cause unless it is in the way we have stated. **(1075b10)** For the art of medicine is also a principle that is a mover, but it moves only when health needs it to, and health is also, in a way, the art of medicine.[415] Nothing prevents[416] the first from being a mover; its moving is for its own sake (as affirmed from the conditions that we stated), and the cause in each of these two [aspects] is one [and the same].[417] **(1075b10-11)** Anaxagoras thinks even more absurdly that good and evil have one and the same principle when he thinks that the intellect is a principle that is a mover, and that matter obeys and accedes to the intellect. But where does evil come from,[418] unless one says (as we have) that evil comes from matter's weakness and from privation? **(1075b11-13)** Anyone who says that the principles contrast each other – like softness and hardness, or association and dissociation – cannot make use of the contraries [so as to provide an account of] the visible order [that is due to] the mover.[419] For you will not find any matters that are sufficient for the coming-to-be of what is begotten from them; rather, they need a cause to move them, arrange them, and form them.[420]

32,30 (1075b13-14) The most outrageous **[33]** ancient statement about natural things is rendering all things – perishable things, non-perishable things, things that come-to-be from them,[421] and things that do not come-to-be – from the same elements.[422] For we have already set apart the principles of celestial bodies; the bodies that go about the earth do not share the same matter with them. For the stars and their motions are efficient causes that move matter, in which coming-to-be occurs, and the same holds for the planets, the sun, and the moon. Of these [i.e. the celestial bodies] it should be said either that they do not have matter at all, or that their matter is different from the matter of things that are susceptible of coming-to-be and perishing (just as the matter of intellect – which is the mover of the [human] body – is not the same as the body's matter).

33,8 (1075b16-17) Further, we do not find our predecessors describe the cause for the non-stop coming-to-be and perishing. We have done so by conceiving this cause as closeness or remoteness of celestial bodies. We also conceived this everlasting varying cause as dependent on a cause that is everlasting in one and the same state. **(1075b14-16)** We find that many predecessors deviated from things that are known[423] to everyone by conceiving coming-to-be [as proceeding] either from what does not exist at all, or from what is in actuality. For the indivisible things that Anaxagoras[424] talked about, and the elements that Empedocles talked about, necessitate existing things to come-to-be from what is in actuality, and this is absurd and repugnant.

33,14 (1075b17-18) Absurd and repugnant as well is the saying of someone who thinks that there is a plurality of principles, whether three, four, or two. Let he who says this explain how all the principles could accord, and why their number is specifically *this* and not another. If some of them are active and some are passive, what thing brought them together, connected them with each other, and put them in accord? For it would be necessary to say that there is another, superior principle therein – even if there were only two [principles] (like God and matter, or hardness and softness). For it would be impossible to say that these two became associated in and of themselves, agreeing that one will act upon the other, while the other would be a recipient of change.

33,21 As for us, since we have already put forth one principle – unmixed with matter, incorporeal, that moves the celestial bodies like an object of desire and love does – and [since] we have learned that coming-to-be and perishing consist in these bodies' motions, it follows that our statement is safeguarded from this doubt.[425] For we do not posit matter as equal in excellence and priority to the first cause, nor did we connect the last nature to the first nature immediately.[426] Rather, we posited matter as that which yearns, the celestial bodies as moved due to the first cause and likeness to it, and the place that is around the earth as the necessary medial place (for a thing that revolves in a cycle must have something like earth, which is naturally stationary). And since things in the middle of the world cannot persist forever as one in number, God finished the world and completed it according to unity by rendering coming-to-be everlasting, so that matter exists as yearning for the first cause.

33,30 This argument refutes not only someone who posits a plurality of corporeal principles, or someone who posits them [i.e. the principles] as God and matter, but also someone who posits Ideas as the principles of things. **(1075b18-20)** For the Ideas would also need another, superior principle to be their agent of coming-to-be[427] and to connect them with each **[34]** other and with things that are susceptible of coming-to-be and perishing. Anyone who expressed these opinions, and also those who posited contrary things [as principles], must necessarily posit another principle that is opposed to them, for contraries are opposites (hot to cold, dense to spongy, and association to dissociation).[428] **(1075b21-2)** Only our claim escapes this refutation, for we do not posit anything contrary to the first cause. For all contrary things are material and are potentially the same as other things, since some of them turn into the others.

34,6 (1075b20-1) Someone who argues that the first cause is contrary to these [things] arrives at absurdity not only because he does not [in fact] posit it as a first principle (as he posits alongside it another principle that is equal to it in excellence and priority); it also follows that the knowledge that is called science would have another, contrary science, and that would be knowledge of their [i.e. the objects of knowledge's] contrary. (Hot is contrary to cold, and likewise sensation of hot is contrary to sensation of cold – for the forms of sensory objects are imprinted in the senses.) **(1075b23-5)** But instead of a different knowledge, we should [rather] posit ignorance as a contrary to knowledge.

34,11 (1075b25-7) Generally, we should know that if a person does not posit, besides the objects of the senses, another substance which is superior to sense, he would not be able to find a first principle, because all sensory objects are composite. Moreover, he would be unable to establish order, coming-to-be, or that the motion of the celestial bodies necessarily depends on the principle. For any corporeal principle he posits would need another principle, as in the case of a theologian who says that existing things are born out of chaos (for they must enquire into the existence of chaos). The same holds for a natural scientist who says that things are made of water and air, since air and water are composite bodies – not completely simple.

34,19 (1075b27-8) If someone posits, apart from sensibles and bodies, a different principle that is immaterial [and] intelligible, but[429] posits it as numbers or Ideas, his statement inclines him to posit idle and inactive principles. For Ideas are models, and we do not find iron or a stone to move towards the model without being moved by art. **(1075b28-30)** Herein follows another refutation for someone who posits the principles as numbers, for it would follow that a magnitude comes-to-be from something without magnitude, and a contiguous [thing] from a dispersed [thing]. Nor would determining the moving cause be sufficient for him, for he would also need to determine the cause that gives the form so it would not be thought that it itself [i.e. the moving cause] creates the form (but a discrete nature cannot create the form of a contiguous nature or [others of] its kind).[430]

34,26 (1075b30-2) Generally, positing the principles as contraries is unfitting, because wherever there is a contrary, there is potentiality.[431] **(1075b32-3)** Hence, actuality would be posterior to it and would succeed it. **(1075b33-4)** Therefore, it would follow that existing things could not be eternal [and] everlasting, as we have explained many times. Therefore, a contrary must be rejected from [being counted as] a principle. We have already spoken sufficiently about rejecting them [i.e. the contraries as principles], and how we should set out to do so.[432]

34,30 The general doubt that opposes all of them [i.e. our predecessors], especially someone who **[35]** posits plurality in principles is, I say, that **(1075b34-7)** we should investigate how[433] plurality comes from the one. We find this frequently in numbers, for the form of three is created out of the one, as do [the forms] of four and ten. Whatever their number amounts to, you will find the form of the one within their plurality. It is also like this in soul and body, for unless they both have one and the same principle, one [of them] will have no function,[434] and an animal could not be created out of both together. Generally, it would not be possible for form and matter to be combined as to create a 'one' – be it a plant or an animal – without having the one (rather than plurality) as a principle from the outset, distinct in its uniqueness.

35,7 We find that no predecessor speaks of any of this. Also, I do not think that an account for this can be given, except in the way we stated, [i.e.] that the first moving nature is clean, distilled, without parts, unmixed, indivisible, and truly one;[435] it moves all things orderly, a motion that is not interrupted and does not perish, throughout eternity. They aim at this 'one', their rectitude is due to it,[436] and its oneness renders the world one. Every single animal in it is 'one' [in a certain respect], and it [i.e. the one] sets it [i.e. the animal] – along with its oneness – also as yearning for it.[437] For every single thing's end is [to be] like only the one [actually] is.

35,13 (1075b37-1076a3) As for those who posited mathematical number as the first principle, and then composed a surface out of it, and from the surface a body – the principles of existing things in their statement are episodic;[438] they do not cause change to one another or associate with one another.

Someone who does this renders the substance of the entire world as episodic,[439] and it would only include principles of numbers, principles of contiguous bodies, principles of *these* bodies,[440] and principles of forms. **(1076a3-4)** No existing thing needs its governance to proceed wrongly; moreover, there is no good in a plurality of leaders.[441]

Notes

1 This chapter is preserved in its entirety in Arabic (MS Ẓāhiriyya 4871, Damascus, 38*r*1-*v*30) and was originally published in, 'Abd al-Raḥman Badawī, *Arisṭū 'inda al-'Arab* (Cairo: Maktabat al-Nahḍa al-Miṣriyya, 1947), pp. 329–33. A revised, critical version of the Arabic text faces the Hebrew text produced in Yoav Meyrav, *Themistius' Paraphrase of Aristotle's* Metaphysics *12: A Critical Hebrew-Arabic Edition of the Surviving Textual Evidence, with an Introduction, Preliminary Studies, and a Commentary* (Leiden: Brill, 2019). For a discussion of this manuscript and Badawī's edition, along with further references, see Meyrav, *Themistius*, pp. 31–3.

2 Themistius quotes Aristotle's general statement about 'existent', which occurs several times in the *Metaphysics* (but not in Book 12), effectively orientating the entire discussion within the broader project of enquiry into being. For discussion see above, introduction, pp. 5–6, and Meyrav, *Themistius*, p. 136, p. 327.

3 In many cases in the present text, the Arabic verb *qaṣada* (translated, in turn, into the Hebrew *kivven* or similar formulations) is probably a translation of the Greek verb *protithēmi*, which Themistius occasionally uses in the context of what he intends to investigate (see, for example, in *On the Soul* 74,21 = 123,10 in the Arabic (in M. C. Lyons, *An Arabic Translation of Themistius' Commentary on Aristoteles De Anima* (London: Cassirer, 1973); 117,27 = 216,7). The literal translation from the Arabic would be 'to intend'.

4 This translation is following the Hebrew *yoter ra'ui mi-kol*, assuming the Arabic was *awlā* and the Greek *malista* (as for example in the case below, 2,14, reflecting *mallon* in *Metaph.* 1069a28, where the Hebrew is appropriately in the comparative). For a discussion of the Arabic *awwal wa-aḥqq* ('the first and most true') and how it could have come about see Meyrav, *Themistius*, p. 331.

5 Assuming *bi-hadhā al-ma'anā* is a standard formula to translate *touto* or *tauta*. See D. Gutas, *Theophrastus*: On First Principles *(known as his* Metaphysics*)* (Leiden: Brill, 2010), s.v. *ma'nan* (p. 460). The literal translation from the Arabic would be 'in this meaning'.

6 This paragraph and the next one (1,5-13) are also quoted in Averroes' long commentary on Aristotle's *Metaphysics* (in Bouyges' *Tafsīr Mā ba'd al-Ṭabī'a*, 3 vols (Beirut: Dar el-Machreq, 1948), 1410,5-15).

7 I assume *jamīʿān* (Heb. *kullam*) translates *amphoteros* here. An example for this translation is found in Themistius, in *On the Soul* 54,14 (Arabic 77,17). The literal translation in Arabic and Hebrew would be 'in all of them'.

8 The text here is occasionally employed to reflect a variant in the manuscript tradition of Aristotle's Greek text, referring to 1096a21, which reads either *eita to poion eita to poson* or *eita to poion ē poson*. I am translating according to the Arabic and Hebrew and do not think that the text can be confidently shown to reflect one version or the other. See the discussion in Meyrav, *Themistius*, p. 333, and in general, M. Frede, '*Metaphysics* Λ 1', in M. Frede and D. Charles, eds, *Aristotle's Metaphysics Lambda* (Oxford: Clarendon Press, 2000), pp. 66–7; S. Alexandru, *Aristotle's* Metaphysics *Lambda* (Leiden & Boston: Brill, 2014), p. 87; and R. Brague, *Thémistius: Paraphrase de la* Métaphysique *d'Aristote (livre Lambda)* (Paris: Vrin, 1999), p. 130, n. 5.

9 Reading *ha-sugim*, with the Hebrew, which is a translation of the Arabic *al-ajnās*. The Arabic text, as Badawī reads it, has *al-ashyā'* ('things'), and is a plausible option. However, the Arabic manuscript is somewhat corrupt and permits reading *al-ajnās* as well, so perhaps there is no discrepancy between the Arabic and the Hebrew. See Meyrav, *Themistius*, p. 334.

10 I assume the underlying Greek here is *moira* (see analogous instance in Themistius, *On the Soul* 103,5 = Arabic 187,3). The literal translation from the Arabic (*ḥaẓẓ*) and Hebrew (*ḥeleq*) would be 'their part', but the Arabic has a stronger positive connotation.

11 I take *iḍāfa* here to translate *schesis* (e.g. Themistius *On the Soul*, 60,22 = Arabic 92,12). The present translation also works well with the Arabic. The Hebrew *semikhut* can have this meaning, but the immediate meaning would be 'attachment'.

12 Reading in the singular, with the Hebrew *'etzem*. Arabic has 'substances' (*jawāhir*). See R. M. Frank, 'Some Textual Notes on the Oriental Versions of Themistius' Paraphrase of Book l of the *Metaphysics*', *Cahiers de Byrsa* 8 (1958/9), §14.

13 The Hebrew adds *lavan* ('white'), rendering the text 'our "is white"'. This is most likely an error.

14 The string 'when we say "this is not straight"' is absent in the Arabic, probably due to a scribal error.

15 Reading *'an al-'iyān*, with the Arabic, which is reflected in some Hebrew manuscripts as *be-'iyyun*. However, a variant in the Hebrew, *be-'inyan*, could be a translation of the Arabic *'an al-'ayn*, namely 'in an individual thing'. If this was indeed the original Arabic, then the translation should be changed to 'let alone in an individual thing'.

16 Literally: 'firsts' (*awā'il*; *reshiyot*), probably translating *ta prōta*.

17 Literally: 'from this place'; perhaps *min hadhā al-mawḍiʿ* here should be understood as 'from this part of the text'.

18 Perhaps Themistius is alluding to the persistence of notions in thought as presented in Aristotle's *Posterior Analytics* 2.19.

19 The Hebrew version has *ḥokhmat ha-higayon* ('science of logic'). Perhaps 'logical exercise' (*al-riyāḍa bi-l-manṭiq*) is Themistius' explication of the pedagogical context of *logikōs* in the Platonic tradition. See the useful survey of in C.D.C. Reeve, *Aristotle: Metaphysics* (Indianapolis & Cambridge: Hackett, 2016), pp. 404–7, and the note in L. Elders, *Aristotle's Theology* (Assen: Van Gorcum, 1972), pp. 79–80.

20 The string 'general things as more fitting than particulars to be substances, so that they even posit general things as the principles' is absent from the Arabic manuscript (probably a copyist error) and restored according to the Hebrew, based on the suggestions in Frank, 'Notes', 219, §28, with a few minor modifications.

21 The difference between *ʿāmīy* ('general' or 'in general'; Heb. *kolel*) and *kullīy* ('universal'; Heb. *kelali*) is probably the result of Aristote's text having *to koinon sōma* (probably echoing Plato; see Alexandru, *Metaphysics*, p. 116) at 1069a30 after having *katholou* at 1069a28.

22 The order in Hebrew is 'earth, fire'.

23 The Hebrew translation has, probably erroneously, 'nor did they posit body in general as the element of *this* fire', etc. See Meyrav, *Themistius*, p. 340.

24 I assume *amʿannā* ('we continue') to be a somewhat amplifying translation of *epi pleon* (see Gutas, *Theophrastus*, 8b15-16). Heb. has *neṭiv leʿayyen*, which means 'to theorize well'; see note ad loc. in Meyrav, *Themistius*, p. 341, for conjectures as to how this came about.

25 'That which is perduring' is missing in the Arabic and restored according to Badawī's suggestion, despite some complications, which have no bearing on the understanding of the text. See Meyrav, *Themistius*, p. 342.

26 I take *yalī* here to translate *peri*, which I render here as 'goes about on'. See Gutas, *Theophrastus*, 5b12 and p. 121, n. 37 for an analogous case. A literal translation of the Arabic would be something like 'whatever is near the earth'. The literal translation of the Hebrew *yihye* is either 'whatever is on the earth' or 'whatever comes to be on the earth', etc. Brague, *Thémistius*, p. 51, n. 4, following Frank ('Notes', p. 219, §34), assumes that the Hebrew translates *fī*, of which *yalī* is a corruption, but this would be difficult to defend (see Meyrav, *Themistius*, p. 342).

27 I translate the Arabic *min* in the sense of 'the definition or explanation of a general or universal by a special or particular term, the latter being one of several objects that go to make up the former' (W. A. Wright, *Grammar of the Arabic Language*, 3rd edn, 2 vols (Cambridge: Cambridge University Press, 1898), vol. 2, §48(g), p. 137). This reading echoes Aristotle's *hoion ta phuta kai ta zōia* at 1069a30-1.

This structure is repeated at 3,3-4. The question whether non-living things can count as substances in discussed by Aristotle in *Metaph.* 7.16.

28 For the scholarly debate surrounding Aristotle's clause that Themistius is paraphrasing here see Meyrav, *Themistius*, pp. 342–3, referring to S. Fazzo, 'Heavenly Matter in Aristotle, *Metaphysics* Lambda 2', *Phronesis* 58, no. 2 (2013), 162-6; Frede, '*Metaphysics* Λ 1', pp. 78–80.

29 It is unclear what these 'earlier discussions' are, Brague suggests, with some reservation, that Themistius is referring to discussions of the ancients he introduced earlier (Brague, *Thémistius*, p. 51; p. 130, n. 11). It is possible that Themistius is referring to discussions in the *Physics*. Another option is to translate the sentence in the present tense: 'this substance alone is the substance whose elements are enquired into in the first discussions', referring to the first parts of *Metaphysics* 12, which mostly focus on perishable sensible substance.

30 'That it is' is absent from the Arabic and *anahu* is restored according to the Hebrew *she-hu*'.

31 Reading with the Arabic *aw* ('or'). The Hebrew has *ve-* ('and'), which cannot be correct.

32 Reading with the Heb. (*yoter peshuṭim*). The Arabic has *al-basīṭ* ('the simple'), perhaps a corruption of *absaṭ*, which would align the Arabic with the Hebrew. See Frank, 'Notes', p. 219, §35; Brague, *Thémistius*, p. 51 and ibid., n. 5.

33 See Aristotle, *On the Heavens* 3.5, where Aristotle discusses and dismisses thinkers who posit a single element with features similar to what Themistius describes here. See also *Physics* 1.4.

34 The Hebrew adds the emphasis 'at all' (*kelal*, perhaps reflecting *aṣlān*, absent in the Arabic we have).

35 In other words, this is the distinctive feature of a celestial body. I am reading the text with the Arabic (*wa-'alā hadhā mabnīy amr ṭabī'atihi*) and assume *amr ṭabī'atihi* to translate the Greek *tēs phuseōs*. Hebrew has *ve-'al ze nivna 'inyan ha-ṭeva'* (reading *al-ṭabī'a* for *ṭabī'atahu*, which our Arabic has). The translation in this case would be 'upon this [the science of] nature is founded', and will have this expression refer to the preceding discussion as a whole rather than focusing only on celestial bodies.

36 I take *khārij 'an* (Heb. *yotze' mi-*) here to translate *exō*, as in Themistius, *On the Soul* 22,2 (=Arabic 5,2). The literal meaning of the Arabic (and Hebrew) is 'the unmoved and incorporeal substance is external to any change'.

37 Themistius may be alluding to Aristotle's definition of place, meaning that a thing that is not confined by corporeal boundaries cannot be said to be in a certain place.

38 In the present text, the Arabic *sā'ir* usually means 'the rest' but sometimes 'all', a dual meaning common in Arabic. See Wright, *Grammar*, vol. 2, pp. 206–7;

E. W. Lane, *Arabic-English Lexicon*, 8 vols (London, 1863-1893), s.v. *sā'ir*. This causes problems in the Hebrew manuscript tradition, which sometimes disagrees about whether to translate *she'ar* ('the rest of') or *kol* ('all of'); see also 18,19 below. Here I chose to translate 'all', with most Hebrew manuscripts.

39 'And' is omitted in the Arabic.

40 Literally: 'all things that are of sensible substances'.

41 The Arabic text adds *mubāyin lahu* ('[and] differentiated from it'). Frank, 'Notes', §41 suggests this is a gloss, and I agree.

42 'At all' (*al-batta*) is absent from the Hebrew.

43 The Hebrew adds 'first' (*ha-rishon*; 'this first substance'). I agree with Frank, 'Notes', §42, who presumes this is a gloss, but this cannot be ascertained.

44 'Into two' (or, more literally, 'a twofold division'; *qismayn*) is absent from the Hebrew.

45 'Mathematical extensions' is a literal translation of the Arabic *al-ab'ād al-ta'līmiyya* (Hebrew: *ha-merḥaqim ha-limudiyim*; 'mathematical distances'). Aristotle in this context has *ta mathēmatika* (1069a35), which is usually translated as 'mathematical objects', and in the Arabic translation of the *Metaphysics*: simply *al-ta'līmiyya* ('the mathematicals'). Perhaps the Arabic in the present case is an unpacking of *ta mathēmatika*, but Isḥāq usually unpacks instances like this in a different way (see Meyrav, *Themistius*, p. 347). A case can be made to translate this expression as 'mathematical objects'. Another option is that *ab'ād* is a translation of the Greek term *diaistēmata*.

46 The Hebrew does not have 'intelligible substances' but simply 'substances'. Frank ('Notes', §44) suggests that the Hebrew should be followed and that *al-ma'qūla* ('intelligible') is a gloss. Brague (*Thémistius*, p. 53, n. 1) is undecided. It is difficult to defend one view or the other, but since the next sentence explicates these substances as intelligible, and both versions agree on this, the implications for the meaning of Themistius' argument are marginal.

47 This sentence changes into the singular halfway through the Arabic (and Hebrew). The literal, ungrammatical translation is 'Those who posited that there is one [kind of] intelligible substance are *he* who presumed that the mathematical extensions are the substances and gave up on Ideas'. I corrected the grammar and rendered the sentence plural, but this is only one option of understanding the text, and not necessarily the best one. It seems that something is missing in the text: in its present form, it has Themistius ignoring Aristotle's mention of people who say that Ideas and mathematical objects have the same nature. Perhaps some text was lost and the grammatical problem in the Arabic is a remnant of this. See further discussion in Meyrav, *Themistius*, p. 348.

48 The Hebrew omits 'not a place... change'. Frank, 'Notes', §45 considers this a homoeoteleuton.

49 'Also' (*aiḍān*) is omitted from the Hebrew.

50 It is unclear whether or not Themistius follows Aristotle's terminology (1069b4-5) in distinguishing between *antikeimenos* ('opposite') and *enantios* ('contrary'), the latter a kind of the former. If he does, then the Arabic common translation *ḍidd* (Heb. *hefekh*) blurs this and the reflection of the distinction is in the qualification *al-mushākila al-qarība* (Heb. *ha-mitdamim ha-qerovim*), literally 'proper proximate', to signify 'contrary'.

51 The first lines of this chapter are preserved in Arabic (MS Ẓāhiriyya 4871, Damascus, 38*v*30-38); the details and references given at n. 1 above hold to this portion as well. The text terminates at Heb. 4,13: 'according to opposition' (Ar. *'alā jihat al-muqābala*; Heb. *'al tzad ha-hitnagdut*), marked at n. 58 below.

52 For this term see Meyrav, *Themistius*, p. 356.

53 Aristotle first lists the four types of change (1069b9-10) and then explains in what respect each is a change (1069b10-13). Themistius elaborates on each type immediately after mentioning it.

54 Literally, 'by which what it is is made known'.

55 Translated according to the Arabic. The Hebrew has 'we call this change'.

56 'Last' (Heb. *aḥaron*) is absent from the Arabic. See Frank, 'Notes', §50.

57 i.e. like all sensible substances.

58 Here the Arabic text of MS Ẓāhiriyya 4871 terminates. The next portion of the Arabic is available at the appendix to Chapter 3, which Averroes quotes (see below, n. 108).

59 Here I take *tzad* (literally: 'side' or 'aspect') to translate *jiha*, which at present I assume translates *tropos* in the sense of 'direction'.

60 i.e. can change in all four kinds of change.

61 Hebrew *matzav*, and this is the only occurrence of the term in the present text. My translation follows Brague. *matzav* usually translates the Arabic *waḍ'* in this context, probably reflecting the Greek *thesis* (see e.g. Themistius, *in De Anima* 25,2 = Ar. 11,15).

62 These three examples reflect, respectively, the other three types of change: change in quality, change in quantity, and change in substance.

63 Literally, 'doubt', but I assume *safeq* here translates the Arabic *shakk* according to Isḥāq's standard translation for the Greek *aporia* (see e.g. Gutas, *Theophrastus*, s.v., *škk*; Themistius, *in De Anima* 35,36 = Ar. 35, 4).

64 Themistius skips 1096b20-21, to which he returns at 5,14 below.

65 Themistius' division is different from Aristotle's at 1067b25-30: the false; the contrary to what is; the contrary to what is something (the latter two are types of potentiality; see the discussion in D. Charles, '*Metaphysics* Λ 2', in Michael Frede and David Charles, eds, *Aristotle's Metaphysics Lambda* (Oxford: Clarendon Press, 2000), p. 89, n. 2; cf. Brague, *Thémistius*, p. 132, §7 for more references).

66 Literally, 'that which comes-to-be'.

67 This is my guess for the odd Heb. expression *ve-hu' 'omed*, which can be understood in different ways. *ve-hu'* ('and it') can refer either to the thing that comes-to-be or to the privation, and *'omed* can translate here (at least) *qā'im* ('stands'), *thābit* ('is affirmed'), or *bāqī* ('persists') if it refers to the thing that comes-to-be, or (at least) *lābith* ('remains' or 'persists') or *sākin* ('rests' or 'dwells') if it is referring to the privation. If the clause is referring to the privation, then *ve-hu' 'omed* might be a repetition of sorts to *ha-munaḥ* ('which stand'), which describes the privation a few lines earlier and renders it static, which (perhaps) would explain why nothing can come-to-be from it (cf. 13,28-30, where the Ideas are rendered useless through similar argumentation). Brague (*Thémistius*) in his translation ('et que celle-ci subsiste') understands the text as referring to the thing that comes-to-be and has Themistius say that it subsists, which (I assume) serves as an explanation as to why it cannot come-to-be from the completely non-existent and the privation, which do not subsist. This would go well with the term *thābit*. My own guess – which is close to Brague's – is that the text is referring to the things that comes-to-be and that Themistius is referring to persistence (*hupomenein*), which is one of the characteristics that distinguish matter from privation and enables to explain why (non-incidental) coming-to-be is from the former, not the latter (See Themistius, *Physics* 24,15-25,23; Robert Todd, *Themistius: On Aristotle's* Physics *1-3* (London: Bloomsbury, 2012), pp. 41–3). See more discussion with further examples in Meyrav, *Themistius*, p. 359.

68 Literally, 'that which comes-to-be'.

69 Adding another *hu'* ('it') to the end of the sentence, in accordance with some Hebrew manuscripts. I now think that it should be part of the body of the text.

70 This is a slightly paraphrastic translation of a Hebrew formulation (*ei ze geshem she-yiqre*) that I find impossible to translate literally. A more elegant translation would perhaps be 'any random body'. The verb *qara* here likely ultimately derives from the Greek *tunchanō*, probably via the Arabic *ittafaqa* (e.g. Themistius, *in De Anima* 23,26 = Ar. 9,2).

71 Literally, 'the same one in all its states'.

72 The Hebrew word *yaḥas* probably translates the Arabic *nasab* (or *nisba*), which in turn translates *logos* (as a formative principle). Themistius is anticipating his discussion of the *logoi* as pre-existing in matter in his appendix to his paraphrase of Chapter 3 (especially starting from 8,2; cf. Brague, *Thémistius*, p. 132, §9, for reference to Stoic precedents). For further context see the notes to the last part of Chapter 3.

73 See Aristotle, *Physics* 8.1, 250b24-6.

74 While Aristotle originally discussed in this passage Anaxagoras, Empedocles, Anaximander, and Democritus, Themistius only mentions Anaxagoras, as a stepping stone for his own view, introduced in 5,18.

75 For this highly interesting passage see Meyrav, *Themistius*, pp. 353–5; G. Guldentops, 'La science suprême selon Thémistius', *Revue de philosophie ancienne* 19, no. 1 (2001), 112. It warrants a much more detailed investigation. To my knowledge, this passage was never included (or considered for inclusion) in surveys of testimonia about Anaxagoras.

76 With only the Hebrew present and without precedents, it is impossible to say anything certain about Themistius' terminology here, but in my opinion it is very likely that he is reproducing Anaxagoras' respective technical terms *apokrinesthai* ('to separate off'), *proskrinesthai* ('to conjoin'), *sunkrinesthai* ('to connect'), and *sumpēgnusthai* ('to compound'). See the discussion in P. Curd, *Anaxagoras of Clazomenae: Fragments and Testimonia* (Toronto: University of Toronto Press, 2007), pp. 192–205.

77 'Craftsman' here translates *tzoref* (most likely reflecting the Arabic *ṣā'igh*; *dēmiourgeō* is translated as *ṣāgha* at Themistius, *On the Soul* 99,25 = Ar. 180,8), and is appropriate to the 'demiurgic' description of the Divine Mind.

78 Themistius does not paraphrase 1069b32-34, which discuss form, privation, and matter as principles. He takes up this issue at his paraphrase of 1070b11 ff. (9,25 etc. below), where Aristotle elaborates on this division.

79 The beginning of this chapter survives only in Hebrew, but its last part (starting at 7,27) is quoted in Averroes' long commentary on Aristotle's *Metaphysics* (in Bouyges' edition, 1492,3-1494,5). The Arabic quotation is critically edited facing the Hebrew in Meyrav, *Themistius*.

80 There is confusion within the Hebrew manuscripts as to whether the text has 'form' or 'forms'. It seems that initially it was translated in the singular, and was then revised to the plural. Without the Arabic it is impossible to know which is correct, but I believe that the original plural is the correct reading, if we take the discussion to be a direct continuation of the previous chapter, where forms were discussed in the plural.

81 Brague (*Thémistius*, p. 59, n. 1) suggests that the word *levad* should be omitted, probably being erroneously copied from the next line (5,27). If this is correct, then the words 'by themselves' in the translation should be omitted. However, I think the present text should be retained, having Themistius mean that a form cannot come-to-be without being accompanied by matter, as the immediately following example tries to show.

82 See Aristotle, *Physics* 1.9. But the argument put forth here seems to be based on an argument at *Metaph.* 7.8, of which Aristotle's discussion at 1069b35-1070a4 is an abbreviation (or the former is an expansion upon the latter, depending on the order of composition). The affinity between *Metaph.* 12.3 and 7.7-9 has long been noticed (See L. Judson, 'Formlessness and the Priority of Form: *Metaphysics*: Z 7-9

and Λ 3', in M. Frede and D. Charles, eds, *Aristotle's Metaphysics Lambda* (Oxford: Clarendon Press, 2000), pp. 111–35, esp. pp. 111–24, for an overview and discussion), so Themistius' employment of these chapters in his paraphrase of this chapter is not surprising (see ibid., pp. 125–6, for the present passage).

83 Themistius uses 'craftsman' (*tzoref*; see above, n. 78) for the sake of continuity with the previous discussion. Aristotle has 'the direct mover' (*tou prōtou kinountos*; see Reeve, *Metaphysics*, p. 515, §1297) at 1070a1; 1033a34 refers to a producer.

84 Themistius is limiting the sense of sameness in coming-to-be of things that share a form, perhaps echoing Aristotle's qualification at *Metaph.* 7, 1033b30-2: 'In some cases it is even evident that the begetter is of this same sort as the begotten (not that they are the same things, certainly, nor one in number, but one in form)' (tr. Reeve). Brague (*Thémistius*, p. 59, n. 3) assumes that the Arabic for *levado* was *faqaṭ* ('only'), and this is possible of course, but since the Hebrew has a possessive suffix, perhaps the Arabic was *waḥdahu* ('it, solely'). A case could also be made for *levado* functioning as a limit to coming-to-be, not only to the name. In other words, an alternative translation could be something like 'every individual natural thing *only* comes-to-be from something like it whose name applies to it'.

85 i.e. the form of the house in the carpenter's thought.

86 Heb. *me-heyot holekh 'al darko* ('from going its way').

87 Brague (*Thémistius*, p. 133, §2) notes a similar example in Themistius' paraphrase of the *Physics* 45,12. 'Pilot' is a translation of *manhig*, itself translating *mudabbir* or *rubbān*, reflecting the Greek *kubernētēs*.

88 Themistius repeats Aristotle's original division of substance in Chapter 1, making it clear that the division of substance in Chapter 3 is a further subdivision. Aristotle's division of substance here refers to the perceptible substance (see Judson, 'Formlessness', p. 128), and Themistius has the subdivision referring specifically to *perishable* perceptible substances.

89 This is the first time the term 'matter' occurs in the text, effectively relegating it to the perishable sensible substance (although Themistius is not entirely consistent with this). Up to this point in the text, Themistius preferred either 'body' or 'recipient', even when Aristotle's text explicitly used the term 'matter'. The translation of the term *hulē* in the present text is problematic because the Arabic is *'unṣur*, which is also used to translate *stoicheion* ('element'), creating much confusion. This problem is discussed in detail in Meyrav, *Themistius*, pp. 527–31.

90 Brague, *Thémistius*, has already shown that *ramuz elav be-nafsho* translates the Arabic *mushārān ilaihi bi-dhātihi*, which reflects the Greek *tode ti kath' hautēn*, hence the translation 'this-something in itself', which aligns to Aristotle's text. The literal translation of the Hebrew would be, approximately, something like 'essentially self-referring'.

91 The Hebrew has the very difficult *lo' tihye ha-remiza elav ela' 'al ze* and the translation depends on how one understands the expression *ha-remiza elav*. I take it to reflect a verbal noun construction out of the form *ramuz elav* (being a 'this-something') explained in the previous note. However, since *remiza* can also mean 'reference', a case could be made for understanding the sentence to say that the fact that one is able to point to an attribute in a thing is due to that thing being a 'this-something'. For further discussion of this issue, see Meyrav, *Themistius*, pp. 369–70.

92 Compare Themistius' paraphrase of *On the Soul*: 'substance as matter is a substance in potentiality and not yet in itself a "this something", but like a natural disposition for it, and a preparation to becoming a "this something"' (39,7-9; Quoting Todd's translation *Themistius: On Aristotle's On the Soul* (Ithaca: Cornell University Press, 1996), p. 56, slightly modified for terminological conformity; cf. Aristotle, *Metaphysics* 1042a27-28 for a similar approach).

93 The literal meaning of the Hebrew *'ad she-* is 'until', but I assume that the underlying Arabic is *ḥattā* in the sense of indicating an exception. Both options are possible. For elaboration, see Meyrav, *Themistius*, pp. 370–1.

94 As already noted by Brague (*Thémistius*, p. 134, §7), this is explained in the *Physics*: 'The underlying nature can be known by analogy. For as the bronze is to the statue, the wood to the bed, or the formless before receiving form to any thing which has form, i.e. the "this something" or existent' (1.7, 191a7-12; tr. Hardie & Gaye with minor revisions, omitting *hē hulē* with Ross at 191a10).

95 Heb. *mezuyyaf* (probably translating the Arabic *zūr*) is literally 'counterfeit' or 'fake', but here I follow Brague's suggestion (*Thémistius*, p. 134, §7) that Themistius is alluding to Plato's 'bastard' (*nothos*) reasoning in the *Timaeus*. This is, in fact, the connection Themistius makes in his paraphrase of *On the Soul*, which refers to 'Plato's claim that matter is "to be grasped by bastard reasoning", for it is precisely a "bastard" activity of both the intellect and sense-perception in that it occurs not in respect of a [direct] impacting of form [on the intellect] but in respect of a process of withdrawal' (111,24-26, tr. Todd, *On the Soul*, p. 137). In this passage, *nothos* is translated into *zūr* (Ar. 203,14–15).

96 Heb. *mitra'e be-ma she-ein bo*, literally 'displays what it does not have', which is probably a translation of *mutaẓāhir bi-mā laysa lahu*.

97 Literally, 'rolls' (Heb. *yitgalgel*).

98 Originally, I thought that by 'the first matter' (Heb. *ha-yesod ha-rishon*) Themistius is alluding to prime matter (see Meyrav, *Themistius*, p. 364), but now I think that this expression reflects *prōton* in the sense of proximity, like a golden ring which turns into the mineral gold when the ring is destroyed.

99 Literally, 'enquire and seek' (*naḥqor ve-nevaqesh*), which most likely translates the Arabic *nabḥathu wa-naṭlubu*, a hendiadys translation of the verb *zēteō* (see Gutas, *Theophrastus*, s.v. *ṭlb*, p. 457).

100 The Hebrew has *she-teḥashev ba-dimyon*, which literally should be translated as 'to be thought in the imagination'. But since the context here is artificial things whose forms exist in the thought of the craftsman, the literal translation would be misleading, as Themistius is probably not talking about *phantasia*. The more plausible explanation for the Hebrew construction is the translator's uncertainty about how to translate the Arabic root *w-h-m* and the different parts of speech it construes. The different Hebrew manuscripts alternate, not always consistently, between the roots *ḥ-sh-b* ('to think') and *d-m-h* ('to imagine' or 'to presume') (see, e.g. 3,11; 13,19). In my opinion, the present construct is a result of this problem; the Arabic had some form of *w-h-m* with reference to the verb *noeō* that was unpacked in the Hebrew version.

101 Literally: 'These things have neither coming-to-be nor perishing, but they are either existents or are non-existent in a different respect'. To paraphrase the somewhat odd Hebrew rendering of the text, if forms of artificial things exist, it is not by virtue of coming-to-be, and if they do not exist, it is not by virtue of perishing. The 'different respect' in which forms of artificial things exist or not is in so far as they are present or absent in the craftsman's thought.

102 This is a literal translation from the Hebrew *mufshaṭot*, but perhaps somewhat distorts the meaning. Desired translations are 'without' (if the Greek had *aneu*) or 'bare' (if the Greek had *psilos*).

103 Aristotle's generally adopted text in 1070a18 has him explicitly mentioning Plato, and this has raised a potential problem of interpretation, as Plato is generally considered to have accepted Ideas of artifacts, and in the present passage Aristotle has him denying that (see Elders, *Aristotle's Theology*, p. 107, for an overview of this problem). Themistius' reference to 'those who posited the Ideas' is not his own interpretative innovation to mitigate this problem, but rather a reflection of an alternative textual tradition which is preserved also in Alexander of Aphrodisias' commentary on this passage (quoted by Averroes in his *Tafsīr*, 1481), as well as in Abū Bishr Mattā's Arabic translation, also quoted by Averroes (ibid., 1480; Usṭāth's translation, quoted in the margins of the manuscript of Averroes' *Tafsīr*, ibid., reflects the accepted tradition). Furthermore, Alexander was aware of the textual tradition explicitly mentioning Plato. Kotwick, who discusses this issue at length, with plenty of further reference, suggests that the textual tradition Alexander and Themistius follow had *hoi ta eidē tithentes ephasan* for the received *Platōn ephē*. This reading would have Aristotle referring

to Plato's successors rather than to Plato himself, effectively eliminating the problem. See M. E. Kotwick, *Alexander of Aphrodisias and the Text of Aristotle's* Metaphysics (Berkeley: California Classical Studies, 2016), pp. 75–8.

104 This is a literal translation of the Hebrew *mesubbakhot ba-geshem*. See discussion in Meyrav, *Themistius*, p. 372.

105 Moses ibn Tibbon replaces Themistius' original example, which was probably Polycleitus or Phidias, with Terah, Abraham's father, who according to Jewish tradition manufactured idols for a living (for discussion see Brague, *Thémistius*, p. 134, §12). It is impossible to know if the Arabic had a transliteration of a Greek name or its own appropriate substitute.

106 This passage is not so much a paraphrase of Aristotle's text at 1070a27-30, which is telegraphic at best, as it is a restatement of Aristotle's argument against the Ideas in *Metaphysics* 7.7-9. For a systematic analysis and preliminary English translation of this passage see Meyrav, 'Spontaneous Generation', pp. 198–9.

107 The printed Hebrew text at 7,21 has *ha-mityalledet* ('the begotten'), but I have since changed my mind about this and now think that the variant *ha-meyalledet* ('the begetting') should be preferred on the basis of argumentative soundness.

108 From this point until the end of the chapter, the Arabic translation is quoted in Averroes' *Tafsīr*, 1492,3-1494,14 and is included in the critical edition in Meyrav, *Themistius* (see the discussion ibid., p 39), and for the Hebrew tradition(s), pp. 518–22. This part of Themistius' text is perhaps the most discussed in scholarship, and has already been translated into English twice: first, from the Arabic, in C. Genequand, *Ibn Rushd's Metaphysics: A Translation with Introduction of Ibn Rushd's Commentary on Aristotle's* Metaphysics, *Book Lām* (Leiden: Brill, 1986), pp. 105–7, revised in R. Sorabji, ed., *The Philosophy of the Commentators, 200-600* AD (Ithaca: Cornell University Press, 2005), vol. 1, p. 259), and then my own preliminary translation, which is integrated in my 'Spontaneous Generation', pp. 195–210. This chapter is also discussed, analysed, and criticized in D. Henry, 'Themistius and the Problem of Spontaneous Generation', in Richard Sorabji, ed., *Aristotle Re-interpreted* (London: Bloomsbury, 2016), pp. 179–94. See both papers for further references.

109 Unlike Genequand's choice, 'sufficient' (in his *Ibn Rushd*), I am translating the Arabic term *muqniʿ* as 'persuasive'. Brague, *Thémistius,* translates *convaincant* as 'convincing', while A. Martin's *suffire* (in his *Averroès: Grand commentaire de la Métaphysique d'Aristote, livre Lambda* (Paris: Les Belles Lettres, 1984)) sides with Genequand. The original Hebrew version of Averroes' *Long Commentary* has *heletziyi* ('rhetorical'; MS Vatican Heb. 336,183*r*1). *Muqniʿ* by itself can go either way in Arabic, but here it is most likely a translation of the Greek *pithanon*, as

can be gathered from Themistius *in De Anima*, 61,24 = 95,2 in the Arabic edition). Other legitimate options would be 'convincing' or 'plausible'.

110 Reading with the Arabic *aghfala*. The Hebrew has *yaqshe* (or *yuqshe, or yiqshe*) *'alav* which could mean different things, like 'would face difficulty', 'could be asked', or 'would pose him a question'. It is unclear how the Hebrew came about. See the further discussion in Meyrav, *Themistius*, pp. 373–4.

111 *Logos* is the original technical term for formal principles in matter of which the Arabic *nisba* and the Heb. *yaḥas* are translations. See the discussion and analysis in Meyrav, 'Spontaneous Generation', pp. 200–7.

112 Genequand (*Ibn Rushd*) translated *naẓā'ir* as 'models', creating the impression that Themistius is advocating a certain notion of Platonic Ideas, and this has led to some confusion in scholarship, probably also because this is how Averroes understood Themistius' text. However, *naẓīr* is here used for translating *analogos*, as is commonplace in Isḥāq's translation of Themistius' paraphrase of *De Anima* (see the glossary in Lyons, *Themistius*). Martin's French 'equivalents' (*Grand commentaire*, p. 129) is also a good option. The Arabic *naẓīr* is employed in this meaning a few times in the surviving Arabic of the present text in other, less problematic contexts.

113 The final words of this sentence ('would not be brought into actuality'; Heb. *lo' haya yōtze' el ha-po'al*) are omitted from Averroes' Arabic quotation, and subsequently from Genequand's English translation of the text. Restoring them makes a very big difference because it enables us to understand differently the syntax of the sentence, and it suggests that for Themistius the *logos*, rather than the parent, is the formal cause of the offspring.

114 Reading with the Arabic (*wa-lā yughirnaka al-iḥtiqār*). The Hebrew manuscripts have conflicting reports. See the discussion in Meyrav, *Themistius*, pp. 375–6.

115 I take the 'and' in the expression '*logoi* and forms' – here and in its other occurrences in the text – to reflect an epexegetic *kai*. 'Forms' here need not be understood in the Platonic sense.

116 Literally: '*has* no artistry'.

117 For this term and its various Hebrew translations, as well as the logic behind the Arabic *ilhām*, see Meyrav, *Themistius*, pp. 376–8 and 'Spontaneous Generation', p. 206, n. 29.

118 Arabic Grammar permits *minhā* ('than it') also to refer to either nature or the *logoi* (and then the translation should be 'than them'). The Hebrew translation (*me-hem*) understands the reference to be to the *logoi*. I think the reference is to nature because it makes better sense for the argument. This aspect of the present passage caused much confusion in the Arabic and Hebrew tradition regarding the causal relation between the different components of the argument.

119 For 'the soul that is in the earth' (Arabic: *al-nafs al-latī fī al-arḍ*; Hebrew: *ha-nefesh asher ba-aretz*) see Meyrav, 'Spontaneous Generation', p. 205, n. 26; p. 206, n. 28, and the further references there.

120 The Hebrew has 'desires' (*mishtoqeq*), misreading the Arabic *mustāqa* for the theoretical *mushtāqa*.

121 Genequand (*Ibn Rushd*) has 'we need' for *iḥtajnā ilā*, which is possible, and this is also how Moses ibn Tibbon understood the Arabic, but 'we enquire into' makes better sense, and the Arabic could be translating the Greek *zētoumen* (this is what Isḥāq does, e.g. in his Arabic translation of Theophrastus' *On First Principles* 7b6; see D. Gutas, *Theophrastus*, p. 132; p. 192.).

122 My translation of this sentence is very different from Genequand's (in his *Ibn Rushd*), who has: 'But when we need any form, we act in such a way that we know that this form cannot be produced by this act alone'. Genequand's translation is a good reflection of the Arabic published in Bouyges' *Tafsīr* (1494,11-13). The new edition emends the text heavily. See discussion in Meyrav, *Themistius*, p. 379.

123 This chapter begins only with Hebrew, but Ibn Taymiyya quotes the Arabic translation of its latter half, starting at 9,24, along with the first half of Chapter 5 (ending at 11,4), in his *Minhāj al-Sunna al-Nabawiyya*, ed. M. Rashad Sālim (Al-Riyāḍ, 1986); For Ibn Taymiyya as a source see Meyrav, *Themistius*, p. 48.

124 Themistius skips Aristotle's opening statement at 1070a31-3 ('The causes and principles of distinct things are distinct in a way, but in a way – if we are to speak universally and analogically – they are the same for all'; tr. Reeve, slightly modified), and heads straight into the aporetic discussion.

125 This is Themistius' way to explain Aristotle's seamless transition from discussing principles to discussing elements, noted by the epexegetical use of *kai* in his expression 'principles and elements' (*archai kai stoicheiai*) when formulating the question at 1070a34. See M. Crubellier, '*Metaphysics* Λ 4', in M. Frede and D. Charles, eds, *Aristotle's Metaphysics Lambda* (Oxford: Clarendon Press, 2000), p. 142 for this expression.

126 Literally: 'say to them'.

127 See above, 1,8 ff.

128 Literally, 'from him'.

129 This translation is a mere guess, as the Hebrew is obscure (*ve-lo'/va-lo' ha-nimtza' ha-eḥad shenei nimtza'im*). Perhaps Themistius' point is that 'existence' would be predicated differently of the categories in themselves and of the things that partake in them, consequently 'doubling' existence. Another translation option would be 'and the "one existent" is not two existents', perhaps because it would revert to two common principles – 'one' and 'existing'. One Hebrew manuscript

has the (maybe desirable) formulation 'the one and the existent are not two [different] existents' (*hine ein ha-nimtza ve-ha-eḥad shenei nimtza'im*), but this may be a local initiative to restore sense.

130 Here begins the Arabic quotation in ibn Taymiyya's *Minhāj al-Sunna al-Nabawiyya.*

131 The Arabic has *'alā ṭarīq al-munāsaba wa-l-muqāyasa* (Heb. *'al derekh ha-yaḥas ve-ha-heqesh*, literally 'in the manner of proportion and comparison'). I assume the original to be some form of *analogos* (see 9,24) and the Arabic to be either a hendiadys or containing a gloss.

132 At this point, 'principle' and 'element' (the latter as one of the meanings of the former) cease to be used interchangeably as they were for the sake of Themistius' discussion (reflecting what he takes to be Aristotle's logic as of 9,1), and are differentiated afresh.

133 That the moving cause is one of the senses of 'principle' has been asserted above, at 9,1-2.

134 Literally, 'be'.

135 Reading with the Hebrew (*hinne eino yesod be-lo' safeq*) rather than the Arabic (*fa-laysa lahu 'unṣur lā maḥāla*; 'undoubtedly it does not have an element'). I take Themistius to be arguing that every element is a principle, but not every principle is an element, and *lahu* to be a misreading or corruption of *huwa.*

136 Correcting the Arabic from *al-muḥarrik* ('the mover') to *al-mutaḥarrik* ('the moved'), reflecting the Hebrew (*ha-mitno'e'a*). For further discussion see Meyrav, *Themistius*, p. 387.

137 Reading with the Hebrew (*aval ha-meni'a ha-qarov ba-devarim ha-ṭiv'iyyim*). The Arabic has 'but the mover that is proximate to natural things' (*wa-lakina al-muḥarrik al-qarīb min al-ashyā' al-ṭabī'iyya*).

138 The Arabic has *al-'ashyā' al-wahmiyya*, probably reflecting the Greek *tois apo dianoias*. Hebrew has the hendiadys *ha-devarim he-melakhutiyim ha-maḥshaviyim* (literally: 'the artificial things which are products of calculation'), probably trying to move the argumentation closer to the distinction between nature and art.

139 Reading with the Hebrew. The Arabic is slightly different, with no significant change in meaning: 'medicine *and* ignorance of it, and carpentry *and* ignorance of it'.

140 Literally, 'the mover'.

141 For the Arabic portion of this chapter see above, n. 123.

142 I am reading with the Arabic (*wa-lam yakun al-tahayyub min al-taṣrīḥ bi-hadhā fīmā taqaddama ṣawābān*). For the problems in the Hebrew *ve-lo' tihye ha-'atzela min ha-be'ur ba-ze be-ma she-qadam yosher* see Meyrav, *Themistius*, p. 392.

143 The Arabic has *aḥdāth wa-aḥwāl* (appropriately translated into *ḥiddushim ve-'inyanim* in Hebrew), which would roughly mean 'accidents and states'.

However, I believe that Themistius is using Aristotle's terminology at 1071a1 here and that this is a hendiadys translation of *pathē*, which here means, according to A. Code ('*Metaphysics* Λ 5', in. M. Frede and D. Charles, eds, *Aristotle's Metaphysics Lambda* (Oxford: Clarendon Press, 2000), p. 162), 'modification'. The term *pathos* occurs twice more in *Metaphysics* 12, each in a place where Themistius' paraphrase is close to Aristotle's text and in which we have both the Arabic and the Hebrew: 1069b12 and 1071b10. The first is translated into *ḥāl* (Heb. *'inyan*; 4,9), and the second into *ḥadath* (Heb. *ḥiddush*; 12,21), so in the present passage it was either a gloss or a hendiadys to widen the semantic field of the term.

144 Literally: 'to judge'.

145 Taking *talzamu* (literally, 'necessitated'; Heb. *yitḥaivu*) to translate *sumbainō*, as is frequent in Isḥāq.

146 For this sentence and the textual problems associated with is see Meyrav, *Themistius*, p. 393.

147 Here it is very likely that Themistius reads *ē* for the traditional *kai* in Aristotle's text at 1071a9 (see the apparatus in Alexandru, *Metaphysics*, p. 94).

148 The Arabic does not give two options, but has *min* instead of the Hebrew *o* (=Ar. *aw*; 'or'). In that case the translation would be: 'By "form" we mean the form which can be separated from the composition of form and matter'.

149 Here 'elements', as in the previous chapter, in the sense of immanent principles. Themistius means that things can differ from each other in matter or in form.

150 Reading with the Hebrew (*aval ba-devarim gam ken ha-yotz'im min ha-davar ha-meni'im oto*). The Arabic is corrupt (*lakina fī al-ashyā' al-khārija 'an al-ashyā' al-murakkaba ayḍān*) and has something like 'in things that are external to composite things as well'. *al-murakkaba* is probably a corruption of *al-muḥarrika*, or a miscopy from the previous line, which also has *al-murakkaba*, but in a proper context and in alignment with the Hebrew *ha-murkavim*.

151 Ar. *muwāfiqa fī al-ṣūra* ('accord in form'; Heb. *na'otot ba-tzura*), most likely translating *homoeidēs*, as can be gathered from 11,3, which reflects 1070a17.

152 The Hebrew mistakenly reads *wa-ba'dahā* (*ve-aḥareihem*; 'and after them') instead of the Arabic *wa-ba'ḍhā* ('and some of them'), creating confusion within the different manuscripts as to the contents of this sentence.

153 Aristotle states the inclined circle and the sun as a joint cause. Perhaps Themistius writes that the inclined circle is a farther away cause then the sun because of the sun's four spheres in Aristotle's astronomy, the inclined course is the second, whereas the sun itself is in the fourth (which is closer to Earth). But there is also a more elaborate explanation, namely that while the sun generates heat, its course is determined by the inclined circle, and this causes the changing

seasons and the cycle of coming-to-be and perishing. I would like to thank Stephen Menn for this point.

154 Here terminates the Arabic quotation in ibn Taymiyya, *Minhāj al-Sunna al-Nabawiyya*.

155 The expression *ha-nifradot ha-praṭiyot* ('particular [and] individual') appears twice in the present line and reflects Aristotle's to *kath' hekaston* ('individual') at 1071a20-1, which Themistius here follows. There is a good chance that the Hebrew reflects either a gloss or a hendiadys in the Arabic.

156 Literally, 'this water is the cause of this water' (!). The reason for this strange course of events is that the Hebrew *mayim* ('water') translates the Arabic *mā'*, which is graphically similar to *bā'*, the second letter of the Arabic alphabet, translating B, and the Arabic *B'* would reflect the combination BA. Aristotle's example at 1071a22 is of a particular B as a principle of a particular BA.

157 Literally, 'and likewise the mover'.

158 Literally, 'not one'.

159 See above, n. 131.

160 See above, 1,13–24.

161 Chapters 6-9 are abridged in the Arabic version. See above, Introduction, p. 10, and for a comprehensive discussion with further references see Meyrav, *Themistius*, pp. 48–62.

162 Heb. *naḥqor ve-nevaqqesh* (literally: 'investigate and enquire'), which translates the Arabic *nabḥathu wa-naṭlubu*, which is a hendiadys translation of the Greek *zēteō* (see above, 6,32). The Arabic abridgement only retains *naṭlubu*.

163 Reading in the singular with the Hebrew. The Arabic is in the plural ('changes and alterations').

164 Reading *allatī hiya*, with the Arabic. The Hebrew has *kelomar* ('i.e.').

165 Heb. has *'inyanim*, which is corroborated by *al-ma'nayayn* in an Arabic quote of this sentence by 'Abd al-Laṭīf al-Baghdādī. The Arabic abridgement adds *ṣifatān* at the end of the sentence to restore sense to the part it abridged (see next note). *ma'nā* is translated into *'inyan* elsewhere in the text (1,5), although with a different meaning. *ṣifa* does not appear anywhere in the text we have.

166 The Arabic has *nanẓuru* ('theorize') which the Hebrew usually reserves for *ne'ayyen*. Here the Hebrew has *naḥqor* ('enquire'), which is usually translated *nabḥathu*. Since the Arabic here comes after a long omission in the abridgement, I take it to be inserting the verb for continuation rather than this being a case of inconsistent Hebrew translation, which probably had *nabḥathu* in front of it. The difference of meaning is negligible.

167 The Arabic continues: 'and these two are the two properties of the first principle' (*wa-hātān ṣifatān li-l-mabda' al-awwal*). Frank ('Notes', p. 220, §60) suggests a

gloss, but this is in fact the Arabic abridger's compensation for the compression of the sentence.

168 The present chapter will thus deal with the subject of eternity. Themistius will have Chapter 7 deal with immovability. See below, 16,9-10.

169 Literally: 'order and correctness' (*seder ve-yosher*). The recurring formula *seder ve-yosher* (sometimes inverted) is a hendiadys translation of the Greek *taxis*, hence I only translate 'order'.

170 The Hebrew text has *hinhig. . .hanhaga* (literally, 'governed a governance'), which is meaningless in this context. In my translation I am adopting Brague's conjecture (*Thémistius*, p. 74, n. 4) according to which the Arabic root *d-b-r*, some forms of which have the sense of governance, was employed here in the sense of reflection and misunderstood by the Hebrew translator.

171 Reading *hena kevar* (the Hebrew edition relegates *kevar* to the apparatus, but now I think it should be reinstated in the body of the text), which translates *hunnā qad*. The Arabic abridgement omits *qad* and has *kannā* ('we have'). The Hebrew first read *kannā* and translated *hayyinu*, but in the revision read *hunnā*, which is graphically similar.

172 I am following Shem Tov Falaquera's Hebrew version of this sentence (*ha-tenuʿa eina ṭevaʿ meshullal*), which was translated from the Arabic independently of Moses ibn Tibbon's translation (*ha-tenuʿa eina ṭivʿit meshullelet*; 'motion is not natural [and] abstract'). The Arabic sentence is lost. See Meyrav, *Themistius*, 98–102.

173 The literal translation is: 'and even more so is time not like this'.

174 See above, n. 143.

175 Brague, *Thémistius*, translates differently: 'même si l'on est extrêmement amatuer de dispute et de chicane'.

176 Reading *takhallafa* with the Arabic. Heb. has *yihye*, which would render the translation 'it would then *be* [or even: *come-to-be*] after it perished'.

177 Literally, roughly, 'the argument would not allow us to assume this' (the difficult Hebrew is *ve-lo' yaniaḥ lanu ha-heqesh hanaḥato*). The term *heqesh* (here 'argument', most likely translating the Arabic *qiyās*) could also mean 'analogy', 'reason', or 'syllogism'.

178 In other words, the elements of the utterance contradict the proposition that the utterance tries to advance.

179 Arabic has: 'for the meanings (*ma'ānī*) of these utterances. . .' (see Frank, 'Notes', p. 220, n. 63). But this is not a problem of textual transmission; the Arabic is not part of the original text, but a paraphrase that compensates for the abridger's omission of the examples.

180 Themistius changes the first part of Aristotle's argument here, replacing Aristotle's 'the same thing' with 'quantity'. In a way, Themistius limits the scope of Aristotle's

claim, which aims to show that motion is eternal whether it and time are the same – a position he does not adopt but ascribes to other thinkers, usually taken to be Plato (see E. Berti, 'Unmoved Mover(s) as Efficient Cause(s) in *Metaphysics* Λ 6', in M. Frede and D. Charles, eds, *Aristotle's Metaphysics Lambda* (Oxford: Clarendon Press, 2000), pp. 184–5) – or time is its modification. In other words, Aristotle tries to make the point that the eternity of motion follows also from positions other than his own, whereas Themistius has Aristotle elaborating only upon his own view.

181 Here Themistius departs from Aristotle's text to introduce an independent argument for the eternity of motion, which is not based upon the eternity of time but examines the concept of motion. For discussion see Meyrav, *Themistius*, pp. 400–1.

182 The expression 'for us to say' (*an naqūl*) is omitted from the Hebrew.

183 The expression 'from it' (*'annahu*) is omitted from the Hebrew.

184 The Arabic is in the third person.

185 The Hebrew has 'that which moves', which is certainly an error. For the philological state of affairs see Meyrav, *Themistius*, pp. 412–13.

186 It will become clear as the discussion progresses that 'the body' in question is the universe as a whole.

187 Reading with the Hebrew. The Arabic has it the other way around: 'then the body would have been created before its motion'.

188 I take *hatḥala* here not to mean 'principle', but in the sense of a concrete starting point, perhaps translating *ibtidā'* (see, e.g. 11,4).

189 Literally, 'the motions in the other descriptions' (*ha-tenu'ot bi-she'ar ha-te'arim*).

190 Literally, 'only in it is the continuous way' (*wa-l-ittiṣāl lā yakūn illā fīhā*; *ve-ofen ha-devequt lo' yihye ela bo'*).

191 Literally: 'what has been said in the *Physics* in a necessary demonstration'. For the argument see Aristotle, *Physics* 8.8.

192 I take this to mean 'something that changes from motion to stop'.

193 This sentence bridges the gap between Aristotle's proof of the existence of an eternal moving substance and his discussion of moving substances starting at 1071b12.

194 Hebrew: *she-yani'a hana'a temidit ve-ya'ase ha-po'al ha-ze* (the Arabic only has the first part of this expression). The literal sense would be 'that it everlastingly causes motion and performs this activity', but the manuscripts reflect a difficulty with the transmission of the text, which seems to be a positive version of *poiētikon. . .energoun de ti* at 1071b12-13.

195 In the sense of causing motion.

196 The logic of this is somewhat strange, but Themistius seems to distinguish between the activity in itself and the causing of the activity.

197 The connection here is that if eternal substances do not cause motion, they are not active in this respect, hence they are no better than stationary Ideas.

198 Reading with the Hebrew (*be-lo po'al baṭel*). The Arabic has 'neither inactive nor idle' (*bi-lā fi'l wa-lā muta'aṭṭila*)

199 Reading with the Hebrew (*nimtzet be-teva' ma she-hu' ba-koaḥ*). The Arabic means something like 'an existent whose nature includes potentiality' (*mawjūd fī ṭabī'atihi mā huwa bi-l-quwwa*). The difference is slight but not insignificant. The Hebrew has Themistius say that the first principle is of a different class than things that have potentiality, whereas the Arabic simply denies potentiality of the first principle.

200 Reading *al-jawhar fi'lhu* with the Arabic. Brague (*Thémistius*, p. 79, n. 3) and Frank ('Notes', n. 103) think that the better reading is in the Hebrew (*ein etzem lefaneha*; 'there is no substance before it'), but the Arabic is much closer to Aristotle's Greek at 1071b20 (*hēs hē ousia energeia*; 'whose substance/essence is actuality'), perhaps somewhat mistranslated. For how the Hebrew came about see Meyrav, *Themistius*, p. 417.

201 Literally 'perhaps someone will act according to speech' (*hine efshar mi she-ya'ase derekh ha-dibbur*). I assume that the Hebrew *derekh ha-dibbur* translates *ṭarīq al-kalām*. It can mean also 'logically'. From the proceeding discussion, it seems that Themistius means a discussion that is based on how potentiality and actuality are used in ordinary language.

202 The Hebrew has 'air' (*avir*), but I follow Brague's correction according to 'Abd al-Laṭīf al-Baghdādī (see Brague, *Thémistius*, p. 80, n. 1), who has the Arabic *al-hāwiyya*.

203 It is notable that Themistius changes Aristotle's argument here. While Aristotle maintains that the semen and the seed are the respective movers of the menstrual blood and earth (both as matter), Themistius has all of them moved by the sun, as their moving cause. This position is consistent with the one he advances in the appendix of Chapter 3. Note also that this goes against Aristotle's basic definition of nature in the *Physics* 2.1 as an internal principle of change. It would seem to suggest that there is no such thing as nature (I would like to thank Yehuda Halper for this observation).

204 This is Plato's 'confused' (*plēmmelōs*) motion, introduced in *Timaeus* 30a4. See also n. 209.

205 I agree with Brague (*Thémistius*, p. 80, n 3) that the Hebrew *'inyan* (here in the meaning of 'issue') is probably a mistranslation of the Arabic *amr*, which in the present context should have been understood as 'command'.

206 I translate according to the assumption that the Arabic was *yukhabbiru*, which the Hebrew (mis-)read as *nukhabbiru* (translated to *nesapper*), which would

change the translation to 'we should make known the cause of this eternal motion', etc.

207 The Hebrew *be-miqre* (literally, 'accidentally'), in the present context, is probably translating *bi-l-ittifāq*, which is probably a translation of *apo tuchēs*.

208 The literal meaning of the Hebrew is 'and all this differs strongly' (*ve-kol ze yitḥallef ḥilluf ḥazaq*), which would mean that the difference between the various kinds of motion is considerable. But Aristotle's Greek that Themistius is paraphrasing has *diapherei gar amēchanon hoson* (1071b37), and *diapherei* is used in the impersonal sense of importance. The Arabic was probably translated with some form of the verb *ikhtalafa* ('to be different'), raising confusion in the Hebrew.

209 'Confused and disorderly' (*ha-mevulbelet she-ein la sedder*) might reflect Plato's expression *plēmmenōs kai ataktōs*, at *Timaeus* 30a4.

210 I take *min qibalihā* ('from itself'; Hebrew: *mi-tzidda*) as a translation of *kath' hauto*, reflecting Aristotle at 1072a12.

211 As will become clear, the 'first cause' here is not the first cause absolutely (i.e. God), but the first of two causes discussed here, namely the sphere of the fixed stars and the planetary sphere.

212 Literally 'all of them'. See above, n. 7.

213 Heb. *yibbadel*; the literal meaning would be 'distinct', but here I think this is a translation of the Arabic *yutabāyan*, in the sense of opposition.

214 Strictly speaking, the second half of this sentence belongs to Chapter 7, but Themistius' text, which was written long before the renaissance division into chapters, runs through them continuously.

215 Themistius replaces Aristotle's 'all things together' with a technical expression of Anaxagoras' *migma* (Heb. *'eruv*), namely the primeval mixture.

216 For information about the Arabic abridgement of this chapter see above, p. 10. The last part of this chapter in Arabic is quoted in Averroes' long commentary on the *Metaphysics*. See below, n. 291.

217 Themistius explains that he is following the plan he offered in the beginning of Chapter 6 (see above, 11,28-30).

218 Themistius is referring to his paraphrase on the *Physics*, where he notes: 'in all cases of things being combined from two [constituents] it could be learnt that if one of the things in the mixture can exist per se, then the other can exist per se too' (223,1-3; tr. Todd, *Themistius: On Aristotle's* Physics 5-8 (London: Bloomsbury, 2008), p. 83).

219 Reading with the Arabic: *wa-huwa fī al-ṭabī'a*, etc. The Hebrew has 'that which exists in a completely immaterial nature' (*we-ze she-hu' nimtza' be-ṭeva'*, etc.).

220 Reading with the Arabic (*al-fi'l*). The Hebrew reads '*in* actuality' (*ba-po'al*). This seems to be an error in the Hebrew translation (see a parallel case at 21,23; Moses ibn Tibbon seems to have had trouble grasping the notion of unqualified actuality). According to Alexandru's critical apparatus (in his *Metaphysics*), the Hebrew reflects a reading of *energeiai* at 1072a25, whereas the Arabic reflects the accepted *energeia*, but this would assume two different Greek textual traditions for the Hebrew and for the Arabic, and this ignores the fact that the Hebrew translates the Arabic with no involvement of the Greek. For the general problem see Meyrav, *Themistius*, p. 436, and for the Greek, see S. Fazzo, 'Unmoved Mover as Pure Act or Unmoved Mover in Act? The Mystery of a Subscript Iota', in C. Horn, ed., *Aristotle's "Metaphysics" Lambda: New Essays* (Berlin & Boston: De Gruyter, 2061), pp. 181–2.

221 Literally: 'the object of desire and the object of intelligizing in us are not united together'. I am reading 'united' according to the Arabic *yuttaḥidān*. The Hebrew has 'moved' (*yitno'e'u*, probably reading *yataḥarrakān*). One might consider the option, with some Hebrew manuscripts, of reading the active 'move' (*yani'u*). In that case the translation would be 'the object of desire and the object of intellect do not move together' (See Brague, *Thémistius*, p. 84, n. 5 and Frank, 'Notes', p. 222, §119).

222 The Hebrew has '*the* first principles', which causes syntactic problems in the sentence and should be rejected.

223 Reading with the Arabic. The Hebrew has 'because it is an object of intellect and an object of desire', connecting the text to the previous sentence. See Meyrav, *Themistius*, p. 437, for analysis.

224 The Hebrew has 'fancy *and* choose', which could also be considered.

225 Literally: 'how they are in themselves' (*ma she-hem 'alav be-nafshotam*).

226 This is probably an epexegetic 'and', customary of Themistius' style.

227 Reading with the Arabic *mā yu'qalu*, against the Hebrew 'what we intelligize' (*ma she-naskil*, reading the Arabic as *na'qilu*). See Frank, 'Notes', p. 222, §125.

228 The term 'per se' translates the Hebrew *nifrad*, which most likely translates the Arabic *mufrad* in this context. It could be referring either to 'one' or to both 'simple' and 'one'. I translate according to the sense of Themistius' explanation in the rest of the passage and take the term to refer to both 'simple' and 'one'. Other options would be 'separately', 'particularly', or 'simply'.

229 Twetten takes this sentence as indicating that Themistius adopts the Plotinian 'One' ('Aristotelian Cosmology and Causality in Classical Arabic Philosophy and Its Greek Background', in Damien Janos, ed., *Ideas in Motion in Baghdad and Beyond* (Leiden & Boston: Brill, 2016), pp. 329–30), but nothing here suggests that he commits himself to another entity besides Aristotle's unmoved mover, as

the discussion is an elaboration on Aristotle's introduction of the terms 'one' and 'simple' at 1072a32-4.

230 The literal meaning would be 'explained in it' (Heb. *yitba'er bo*), but I think the likely underlying Arabic root, *b-y-n*, is employed in the sense of appearance or visibility in something.

231 This is the first of several political metaphors in the text that are employed for explaining the cosmos. As Twetten ('Aristotelian Cosmology', p. 330) and Guldentops ('La Science', pp. 113–14) have already noticed, Themistius' politicization of the cosmos is a theme that connects the present paraphrase to his orations, in which this is a recurring theme.

232 The Hebrew *sekhel* translates *'aql* as a substantive noun ('intellect'), but here I assume *'aql* functions as a verbal noun ('intelligizing').

233 For the textual problem with this expression (Hebrew has *ḥokhma ve-maḥashav*; Arabic only *'ilm*, but not necessarily abridging), see Meyrav, *Themistius*, pp. 438–9.

234 Literally: 'administration of cities' (Ar. *siyāsat al-mudun*; Heb. *hadrakhat ha-medinot*). I take this to be a translation of the Greek *politeia*.

235 Heb. *ba-kan* is doubtlessly a translation of *hunā* (or *hahunā*), reflecting the Greek *entautha*. There are two ways to understand this sentence, based on what *entautha* means here. Either, as I have translated, Themistius draws an analogy between how the celestial bodies desire the first cause as law, which is the topic of the discussion, and between a person's adherence to the law. Alternatively, *entautha* may mean our world as opposed to the celestial realm. In that case Themistius makes a much stronger claim, namely that in this world, the desire for the first cause should be expressed as a desire for the correct political order. This reflects Themistius' general attitude of the priority of the *via activa* over the *via contemplativa* (see discussion in Schramm, 'Platonic Ethics and Politics in Themistius and Julian', in Ryan C. Fowler, ed., *Plato in the Third Sophistic* (Boston & Berlin: De Gruyter, 2014), pp. 132–5).

236 Reading with the Arabic *jawharān wa-fi'lān*. The Hebrew has 'substance and *intellect*' (*sekhel*), reading *'aqlān*, owing to the graphical similarity between *fi'l* and *'aql* when not dotted, already encountered in the present text. There is no way to know for certain which is the correct text, since both 'intellect' and 'actuality' as divine properties are pertinent to Themistius' argumentation in this passage.

237 The adjective *bāqin* is usually translated as *ha-nish'arim*, which could mean the members of the group that have not been discussed yet, as I translate here, but also 'everlasting'. It is tempting to employ this meaning in the present sentence, as it is hard to see how all things besides the first cause intelligize it, as most things in the world are without intellect. Ascribing the term to the celestial

substances would make more sense in the context of this passage and serve as a counterpart to the immediately following analogy. However, this cannot be done with confidence since all of the other instances of this term in the text are used in the first meaning.

238 The Arabic and Hebrew are difficult here and can be understood in different manners. I translate the sentence as if the first cause's essence is the object of the intelligizing of the things which desire it. It can also be read as if Themistius is writing that the first cause intelligizes its own essence (Brague, *Thémistius,* has Themistius say that the first cause's intelligizing is its essence, but although it is a possible reading, with a stretch, I cannot see how it fits in the context of the discussion). Of course, Themistius believes that the first cause is its own object of intelligizing, and will muse about it quite a bit as the text progresses, but here it seems that the point of discussion is the first cause's function as an unmoved mover, which is an object of desire by virtue of being intelligized. For the problem in the Hebrew see Meyrav, *Themistius*, p. 440.

239 Reading with the Hebrew. The Arabic omits 'activity', which would render the translation 'pursue this intellect'. I think that this omission undermines Themistius' point about the cosmic order as the activity of the first cause.

240 The present sentence has been misused as support for preferring *dē* over *de* in Aristotle's clause *kinei de/dē hōde to orekton*, rendering Aristotle's claim as a logical consequence rather than an addition to the preceding sentence. While there are reasons independent from Themistius to support this reading (see Alexandru, *Metaphysics*, p. 141, and also A. Laks, '*Metaphysics* Λ 7', in M. Frede and D. Charles, eds, *Aristotle's Metaphysics Lambda* (Oxford: Clarendon Press, 2000), p. 220, n. 24, who nevertheless prefers *de*), there are no grounds to conclude that Themistius' text had *dē* (or *de*, for that matter). The Arabic particle *fa-*, translated into Hebrew as *hine*, and in turn into Latin as *igitur* (from which the discussion originally sprung), is used to translate both, as well as several other Greek words which would fit here (e.g. *ge*, *gar*, *oun*, etc.). The argument for *dē* functioning as a logical connection loses its force here too, as the present sentence in Themistius' paraphrase comes after an independent discussion and is dissociated from its original positioning in Aristotle's text.

241 I take this 'and' to be epexegetical, as there is no reason to believe that Themistius departs from Aristotle's view that the sphere of the fixed stars is the first sphere. For discussion Meyrav, *Themistius*, p. 441.

242 Reading with the Arabic, whose possessive suffix points to the first cause. The Hebrew *shelo*, in the masculine, has the correctness as belonging to the first heaven, which seems like a mistake. The translation in this case would be '[its share] of its [own] correctness'.

243 For the reconstruction of the text here see Meyrav, *Themistius*, p. 442.

244 The Arabic *sā'ir* (reflected in the Hebrew *she'ar*) is probably used here in the meaning of 'all'. For this phenomenon see above, n. 38. Alternatively, the translation would be 'the rest of the remaining things'.

245 I take 'nature' here to allude to matter, whereas 'motion' here is probably *kinēsis* in its meaning as 'change', and likewise in the next paragraph.

246 i.e. they have all kinds of motion, not just motion in place.

247 Or, more literally, '"the possible" in each of them is different from ["the possible"] in the other'.

248 Literally, 'qualities' (Hebrew: *'inyanim*).

249 I think Themistius' point here is that 'possible' reflects not only various kinds of things, but also various kinds of motions (or changes). This argument completes, in a way, the enumeration of four kinds of change at the beginning of the paraphrase of Chapter 2.

250 Literally, 'not that it is possible for them [to vary] not in place'.

251 This (Hebrew: *el shnei ha-tzedadim*) can either mean 'be one way or another', or treated as a reference to the discussion of potentiality as something that can either be actualized or not (see above, 14,4-6).

252 I take Themistius to refer to natural substances, who receive contraries in a stronger sense (compare above, 4,10-21, especially the difference between susceptibility to change in place and being 'wholly' susceptible to change).

253 The Hebrew words *ein 'inyan lo* are difficult to understand here, especially without the Arabic, so my translation of the first part of the sentence is hesitant. Another possible translation can be 'does not include quality', which is one type of change that celestial bodies do not undergo. But if we adopt this translation, the question would be why Themistius does not mention the other two types of change of which celestial bodies are exempt.

254 The Hebrew omits 'the first motion'. Perhaps the Arabic *awwal al-ḥarakāt* is a gloss (see Frank, 'Notes', p. 223, §148).

255 Themistius probably inserts this clause to bridge the terminological gap between 'motion' and 'change'.

256 Literally, 'in any other thing' (Arabic: *fī shay' min al-ashyā'*; Hebrew: *be-davar min ha-devarim*).

257 This is somewhat paraphrastic due to translation constraints. The literal translation would be '. . . and if something is not moved the first motion, even less so is it moved the other motions'. Themistius' point is that the first mover causes motion without being moved at all; the hierarchy of motion is such that locomotion is prior to all other types of motions (for example, something cannot decrease or increase if it cannot move in place); hence, if one denies of

something locomotion, one denies of it motion altogether. What is implied is that it is sufficient to show that the first mover does not move in place in order to claim that it is completely unmoved.

258 This sentence is barely intelligible in Hebrew. Perhaps Themistius is trying to isolate the 'necessary' component from the 'existing' component in the first principle.

259 Literally: 'since it is outside what is aimed by it' (Hebrew: *mipnei she-hu' ḥutz min ha-mekhuvvan mimeno*).

260 In other words, it is impossible for it not to exist because 'existence' in it is that which cannot be otherwise.

261 Literally, 'a portion of time' (Arabic: *mudda min al-zamān*; Hebrew: *midda min ha-zeman*).

262 My translation requires concessions from both the Arabic and the Hebrew. The Hebrew *me'aṭ* should be relinquished in favour of the Arabic *bi-kadd*, whereas the Arabic *bi-jidd* was emended to *najid*. At present, the Arabic is reflected in this translation. The Hebrew means: 'we find [only] a small portion of the path towards knowledge', a skeptical attitude that does not seem to accord with Themistius' argumentation. See further discussion in Meyrav, *Themistius*, p. 444.

263 Reading with the Hebrew *be-rov ha-'ittim*. The Arabic has 'mostly' (*fī akthar al-amr*).

264 From here until 21,27, I consulted Pines' English translation of the Arabic abridgement of these passages (Pines, 'Some Distinctive Metaphysical Conceptions in Themistius' Commentary on Book Lambda and their Place in the History of Philosophy', in Jürgen Weisner, ed., *Aristoteles: Werk und Wirkung*, 2 vols, (Berlin, New York: De Gruyter, 1987), vol. 2, pp. 180–2), which occasionally completes missing portions according to the Hebrew translation.

265 Literally, 'in all things'.

266 Literally, 'What relation does it have. . .' (Arabic: *ay nisba tūjad lahu*; Hebrew: *ei ze yaḥas yimmatze' lo*).

267 Reading with the Hebrew (literally, 'the joy that it enjoys'; *ha-simḥa asher yismaḥ ba*, the subject being 'something whose nature is only actuality'). The Arabic has 'the joy that *God* enjoys' (*al-surūr alladhī yasurrhu allah*). 'Abd al-Laṭīf al-Baghdādī, in his paraphrase of this part, also has *allah* (39,8), but Neuwirth (*'Abd al-Laṭīf al-Baġdādī's Bearbeitung von Buch Lambda der Aristotelischen Metaphysik* (Weidbaden: Steiner, 1976), p. 140, §66) is uncomfortable with this, as is Brague (*Thémistius*, p. 91, n. 3), who prefers reading with the Hebrew. I agree with both, because the context of the discussion is meant to assert to the superiority of intellectual pleasure over sensual pleasures. See further discussion in Meyrav, *Themistius*, p. 445.

268 The Arabic adds here: 'than the senses from their perceptions' (*min al-ḥawāss bi-mudrakāthā*). Since the Arabic omits the part of the text relating to the individual senses above, it seems to me that this addition is a gloss intended to compensate for the omission of the examples at 19,30-20,1 rather than an integral part of the original text.

269 Reading with the Hebrew (*ya'iqahu*). The Arabic has 'intelligize it' (*ya'quluhu*; probably a corruption of *ya'ūquhu*).

270 The text is confusing, but I think that Themistius' point is that objects of intellect that are the result of abstraction from the senses always need to be emptied of them when thought about, in contrast to things that are by nature objects of intelligizing, which are discussed in the next sentence.

271 'Abd al-Laṭīf al-Baghdādī alludes to this sentence (41,1) and has the term *mulābis* (Heb. *lovesh*), which Neuwirth (*'Abd al-Laṭīf al-Baġdādī*) presents as a translation of *thinganō* ('to touch') in her glossary (see also Brague, *Thémistius*, p. 92, n. 2), because of the connection the present discussion has with *Metaphysics* 12, 1073b21. However, I did not find a precedent for this pairing. Perhaps a better option is *ephaptesthai*, which is translated into the verb *lābasa* in Themistius' paraphrase of *On the Soul* 107,23 (Arabic 195,9).

272 'Upon it' (*fīhi*) is missing in the Hebrew.

273 Literally, 'from thing to thing' (Arabic: *min shay' ilā shay'*; Hebrew: *mi-davar el davar*).

274 Literally, 'because of the multiplicity of that which is mixed with it of that which is in potentiality' (Arabic: *li-kuthrat mā yukhtaliṭu bihi mi-mā bi-l-quwwa*; Hebrew: *le-ribbui ma she-yit'arev bo mi-ma she-hu' ba-koaḥ*).

275 The translation is according to 'Abd al-Laṭīf al-Baghdādī's quotation, which makes more sense. The Hebrew translation is approximately, 'If there is nothing puzzling about our intellect being the thing that it [i.e. the first intellect] intelligizes, all the more should we consider the first intellect to be so'. See the discussion in Meyrav, *Themistius*, pp. 447–8.

276 Reading with the Hebrew (*ve-taskil 'atzmuta*). The Arabic has 'intelligizes *in* itself' (*wa-ta'qilu fī dhātihā*).

277 Hebrew has *miqrim ve-ḥiddushim*. Both terms' literal meaning is 'accidents'. For my translation 'modification' see above, n. 143.

278 Following the Arabic (*wa-lahu akthar*), which reflects Themistius' close approximation of 1072b24-25. The Hebrew is corrupt (see Brague, *Thémistius*, p. 94, n.1; Frank, 'Notes', n. 172 and n. 173, and Meyrav, *Themistius*, pp. 448–9).

279 Literally, his 'abundance' (*kathra*). The Hebrew is still corrupt (see previous note).

280 The Arabic adds: 'and creates them' (*wa-yaḥduthuhā*), which is probably a gloss.

281 Or, alternatively, 'He is what they are' (Arabic: *wa-allatī hiya huwa*; Hebrew: *ve-asher hem hu'*).

282 Reading with the Hebrew (*ve-heqesh*), omitted in the Arabic. Brague (*Thémistius*, p. 94, n. 3) suggests that the underlying Greek was *logos*.

283 Preferring the Hebrew *yidda' be-'atzmuto ve-yaskil be-'atzmuto*, unlike Brague (*Thémistius*, p. 94, n. 5) and Frank ('Notes', p. 224, §177), who prefer the Arabic: *yarā dhātahu wa-ya'qilu dhātahu* ('knows itself and intelligizes itself'). Both readings are possible, depending on how one understands Themistius' argument. For the Hebrew Themistius suggests that the reader imagine the law as if it were able to have the cognitive faculties of the lawgiver, whereas the Arabic has Themistius go further by saying that the law would be able to intelligize itself. The following example of Lycurgus shows a case where the lawgiver and the law are separate, the former knowing the latter. When Lycurgus dies, the law remains but will eventually also 'die', probably since nothing would be able to sustain it, as no one knew it as well as Lycurgus had. If this is the logic, then the Arabic should be preferred, because the main point here would not be the law's ability to know, but the law's ability to know itself. To take things further to Themistius' desired outcome – if the law is always alive, then lawgiving is always present, hence the cosmos never ceases to be ordered.

284 Heb. has the string *'-p-v-r-g-v-sh*. For the identification as Lycurgus see Brague, *Thémistius*, p. 143, §29).

285 Reading with the Arabic *waqt ba'da waqt*. The Hebrew has *be-'et zulat 'et* ('at different moments'). The difference of meaning is marginal.

286 The Hebrew is *adonei ha-ḥayyim* ('masters of life'), which is probably an elevation of the standard *ba'al ḥayyim* (etymologically, 'possessor of life', but simply meaning 'animal'), which would otherwise have been used for the Arabic *al-ḥayā* in this context. I do not understand Brague's translation *les plaisirs de la vie* (in his *Thémistius*, p. 94).

287 The identification of Speusippus is based on Aristotle's text at 1072b31. The Hebrew manuscripts have various corruptions of the name.

288 Literally, 'with them' (Hebrew: *'immahem*).

289 See the discussion of this in Meyrav, *Themistius*, pp. 450–1. The construction *lā yaqbalu al-ta'thīr* (Hebrew: *lo' yeqabbel ha-shinnui*) ultimately reflects Aristotle's *apathes* at 1073a11.

290 Most Hebrew manuscripts, as well as the printed version, have *hana'atam*, which would render the translation as something like 'especially if they would enable it *to move* as an ensouled body [moves]'. However, now I think the variant *hanaḥatam* should be preferred, and the expression *hanaḥatam lo* to mean 'their ascription to it'.

291 From this point, and until the end of the chapter, we possess a full Arabic quotation in Averroes, *Tafsīr*, 1635,4-1636,13.

292 I am reading with the Hebrew *tesovev otam* (also adopted by Brague, *Thémistius*), assuming that the Arabic had *tudīrhā*. The printed edition of the *Tafsīr*, and Badawī read *tudabbirhā* ('governs them'). The Arabic manuscripts are not dotted so could go either way.

293 The Arabic has 'motion' (in the singular).

294 For the Arabic abridgement of this chapter see above, p. 10.

295 Reading with the Arabic (*wāḥida aw [. . .] kathīra*). The Hebrew has 'one *and* many' (*she-hem eḥad ve-she-hem rabim*).

296 Literally, 'in doubt' (Hebrew: *be-safeq*).

297 Hebrew: *she-lo' yivvada' haga'atam*, perhaps also 'which cannot be counted'. The point here is, I think, that they say that because they do not know how many numbers there are (the options given are ten or infinite), they do not know how many Ideas there are (since Ideas are assumed to be numbers).

298 Reading *yawjabu* with the Arabic. Hebrew has *yamtzi'*, probably reading the Arabic as *yawjadu*. This would be translated as: 'But [the fact] that there are other substances like this beyond the first principle is *produced* by reason and testified by sense'.

299 It is difficult to discern whether Themistius is ostensibly identifying between the unmoved movers of the celestial bodies and souls (hence they are subject to the same account as soul does), drawing an analogy between them and souls, or referring to some argument in *On the Soul*.

300 Literally: 'it is prior to the moved thing' (*hu' yoter qodem min ha-davar ha-mitno'e'a*).

301 Literally, 'the number of motions that each planet is moved' (*mispar ha-tenu'ot asher yitno'e'a otam kol eḥad min ha-kokhavim ha-nevukhim*).

302 Literally, 'govern' (*manhigim*). However, there is also a chance that *manhigim* misreads the Arabic *mudabbira* for the original *mudīra* (an analogous case is found above at 22,15). If this is so, then the translation should be 'rotate'.

303 Literally, 'we should determine' (*ra'uy she-nigzor*). The Arabic probably had something of the root *j-z-m*. Perhaps the Greek was some form of *apophainō*.

304 In the present text, in cases where Arabic is available, the Hebrew root *n-s-g* translates either the root *d-r-k* or the root *l-ḥ-q*. Here, if it is indeed one of the two, then *l-ḥ-q* is better as a translation of, e.g. *sumbainō*.

305 Hebrew has *mevo'ar nir'e* (literally, 'clear [and] visible'), but *mevo'ar* was probably accidentally copied from the beginning of the sentence ('it is clear. . .'). See my elaboration in Meyrav, *Themistius*, pp. 459–60.

306 Literally, '*in* four spheres' (*be-arba'a galgalim*).

307 i.e. the sphere of the fixed stars and the zodiac.

308 The Hebrew has *meyuḥadim* (here, roughly, 'are distinguished'), translating probably *khāṣa*, but this should have been read adverbially as *khāṣatan* ('exclusively', here simplified to 'only').

309 Themistius changes Aristotle's argument here. Aristotle writes that the condition is to accommodate the motion of the planets to the phenomena. Themistius seems to allude to the argument that the sphere of the fixed stars is the cause of constant motion which is always the same in Chapter 6.

310 For the textual tradition that Themistius is following here with regards to 'motions' and, in the next sentence, 'sensible substances', see Meyrav, *Themistius*, pp. 460–1, with further references.

311 The 'and' here is probably epexegetical (like the *kai* in 1074a15), and 'them' is the motions. To paraphrase: Themistius is saying (I think) that the number of unmoved substances which cause the celestial motions is identical to the number of celestial motions. Alternatively, we can drop the 'them' (omitted by some Hebrew manuscripts and Brague, *Thémistius*) and translate 'the substances and unmoved moving principles' (Aristotle has *tas ousias kai tas archas tas akinētous*, an expression that does not include 'movers').

312 See above, n. 310.

313 Themistius argues here for the impossibility of the existence of a *sphere* that is not conducive to a planet's motion. If that was possible, then it would be impossible to count the spheres with certainty.

314 Here and in the next sentence, literally: 'that which has no end' (Hebrew: *ma she-ein takhlit lo*).

315 This could be either read as if Themistius sees the next passage as consequent upon the aforementioned discussion, or as if he is announcing that the paraphrase moves to the next passage of the treatise.

316 The Hebrew and Arabic have 'matter and element' (*ḥomer ve-yesod*; *mādda wa-'unṣur*), but this has to do with a textual problem in the Arabic translation of *hyle* in the present text. See Meyrav, *Themistius*, pp. 527–40.

317 This 'and' is epexegetical.

318 Hebrew has *ha-qodem* ('the prior'), which is an incoherent translation of the Arabic *al-awwalī* in this context.

319 The Hebrew has *qayyam* (in a sense close to 'persists'), probably reading the Arabic as *muthabbita*. I read *munbaththa* with 'Abd al-Laṭīf al-Baghdādī, probably echoing the Greek *diesparmena* (compare Themistius, *On the Soul*, Arabic, 198,18 = Gr. 109,13). This better fits the analogy of the state now given. See the elaboration in Meyrav, *Themistius*, p. 462.

320 The formulation is unclear, but Themistius is essentially saying that the king, like the law, is one.

321 I am paraphrasing the confusing Hebrew *ve-nimtza' haga'at ha-re'iya el ha-qarov me-ha-shelemut ha-'inyan ha-hu' asher yetzavvehu ha-melekh.*

322 Literally, 'from'.

323 The text as reconstructed here is significantly different from Landauer's edition, *Themistii in Aristotelis Metaphysicorum librum Λ paraphrasis hebraice et latine*, Commentaria in Aristotelem Graeca 5.5 (Berlin: Reimer, 1903). See, for discussion, Meyrav, *Themistius*, pp. 462–3.

324 The translation is slightly paraphrastic. The Hebrew has *we-hu' kedei she-yihyu 'al ha-'inyan asher yetzave bo ha-melekh we-yesadrehu.*

325 The Hebrew has *qibbutz min ha-ṭovim.* In my translation I am following Brague.

326 The Hebrew has *yeyuḥad*, whose literal meaning would be something like 'the divine body is proper/exclusive to nature in its entirety'. Themistius' text here seems very close to Aristotle's words, and Aristotle at 1074b3 has *periekhei* (Themistius, *in DA* 58,30 *periekhetai* = Ar. 89.2 *maḥṣūr*).

327 Literally, 'and its truth is for us', reading *emeto.* It could also be read as *imtu.* In this case the translation would be '. . .and verified it for us', but I think that Themistius somehow reflects Aristotle's *phanera* at 1074b14.

328 Themistius does not paraphrase the final part of this chapter (1074b10-14), where Aristotle discusses the cyclical nature of the sciences.

329 For the Arabic abridgement of this chapter see above, p. 10.

330 In this chapter, I consulted Pines' English translation of the Arabic abridgement (Pines, 'Metaphysical Conceptions', pp. 182–6), as well as some parts that survive only in the Hebrew.

331 Literally: 'things' (*ha-devarim*).

332 The Arabic has 'other activity' (literally, 'the rest of the activities'; *sa'ir al-af'āl*), whereas the Hebrew has 'any activity' (literally, 'any thing of the activities'; *davar min he-pe'ulot*, probably reading the Arabic *shay'ān min al-af'āl*). See Frank, 'Notes', p. 225, §194.

333 Reading with the Hebrew (*me-hana'at*). The Arabic *min ḥarakat* has the objects of desire being the ones that are in motion, but the logic of the argument should have them unmoved.

334 Reading *an ya'aqilu al-'aql*, with the Arabic. The Hebrew has *she-ya'ase ha-po'al*, probably reading the Arabic as *an ya'amalu al-fi'l* (this frequently happens due to graphical similarity in the Arabic, especially when it is not dotted in the manuscript). The reading would change the translation to something like 'would control its being active', which is also possible.

335 Reading *shaliṭ* with the Hebrew, assuming the Arabic has *mutasalliṭ*, of which the current *bi-basīṭ* is a corruption.
336 See above, 17,26-7.
337 The Arabic has *ʿāqil* (Hebrew: *maskil*). The point here is that it intelligizes independently, i.e. not conditioned by the existence of an external object to actualize it.
338 Literally: 'from this place' (Hebrew: *mi-ze ha-maqom*).
339 The Hebrew (*siba ve-ʿilla*) and the Arabic (*sabab wa-ʿilla*) have both terms for 'cause'.
340 Here, as well as in the cases of hearing and intelligizing, the Arabic and Hebrew have, respectively, *sabab* and *sibat* ('the cause of'), which would mean that vision is the cause of the visibles, hearing is the cause of sounds, and the intellect is the cause of the intelligibles. But this seems to me the opposite of what Themistius is trying to say, namely that the external object is the cause of the activity of the faculty. Hence I suggest emending the Hebrew to *be-sibbat* and the Arabic (where available) to *bi-sabab*, to switch the causal roles.
341 Hebrew *ʿinyanim*, which could also mean 'things' or 'accidents'.
342 Themistius seems to ask if the intellect would be better or worse than the external object of intelligizing.
343 i.e. individuals (like me or you) intelligize in a lesser manner.
344 'Before receiving' is my assumption, synthesizing the Arabic, which only has *qabūl* ('receiving') with the Hebrew, which only has *qodem* ('before'). I assume that the text originally had *qablu qabūl*, which caused confusion due to these two words' similarity, causing copyists to drop one.
345 This qualification is not very clear. Maybe it means that the identification only pertains to the intellectual aspect and not to other parts of the individual object (e.g. its matter).
346 Reading *mimeno* ('from it'), with the Hebrew. The Arabic has 'from the first' (*ʿan al-awwal*), which I take to be a gloss aimed at restoring sense to the Arabic abridgement.
347 I think that there are two problems addressed here: first, the change would be for the worse (as it starts from being best); and second, that it would admit motion, which is contradictory.
348 The Hebrew has *yitten*, which I take translates the Arabic root *w-h-b* in the sense of yielding.
349 I am reading *shorashim* ('propositions') with the Hebrew, against the Arabic (*aḥwāl*, 'states') which seems to be a corruption of *uṣūl*, whose Hebrew translation is indeed *shorashim*.

350 This means perhaps that in this case the intellect would need something beyond an intelligible to be perfected.
351 This seems to be contradicting what Themistius says in the next passage, where he explicitly argues for God's ability to intelligize all things together. Nevertheless, this position is argued for through the mediation of the position that God intelligizes only one thing (which is identical to all things).
352 The language is somewhat circular, but Themistius seems to stress the logical distinction (but ontological identification) between subject and object both in self-love and in self-intelligizing.
353 The Hebrew version omits 'together' (Arabic: *ma'ān*).
354 Literally: 'cast its intention' (Hebrew: *yashlikh kavanato*).
355 The context of this expression is unclear, but it seems that the end of this paragraph unpacks the 'way of perfection' of divine intelligizing.
356 Sharples took this passage to mean that Themistius advocates a divine intellect that is supernatural and transcends human understanding. See R. W. Sharples, 'Alexander of Aphrodisias and the End of Aristotelian Theology', in T. Kobusch & M. Erler, eds, *Metaphysik und Religion: zur Signatur des spätantiken Denkens* (Munich & Leipzig: Saur, 2002), pp. 9 and 15). I disagree with this analysis at Meyrav, *Themistius*, p. 470, n. 4.
357 For 'yet', reading *'alā an* with 'Abd al-Laṭīf al-Baghdādī rather than *'ad she-* in the Hebrew, which would means 'so that. . .', connecting the two sentences consequentially.
358 This passage is highly unclear, but seems to lead to the next passages where Themistius explains how the first intellect can intelligize many things at once, and then how it can move many things at once.
359 The Arabic *tuthbatu lahu* ('affirmed for it', which is negated) is omitted in the Hebrew, probably accidentally.
360 The Hebrew has *tavin* ('understand'), but I take this as a misunderstanding of the use of the root *b-y-n*, here in the sense of differentiation.
361 The Hebrew has *sekhel* ('intellect'), but I assume that the Arabic had *'aql* as a verbal noun ('intelligizing') rather than a substantial noun ('intellect').
362 The Hebrew has *meḥuyyav* (literally, 'necessary'), which I take to mistranslate *wājib* in the sense of 'proper'.
363 For the Hebrew term *bahir* in this context see Meyrav, *Themistius*, p. 480.
364 Literally: 'in the here'.
365 The Hebrew is not very clear, and there is no Arabic, but Themistius seems to be saying that the first principle is essentially an intellect because it has the same function as an intellect in the natural world when material restrictions are removed from it.

366 Literally: 'things' (Hebrew: *devarim*).

367 Or: 'exist through Him' (Ar. *qawāmihā bahu*; Heb.: *'amidatam bo*).

368 The Hebrew *ḥazaq* ('strong') is an error for the Arabic *yarā*, probably read as *qawī*. This was first noted by E. Wakelnig, *A Philosophy Reader from the Circle of Miskawayh* (Cambridge: Cambridge University Press, 2014), pp. 353–4; see the discussion in Meyrav, *Themistius*, p. 36.

369 The four terms Aristotle uses in the context of this discussion (1074b5) are *epistēmē*, *aisthēsis*, *doxa*, and *dianoia*.

370 Literally: 'are apprehended an apprehension' (*yusgu hasaga*). The Arabic probably had the root *d-r-k*, perhaps reflecting *antilambanō*.

371 In this passage, the Hebrew translated as 'to become aware' alternates between *hirgish* for the sensible aspect and *hevin* for the intellectual aspect, but the textual tradition shows that the original Arabic had the same term (see Meyrav, *Themistius*, p. 481), which I take to be the root *sh-'-r*, which in Themistius' paraphrase of *On the Soul* translates the Greek *hupeidomai* (37,25 = 39,7; see Todd's lexicon in *On the Soul*).

372 Namely, perception and knowledge, when actualized, are aware not only of their objects, but also of their own activity.

373 Here the Hebrew is *heqesh*, probably translating the Arabic *qiyās*, reflecting *logos* in *Metaph.* 1075a3.

374 This could also be epexegetical: 'formula, i.e. intellect'.

375 I assume that the Hebrew *yithappekh* reflects the Arabic verb *yan'akisu*.

376 This is more of a paraphrase. The literal meaning is 'both together are said of it, that it is an intellect and an intelligible' (*ve-ye'amer bi-shneihem yaḥad she-hu' sekhel ve-muskal*).

377 The Arabic abridgement only lists the intellect and the intelligible, omitting thinking. This is, I think, to restore continuation within the narrative created by the abridgement. See the note in Meyrav, *Themistius*, p. 482.

378 The Arabic abridgement adds the term *takaththara* ('to become many'); 'Abd al-Laṭīf al-Baghdādī, quoting the full Arabic, is in tune with the Hebrew and does not include it, so this could be a gloss. If this reading is adopted, then the text in the abridgement seems to suggest that the first intellect 'becomes many' (to use Pines' term, although he is unsure what to make of it; see Pines, 'Metaphysical Conceptions', p. 185 and n. 37) when it intelligizes its essence. If this is the case, then the text should be read with 21,9-11, where Themistius explains how the first mover can be seen as multi-fold despite its simplicity. For the philological aspect see Meyrav, *Themistius*, p. 482.

379 I am reading with the Arabic (the abridgement as well as in 'Abd al-Laṭīf al-Baghdādī). The Hebrew is slightly different, but significantly so, omitting 'that

it is'). According to the Hebrew, the first intellect intelligizes from its essence the cause and principle of all things. In other words, the Arabic has the first intellect acknowledge its own function, whereas the Hebrew expands upon the first intellect as the object of its own intellect. I think the Arabic is to be preferred, based upon the logical construction of the argument of which the present statement is the conclusion.

380 This chapter is only preserved in Hebrew, save a few allusions in ʿAbd al-Laṭīf al-Baghdādī, discussed in Meyrav, *Themistius*, p. 46.

381 'The utmost best' is, as we have seen, equivalent to the divine intellect, or God. Themistius seems to be asking about 'the good' and 'the best' in Aristotle's expression *to agathon kai to ariston* (1075a11-12) as if they were different concepts whose relationship needs to be assessed, rather than the collective subject of the chapter. See Brague, *Thémistius*, p. 149, §1.

382 The Hebrew *muqaf nifrad* seems to reflect some hendiadys translation in the Arabic that traces back to *kechōrismenon* at 1075a12.

383 I am assuming, with Landauer (*Themistius*) and Brague (*Thémistius*), that the Hebrew *ve-omnam* ('and indeed') is a mistake, reading the Arabic as *wa-ammā* instead of *wa-immā* ('or'). Otherwise, Themistius would be contradicting himself.

384 Following Brague (*Thémistius*, p. 117, n. 2), I adopt the Hebrew reading *ha-seder le-kullam*, instead of *ha-nistar mi-kullam* ('The hidden from all'), which would add an out of place aura of mystique to the divinity. This variant misled Guldentops, 'La Science', 111.

385 i.e. the difference is not of measure.

386 For the Hebrew *be-shekhunat ha-sekhel* see Meyrav, *Themistius*, p. 496.

387 I understand Themistius to be taking the items here as examples of different biological 'arrangements'.

388 i.e. in this case, the household.

389 If I understand correctly (there seems to be some corrupt transmission issue), the clarification ('the nature of each and its principle') refers to the compatibility between the lesser members of the household's nature and their contribution to its common aim.

390 There is no doubt that the Arabic used here was *tadbīr*, which was translated to the Hebrew *hanhaga*, but the meaning seems to me to be more about activity according to a rule than an extension of the political analogy (but this could be both).

391 Literally, 'their achieving of the end' (*hagaʿatam el ha-takhlit*), meaning the point where an organism is fully developed.

392 These examples can be explained in two ways: either simply as cases which are accidental, contrasting the previous examples of some utility, or as cases of specifically bad occurrences, which force us to appeal to privation or the

weakness of matter if we want to avoid casting the blame for this on God (this is also revisited below at, e.g. 32,26).

393 The Hebrew is difficult, but Themistius seems to add an affirmative aspect after denying communality: not only are they different from God, they are in fact reprehensible.

394 The Hebrew *'avadim* can also mean 'slaves'.

395 The Hebrew *be-sibba aḥat* ('by/for one cause') could reflect either an efficient cause or a final cause. The context seems to suggest that the term here should be taken in the sense that all things under discussion have the same final cause, but the efficient cause cannot be ruled out.

396 i.e. not to pass away into something else.

397 i.e. eternally and perfectly.

398 The Hebrew expression is *yelkhu etzlo*. I have no idea what the Arabic was but the sense seems to be something between 'follow' and 'imitate' (according to the inner logic of the argument). In classical Hebrew, the term *halakh etzlo* means 'went to him' or 'visited him', but here the meaning does not make sense and the construction seems to build on the Arabic *dh-h-b* or *s-l-k 'inda*.

399 Literally, 'a plurality of numbers' (*mispar rav*).

400 The Hebrew has *mipnei she-* ('because'), which is probably a translation of the Arabic *lammā* as causal rather than restrictive.

401 I borrow this terminology from Brague, *Thémistius*, p. 119.

402 Alternatively, but with a stretch in the Hebrew (which is anyway clumsy), Themistius may be saying that the 'firstness' of the first principle was not explained correctly.

403 Heb. is *'amdu etzel* ('stood at'), which is a literal translation of *waqafū' 'inda*.

404 Literally, 'with matter' (*'imma ha-hiyuli*), but the point is not that the first principle is necessary material, but that there is a material component involved from the outset (e.g. like God and matter as contraries which are jointly the first principle).

405 I take *lo' yeqabbel qetzatam ha-shinnuy me-qetzatam* as reflecting *lā yaqbalu al-ta'thīr ba'ḍihā ba'ḍ*, which traces back to *apathē... hup' allēlōn* at 1075a30-1.

406 'Form' not in an absolute sense, but as a specific form that matter receives in the coming-to-be of an individual substance.

407 This may be epexegetical.

408 The Hebrew has *im nimlaṭ*, so the literal sense is 'if it escapes', but this makes no sense. I think that the Hebrew *im* misread the Arabic *an* ('that') as *in* ('if'). Landauer (*Themistius*) already suspected that this is the case in his original edition. Also, the Hebrew *nimlaṭ* (literally, 'escaped') reflects the Arabic *khilw* or *khalī* in the sense of being free from something.

409 There is certainly a corruption in the Hebrew manuscript tradition here, probably omitting a word or two after *she-hu' yitḥabber* (probably reading passively the originally active *yajtami'u*, which in turn reflects Aristotle's Greek *sunagei* at 1075b2), changing its meaning from 'brings together' to 'linked to', rendering the present text we have as nonsensical, roughly translated as follows: 'it is a principle as a mover, for it is connected to his account that it [is a principle] as matter'. Aristotle's text, which Themistius seems to reflect properly according to the rest of the passage, says that for Empedocles love is a principle both as a mover and as matter.

410 Literally: 'the definition and the "what the thing is" (=*to einai* at 1075b7) are not one and the same' (*aval ha-geder ve-ma hu' ha-davar eino eḥad be-'eino*).

411 In other words, since the material principle and the moving principle are not essentially the same, which of these two types of principles would love be?

412 Hebrew: *yippased takhlit ha-hippased*. See Brague, *Thémistius*, p. 121, notes 2 and 3, for the terminology and for the claim that this is completely the opposite of Aristotle's text at 1075b6, which has *aphtharton* ('*im*perishable'). However, the Greek manuscripts tradition indeed also has the variant *phtharton* ('perishable'; see Alexandru's critical apparatus (*Metaphysics*) at 1075b6), so perhaps Themistius is following an accepted tradition. The reading *phtharton* might be possible if one understands the argument as saying that since strife is a principle, it would be impossible to assume that it is perishable (since then it could not function as a principle).

413 If I understand correctly, Themistius is expressing the required distinction between the efficient cause and the final cause that is absent in Anaxagoras' account. The 'first thing' is *Nous*, but the final cause of motion, the 'mover' in the second part of the sentence, remains unaccounted for.

414 Some Hebrew manuscripts have 'its motion' (*tenu'ato*), but the analogy to medicine's moving seems to support the current reading.

415 The Hebrew has *ve-ha-beri'ut gam ken refu'at ma*, which literally means 'Health is a *kind of* art of medicine', which somehow reflects Aristotle's *pōs* at 1075b10 (*ē gar iatrikē esti pōs hē hugieia*). In any case, the order is inverted; Aristotle writes that the art of medicine is in a way health (see Brague, *Thémistius*, p. 121, n. 4). This could have been a matter of translation rather than originating in Themistius, since both 'health' and the 'art of medicine' are in the substantive and conjoined by a copula.

416 Literally, 'no preventer prevents' (Hebrew: *lo' yimna' mone'a*).

417 In other words, if I understand correctly, Aristotle's conception of the first principle allows it to function both as the moving cause and as the final cause.

418 Themistius seems to be saying that by having matter obey *Nous*, Anaxagoras necessitates that everything happens through *Nous*, including evil. But this would necessitate either saying that there is no evil, or that the first principle is responsible for evil – both of which are absurd ideas. Hence it is better to revert to Aristotle's explanation of evil as deriving from the inherent deficiency of matter. For this passage and the other discussions of evil in the paraphrase see G. Guldentops, 'Themistius on Evil', *Phronesis* 46, no. 2 (2001), 196.

419 If I understand correctly, the point is that positing contraries cannot lead to the desired function of the principle, which would also account for the cosmic order.

420 The point is that neither matter nor the contraries it receives are sufficient for explaining the cosmic order, so if the principles are contraries, the cosmic order remains unexplained.

421 This could refer to either of the former items on the list, or to both. Alternatively, 'from them' (*me-hem*) could be translated as 'among them', referring to the existing things. In that case, the translation of the list would be: 'those which are perishable, those which are not, those among them [i.e. among the existing things] that come-to-be, and those that do not come-to-be'. This perhaps would have been better because then the list focuses on the division of types of existents without adding any explanatory weight introduced by alluding to their causal relations. However, in the second part of the argument Themistius stresses their causal relations as a factor that explains why they have different kinds of matters.

422 The Hebrew *yesodot* here could mean either 'matters' or 'elements'. This argument can be read as specifically referring to natural bodies, and hence focusing on the question if all of them have the same 'kind' of matter. If this is so, it is an extension of the argument already put forth in Chapter 2 about the different kinds of matter. But if we read 'elements', we could see this argument as an extension of the discussion in Chapter 4 concerning immanent principles.

423 Literally, 'things that are intelligized [and] known' (*ha-devarim ha-muskalim ha-noda'im*), which probably translates *al-ashyā' al-ma'qūla al-ma'rūfa*, which is perhaps a hendiadys translation.

424 The manuscript tradition is probably confused between Anaxagoras and Democritus (or Leucippus) here.

425 i.e. the doubt arising from positing more than one principle.

426 The Hebrew *pit'om* most likely translates *duf'atan*, perhaps reflecting the Greek *athroōn* (as in the Arabic translation of Themistius' *On the Soul* 21,6, but in a slightly different meaning).

427 Heb. *ha-mehavva lahem*, literally, 'their bringer-into-being'.

428 I am not sure I understand this argument (Aristotle does not have it). My guess is that Themistius is saying that if there were two contrary principles (e.g. hot

and cold), there would have to be not one but two contrasting principles beyond them (e.g. one which transforms heat into coolness, and one which transforms coolness into heat).

429 Literally, 'and'.

430 In other words, positing numbers as formal causes entails the absurdity of constructing the continuous out of the discrete.

431 The Hebrew is difficult (*ha-hefekh be-ei ze min ha-meqomot haya sham ma she-hu' ba-koaḥ*), but the text can also mean something like 'whatever is a contrary will occasionally be in potentiality'.

432 Literally, 'from which place we should aim at this' (*me-ei ze min ha-meqomot ra'uy she-nekhavven el ze*).

433 Literally, 'from where' (*me-ayin*).

434 Assuming that the Hebrew *ma'ase* (which could also mean 'activity' or 'act') reflects the Arabic *'amal*, translating the Greek *ergon*.

435 I. Hadot takes this suggestion to refer to the Plotinian One (I. Hadot, *Athenian and Alexandrian Neoplatonism and the Harmonization of Aristotle and Plato* (Leiden & Boston: Brill, 2015), pp. 95–6; see also Twetten, 'Aristotelian Cosmology', p. 329), but I see no evidence to support this. See Meyrav, *Themistius*, p. 501.

436 Literally, 'their rectitude is from it' (*ve-yoshram mimeno*).

437 I am reading *nimshakh elav* ('yearning for it') with MS C[1], against all other manuscripts, which have *nimtza'* ('existent'), as does the body of the text, because it renders Themistius' argument more coherent. With the more common reading, the translation would be something like this: '. . .and it renders it – along with its unity – also as an existent'.

438 The literal meaning of the Hebrew *nikhnasim*, which here is translated into 'episodic', is 'entering' or 'included in', but it can be shown how it traces back to Aristotle's *epeisodiōdē* at 1076a1. Isḥāq translated *epeisodiōdēs* into *madkhūl* in Theophrastus (see Gutas, *Theophrastus*, p. 169, n. 7). The Arabic verb *dakhala* also means 'entered', so a Hebrew translator could have taken it in this sense.

439 See the previous note.

440 It is unclear what kinds of bodies Themistius is referring to.

441 Themistius does not complete Aristotle's quotation from Homer, which ends with 'let there be one leader' (*heis koiranos estō*; *Iliad* 2.204).

Bibliography

Achard, Martin, 'Themistius' Paraphrase of Posterior Analytics 71a17-b8: An Example of Rearrangement of an Aristotelian Text', *Laval théologique et philosophique* 64, no. 1 (2008), 19–34

Achard, Martin, 'La paraphrase de Thémistius sur les lignes 71a1-11 des *Seconds Analytiques*', *Dionysius* 23 (2005), 105–16

Adamson, Peter, 'State of Nature: Human and Cosmic Rulership in Ancient Philosophy', in Andreas Höfele and Beate Kellner, eds, *Menschennatur und politische Ordnung* (Paderborn: Wilhelm Fink, 2015), pp. 79–94

Adamson, Peter, 'The Last Philosophers of Late Antiquity in the Arabic Tradition', in Richard Sorabji, ed., *Aristotle Re-interpreted* (London: Bloomsbury, 2016), pp. 453–76

Alexandru, Stefan, *Aristotle's* Metaphysics *Lambda* (Leiden & Boston: Brill, 2014)

Averroes, *Tafsīr Mā ba'd al-Ṭabī'a*, ed. Maurice Bouyges, 3 vols (Beirut: Dar el-Machreq, 1948)

Badawī, 'Abd al-Raḥman, *Arisṭū 'inda al-'Arab* (Cairo: Maktabat al-Nahḍa al-Miṣriyya, 1947)

Berti, Enrico, 'Unmoved Mover(s) as Efficient Cause(s) in *Metaphysics* Λ 6', in Michael Frede and David Charles, eds, *Aristotle's Metaphysics Lambda* (Oxford: Clarendon Press, 2000), pp.181–206

Blumenthal, Henry J, 'Photius on Themistius (cod. 74): Did Themistius Write Commentaries on Aristotle?, *Hermes* 107, no. 2 (1979), 168–82

Brague, Rémi. *Thémistius: Paraphrase de la* Métaphysique *d'Aristote (livre Lambda)* (Paris: Vrin, 1999)

Capone Ciollaro, Maria, 'Osservazioni sulla Parafrasi di Temistio al *De Anima* aristotelico', in Claudio Moreschini, ed., *Esegesi, parafrasi e compilazione in Età Tardoantica, Atti del Terzo Convegno dell'Associazione di Studi Tardoantichi* (Naples: D'Auria, 1995), pp. 79–92

Charles, David, '*Metaphysics* Λ 2', in Michael Frede and David Charles, eds, *Aristotle's Metaphysics Lambda* (Oxford: Clarendon Press, 2000), pp. 81–110

Code, Alan, '*Metaphysics* Λ 5', in Michael Frede and David Charles, eds, *Aristotle's Metaphysics Lambda* (Oxford: Clarendon Press, 2000), pp. 161–79

Crubellier, Michel, '*Metaphysics* Λ 4', in Michael Frede and David Charles, eds, *Aristotle's Metaphysics Lambda* (Oxford: Clarendon Press, 2000), pp. 137–60

Curd, Patricia, *Anaxagoras of Clazomenae: Fragments and Testimonia* (Toronto: University of Toronto Press, 2007)

Elders, Leo, *Aristotle's Theology* (Assen: Van Gorcum, 1972)

Fazzo, Silvia, 'Heavenly Matter in Aristotle, *Metaphysics Lambda 2*', *Phronesis* 58, no. 2 (2013), 160–75

Fazzo, Silvia, 'Unmoved Mover as Pure Act or Unmoved Mover in Act? The Mystery of a Subscript Iota', in Christoph Horn, ed., *Aristotle's "Metaphysics" Lambda: New Essays* (Berlin & Boston: De Gruyter, 2016), pp. 181–205

Finzi, Moses, *Themistius: In Metaphysicorum Librum Duodecimum* (Venice: Hyeronimum Scotum, 1558)

Fraenkel, Carlos, 'Maimonides' God and Spinoza's *Deus sive Natura*', *Journal of the History of Philosophy* 44, no. 2 (2006), 169–215

Frank, Richard M, 'Some Textual Notes on the Oriental Versions of Themistius' Paraphrase of Book l of the *Metaphysics*', *Cahiers de Byrsa* 8 (1958/9), 215–30

Frede, Michael, '*Metaphysics* Λ 1', in Michael Frede and David Charles, eds, *Aristotle's Metaphysics Lambda* (Oxford: Clarendon Press, 2000), pp. 53–80

Genequand, Charles, *Ibn Rushd's Metaphysics: A Translation with Introduction of Ibn Rushd's Commentary on Aristotle's* Metaphysics, *Book Lām* (Leiden: Brill, 1986)

Geoffroy, M., 'Remarques sur la traduction Usṭāṯ Du livre lambda de la *Métaphysique*, Chapitre 6', *Recherches de théologie et philosophie médiévales* 70, no.2 (2003), 417–36.

Golitsis, Pantelis, 'Who Were the Real Authors of the *Metaphysics* Commentary Ascribed to Alexander and Ps. Alexander?, in Richard Sorabji, ed., *Aristotle Re-Interpreted* (London: Bloomsbury, 2016), pp. 565–88

Guldentops, Guy, 'La science suprême selon Thémistius', *Revue de philosophie ancienne* 19, no. 1 (2001), 99–120

Guldentops, Guy, 'Themistius on Evil', *Phronesis* 46, no. 2 (2001), 189–208

Gutas, Dimitri, 'Editing Arabic Philosophical Texts', *Orientalistische Literaturzeitung* 75, no. 3 (1980), 213–22

Gutas, Dimitri, *Theophrastus:* On First Principles *(known as his* Metaphysics) (Leiden: Brill, 2010)

Hadot, Ilsetraut, *Athenian and Alexandrian Neoplatonism and the Harmonization of Aristotle and Plato* (Leiden & Boston: Brill, 2015)

Hardie, R. P., and Gaye, R. K., trans., 'Physics', in Jonathan Barnes, ed., *The Complete Works of Aristotle*, 2 vols (Princeton: Princeton University Press, 1984), vol. 1, pp. 315–446

Heath, Malcolm, 'Theon and the History of the Progymnasmata', *Greek, Roman, and Byzantine Studies* 43 (2002), 129–60

Heather, Peter, 'Themistius: A Political Philosopher', in Mary Whitby, ed., *The Propaganda of Power: The Role of Panegyric in Late Antiquity* (Leiden: Brill, 1998), pp. 125–50

Henry, Devin, 'Themistius and the Problem of Spontaneous Generation', in Richard Sorabji, ed., *Aristotle Re-interpreted* (London: Bloomsbury, 2016), pp. 179–94

Ibn Taymiyya, *Minhāj al-Sunna al-Nabawiyya*, ed. M. Rashad Sālim (Al-Riyāḍ, 1986)

Judson, Lindsay, 'Formlessness and the Priority of Form: *Metaphysics*: Z 7-9 and Λ 3', in Michael Frede and David Charles, eds, *Aristotle's Metaphysics Lambda* (Oxford: Clarendon Press, 2000), pp. 111–35

Kakavelaki, Antonia S., 'On the Origin of Paraphrasis as a Philosophical Exegetical Method' [in Greek], *Philosophia* 45 (2015), 268–76

Kotwick, Mirjam E., *Alexander of Aphrodisias and the Text of Aristotle's* Metaphysics (Berkeley: California Classical Studies, 2016)

Kupreeva, Inna, 'Themistius', in Lloyd L. Gerson, ed., *The Cambridge History of Philosophy in Late Antiquity*, 2 vols (Cambridge: Cambridge University Press, 2010), vol. 1, pp. 397–416

Laks, André, '*Metaphysics* Λ 7', in Michael Frede and David Charles, eds, *Aristotle's Metaphysics Lambda* (Oxford: Clarendon Press, 2000), pp. 207–43

Landauer, Samuel, ed., *Themistii in Aristotelis Metaphysicorum librum Λ paraphrasis hebraice et latine*, Commentaria in Aristotelem Graeca 5.5 (Berlin: Reimer, 1903)

Lane, Edward W., *Arabic-English Lexicon*, 8 vols (London, 1863–1893)

Luna, Concetta, *Trois études sur la tradition des commentaires anciens à la* Métaphysique *d'Aristote* (Leiden: Brill, 2001)

Lyons, M. C., *An Arabic Translation of Themistius' Commentary on Aristoteles De Anima* (London: Cassirer, 1973)

Martin, Aubert, *Averroès: Grand commentaire de la Métaphysique d'Aristote, livre Lambda* (Paris: Les Belles Lettres, 1984)

Martini Bonadeo, Cecilia, *'Abd al-Laṭīf al-Baġdādī's Philosophical Journey: From Aristotle's* Metaphysics *to the 'Metaphysical Science'* (Leiden: Brill, 2013)

Meyrav, Yoav, 'Arabic-into-Hebrew Translation Strategies and Procedures in the Hebrew Manuscript Tradition of Themistius's Paraphrase of Aristotle's Metaphysics XII', in R. Leicht and G. Veltri, eds, *Studies in the Formation of Medieval Hebrew Philosophical Terminology* (Leiden: Brill, 2020), pp. 166–98

Meyrav, Yoav, 'Spontaneous Generation and its Metaphysics in Themistius' Paraphrase of Aristotle's *Metaphysics* 12', in Richard Sorabji, ed., *Aristotle Re-interpreted* (London: Bloomsbury, 2016), pp. 195–210

Meyrav, Yoav, 'Themistius' Paraphrase of Aristotle's *Metaphysics* 12', PhD diss., Tel Aviv University, 2017

Meyrav, Yoav, *Themistius' Paraphrase of Aristotle's* Metaphysics *12: A Critical Hebrew-Arabic Edition of the Surviving Textual Evidence, with an Introduction, Preliminary Studies, and a Commentary* (Leiden: Brill, 2019)

Neuwirth, Angelika, *ʿAbd al-Laṭīf al-Baġdādī's Bearbeitung von Buch Lambda der Aristotelischen Metaphysik* (Weisbaden: Steiner, 1976)

Owen, G. E. L., 'Logic and Metaphysics in Some Early Works of Aristotle', in I. Düring and G. E. L. Owen, eds, *Aristotle and Plato in the Mid-Fourth Century* (Gothenburg: Eilanders, 1960), pp. 163-90

Patillon, Michel, *Aelius Théon: Progymnasmata* (Paris: Les Belles Lettres, 1997)

Penella, Robert J., *The Private Orations of Themistius* (Berkeley: University of California Press, 2000)

Pines, Shlomo, 'Some Distinctive Metaphysical Conceptions in Themistius' Commentary on Book Lambda and their Place in the History of Philosophy', in Jürgen Weisner, ed., *Aristoteles: Werk und Wirkung*, 2 vols (Berlin & New York: De Gruyter, 1987), vol. 2: *Kommentierung, Überlieferung, Nachleben*, pp. 177–204

Reeve, C. D. C., *Aristotle: Metaphysics* (Indianapolis & Cambridge: Hackett, 2016)

Ross, William David, *Aristotle's Metaphysics*, 2 vols (Oxford: Clarendon Press, 1924)

Ross, William David, *Aristotle's Physics*, 2 vols (Oxford: Clarendon Press, 1936)

Schramm, Michael, 'Platonic Ethics and Politics in Themistius and Julian', in Ryan C. Fowler, ed., *Plato in the Third Sophistic* (Boston & Berlin: De Gruyter, 2014), pp. 131–43

Sharples, Robert W., 'Alexander of Aphrodisias and the End of Aristotelian Theology', in Theo Kobusch and Michael Erler, eds, *Metaphysik und Religion: zur Signatur des spätantiken Denkens* (Munich & Leipzig: Saur, 2002), pp. 1–22

Sharples, Robert W., 'Pseudo-Alexander on Aristotle, *Metaphysics Λ*', in Giancarlo Movia, ed., *Alessandro di Afrodisia e la 'Metafisica' di Aristotele* (Milan: Vita e pensiero, 2003), pp. 187–218

Sorabji, Richard, *Time, Creation and the Continuum* (London: Duckworth, 1983)

Sorabji, Richard, *The Philosophy of the Commentators, 200-600 AD*, 3 vols (Ithaca: Cornell University Press, 2005)

Sorabji, Richard, *Aristotle Re-interpreted* (London: Bloomsbury, 2016)

Themistius, *In Aristotelis Physica paraphrasis*, ed. H. Schenkl, Commentaria in Aristotelem Graeca 5.2 (Berlin: Reimer, 1900)

Themistius, *In libros Aristotelis De anima paraphrasis*, ed. R, Heinze. Commentaria in Aristotelem Graeca 5.3 (Berlin: Reimer, 1899)

Todd, Robert B., *Themistius: On Aristotle's On the Soul* (Ithaca: Cornell University Press, 1996)

Todd, Robert B., 'Themistius', *Catalogus Translationum et Commentariorum* 8 (2003), 57–102

Todd, Robert B., *Themistius: On Aristotle's* Physics *4* (London: Bloomsbury, 2003)

Todd, Robert B., *Themistius: On Aristotle's* Physics *5-8* (London: Bloomsbury, 2008)

Todd, Robert B., *Themistius: On Aristotle's* Physics *1-3* (London: Bloomsbury, 2012)

Twetten, David, 'Aristotelian Cosmology and Causality in Classical Arabic Philosophy and Its Greek Background', in Damien Janos, ed., *Ideas in Motion in Baghdad and Beyond* (Leiden & Boston: Brill, 2016), pp. 312–433

Vanderspoel, John, *Themistius and the Imperial Court: Oratory, Civic Duty, and Paideia from Constantius to Theodosius* (Ann Arbor: University of Michigan Press, 1995)

Volpe Cacciatore, Paola, 'La parafrasi di Temistio al secondo libro degli Analitici Posteriori di Aristotele', in Claudio Moreschini, ed., *Esegesi, parafrasi e compilazione in età tardoantica, Atti del Terzo Convegno dell'Associazione di Studi Tardoantichi* (Naples: D'Auria, 1995), pp. 389–95.

Wakelnig, Elvira, *A Philosophy Reader from the Circle of Miskawayh* (Cambridge: Cambridge University Press, 2014)

Watt, John W., 'From Themistius to al-Farabi: Platonic Political Philosophy and Aristotle's *Rhetoric* in the East', *Rhetorica* 13, no. 1 (1995), 17–41

Wilberding, James, 'The Neoplatonic Commentators on "Spontaneous" Generation', in Richard Sorabji, ed., *Aristotle Re-Interpreted* (London: Bloomsbury, 2016), pp. 211–29

Wright, W. A., *Grammar of the Arabic Language*, 3rd edn, 2 vols (Cambridge: Cambridge University Press, 1898)

Zucker, Arnuad, 'Qu'est-ce qu'une *paraphrasis*? L'enfance grecque de la paraphrase', *Rursus* 6 (February 2011)

English–Hebrew–Arabic Glossary

The following glossary contains the English terms used in the present translation for their corresponding Arabic (when available) and Hebrew terms. It has been somewhat simplified and abridged compared to the following Indexes, which include precise locations and more elaborate forms and constructions.

English	Hebrew	Arabic
ability	*yekholet*	*qudra*
absolute	*muḥlaṭ*	
absolutely	*ba-muḥlaṭ*	*ʿalā al-iṭlāq, muṭlaqān*
abstain	*mashakh yado*	
abstract	*meshulal, mufshaṭ*	
absurd	*megunne*	
absurd, virtually	*qarov le-seḥoq*	*muḥāl*
absurdity	*genai, dibba*	*shanāʿa*
abundance	*ribbui*	*kathra*
abyss		*hāwiyya*
accede	*hitratza*	
accident	*ʿinyan, ḥiddush, miqre*	*ḥāl, ḥādath, ḥādith, ʿaraḍ*
accomplish	*hishlim*	*atamma*
accord, bring into	*hiskim*	
according	*naʾot*	
account	*dibbur, heqesh*	
accurateness	*amitut*	
achieve	*hissig*	
acknowledge	*hoda*	*aqarra*
acquire	*qana*	*istafāda*
act (v.)	*ʿasa*	*faʿala*
action	*peʿula*	*fiʿl*
active	*poʿel*	*fāʿil*
activity	*peʿula, poʿal*	*fiʿl*
actuality	*poʿal*	*fiʿl*
actuality, brought into	*yatzaʾ el ha-poʿal*	*kharaja ilā al-fiʿl*
actually, in actuality	*ba-poʿal*	*bi-l-fiʿl*
add	*hosif*	
adherence	*redifa*	
adherent	*daveq*	
adjacency	*shekhuna*	
administration	*hadrakha*	*siyāsa*
admiration	*peleʾ*	*ʿajab*
admit (i.e. susceptible)	*qibbel*	*qabila*
admit (i.e. agree)	*hoda*	
affection	*shinnuy*	*taʾthīr*
affection (category)	*hipaʿalut*	*infiʿāl*
affinity, to have	*hityaḥes*	*jānasa*
affirm	*ḥiyyev, qiyyem*	*thabbata*

agree	*hiskim*	*ittafaqa*
aim	*kavvana*	*gharaḍ*
aim (v.)	*sam kavanato*	
air	*avir*	
allow	*ḥiyyev*	
allusion	*remez*	
alone	*nifrad*	*mufrad*
alter	*shinna*	*aḥāla*
alteration	*shinnuy, hishtanut, hitḥalfut*	*istiḥāla*
altered, to be	*hitḥalef*	
alternate (v.)	*humar*	*tabaddala*
amount (v.)	*haga'a*	
analogy	*heqesh, yaḥas*	*qiyās, munāsaba*
animal	*ḥay, ba'al ḥayyim*	*ḥayawān*
apart	*ḥutz, nifrad*	*mufrad*
apparent, to be	*nir'a*	*ru'iya*
appetite	*ta'ava*	*shahwa*
apply	*halakh, hipil*	*awqa'a*
appoint	*sam*	
apprehend	*hissig*	*adraka*
apprehensiveness	*'atzla*	*tahayyub*
appropriate	*ra'uy bo, ya'ut*	*akhlaqa bihi*
argument	*ma'amar, heqesh*	*qawl*
aristocracy	*qibbutz min ha-ṭovim*	
arithmetic	*ḥeshbon*	
arrange	*sidder*	
arrive	*hissig*	
art	*umanut, melākha*	*ṣinā'a*
art, productive	*umanut ma'asit*	*ṣinā'a 'amaliyya*
articulated	*husam*	
artificial	*melākhuti*	
artisan	*uman*	*ṣāni'*
artistry	*umanut*	*ṣan'*
ascribe	*sam*	
ascribed	*yuḥas*	
ask	*sha'al*	
asleep, sound	*shaqu'a be-shena*	*ghariqa fī al-nawm*
assertion	*be'ur*	*taṣrīḥ*
associate	*hitḥabber*	
association	*qibbutz*	
assume (regarding a proposition)	*hiniaḥ*	*waḍa'a*
assume (i.e. put on)	*lavash*	
assume a form	*tzuyyar*	
assumption	*hanaḥa*	
assured	*hitbarer*	
astronomy	*ḥokhmat ha-kokhavim*	*'ilm al-nujūm*
attached, to be	*nimshakh*	
attain completely	*hissig be-shelemut*	*fāza*
attained	*hussag*	
attribute	*to'ar, 'inyan*	*ma'anā*
author	*ba'al*	*ṣāḥib*
avoid	*mana'*	

avoid, cannot	*lo' nimlaṭ mi-*	*lā yakhlu min*
aware	*ḥashav*	*darā*
aware, to become	*hevin, hirgish*	
bare	*mufshaṭ*	
'bastard'	*mezuyyaf*	
be	*haya*	*kāna, ṣāra*
beauty	*yofi*	*ḥusn*
beget	*holid*	*walada*
beginning	*hatḥala, reshit, teḥila*	*ibtidā', awwal*
benefit from	*qibbel to'elet*	
benefit in	*hayta to'elet*	*intafa'a*
best	*na'ale, nikhbad, ṭov, yoter ṭov*	*faḍīl*
best, utmost	*be-takhlit / 'al takhlit ha-ma'ala*	*fī / 'alā ghāyat al-faḍīla*
better	*yoter ṭov, yoter na'ot*	*awlā, afḍal*
beyond	*ḥutz, na'ale*	
beyond measure	*lo' yisapper me-rov*	*la yukhṣā*
bigger	*gadol*	*akbar, ashaddu*
birth (v.)	*holid*	*walada*
blindness	*'ivvaron*	
blood of the menses	*dam ha-niddot*	*dam al-ṭamth*
body	*guf, geshem*	*badan, jism, juththa*
body, divine	*geshem elohi*	
born	*nolad*	
boundary	*takhlit*	*ghāya*
breadth	*roḥav*	
brief	*qaṭan*	*yasīr*
bring out	*hotzi'*	
bring together	*qibbetz*	
bringer [to actuality]	*motzi'*	*mukhrij*
brought out	*yatza'*	*kharaja*
call	*qara'*	*sammā*
can	*efshar (haya efshar), yakhol, tukkan, yitakhen*	*yajūz (jāza), tahayya'a*
capable	*yakhol*	*qādir*
careful	*nishmar*	*ḥadhira*
carried out	*halakh*	
carry	*nasa'*	*ḥamala*
cast	*hishlikh*	*iṭṭaraḥa*
cause	*sibba, 'illa*	*sabab, 'illa*
cause for the sake of which	*ha-sibba asher ba'avura*	*al-sabab allatī lahu*
cause, efficient	*sibba po'elet, 'illa po'elet*	*'illa fā'ila*
cause, moving	*sibba meni'a, 'illa meni'a*	*sabab muḥarrik, 'illa muḥarrika*
cautious, to be	*nizhar*	*tawaqqā*
cease	*sar*	*zāla*
celestial body	*geshem shememi, gerem shememi*	*jism samāwī*
change	*shinnuy*	*taghayyur*
chaos	*bohu*	
charge	*hishliṭ*	

chief	*rosh*	
choice	*beḥira*	
choose	*baḥar*	*ikhtāra*
chosen	*nivḥar*	*mukhtār*
circular	*ʿal ha-sibuv*	*mustadīr*
city	*medina*	*madīna*
city's governance	*hanhagat ha-medina*	
claim (v.)	*kivven*	*zaʿama*
clean	*naqi*	
clear	*mevo'ar*	*bayyin*
close	*qarov*	*qarīb*
closeness	*qurva*	
coerce (v.)	*anas*	
coerced	*mukhraḥ*	
coercion	*ones, hekhreaḥ*	
cold	*qor*	*bard*
collected	*hitqabbetz*	*ijtamaʿa*
colour	*mar'e*	*lawn*
combination	*ḥibbur*	*ta'līf*
combined, to be	*hitḥabber, hitqabbetz, hurkav*	
come	*shav*	*ṣāra*
come-to-be	*hithava*	
coming-to-be	*haviya*	*kawn*
coming-to-be, agent of	*mehavve*	
coming-to-be, to receive	*meqabbel/yeqabbel ha-haviya*	*qābil/yaqbalu al-kawn*
command	*tzivvui, mitzvah*	
commander	*moshel*	*qā'id*
common	*meshuttaf, nikhlal, kolel*	
common, to have something in	*shittuf*	*mushāraka*
community	*reʿiya*	
compare	*hiqqish*	*qāsa, qāyasa*
comparison	*heqesh*	*muqāyasa*
compelled	*hitzṭarekh*	*uḍṭurra*
complete (v.)	*hishlim*	*kamala*
completeness	*temimut*	*tamām*
completion	*gemar, shelemut*	*inqiḍā'*
compose	*ḥibber*	
composed, composite	*murkav*	*murakkab*
composed, to be	*hitrakkev*	*tarakkaba*
composition	*harkava*	*tarkīb*
compound (v.)	*hirkiv*	
comprehend	*hevin*	*fahima*
concealment	*hester*	
conceive	*tziyyer*	
conception	*tziyyur*	
conclude	*holid*	*antaja*
conclusion	*tolada*	*natīja*
condition	*tenai*	
confront	*ḥalaq*	*ʿānada*
confused	*mevulbal*	*muḍṭarib*
conjoin	*tzaraf*	
connect	*ḥibber*	
consider	*dimma, ḥashav, sam*	*tawahhama, jaʿala*

consider as	*biqqesh*	
considered as, to be	*hunnaḥ, husam*	*ju'ila*
constancy	*temidut*	*dawām*
constituted	*'amad*	*qāma*
contact, to be in	*lavash*	*lābasa*
contain	*hiqqif*	*ḥawā*
containing	*nikhlal*	
content, to be	*'amad*	
contiguous	*daveq*	
continue	*himshikh*	*ittaba'a, am'ana*
continuity	*devequt*	*ittiṣāl*
continuous	*nidbaq, mitdabbeq*	*muttaṣil*
contract (v.)	*niqwatz*	*inqabaḍa*
contradict	*satar*	*nāqaḍa*
contradiction	*setira*	
contrariety	*hipukh*	*taḍādd*
contrary	*hefekh*	*ḍidd*
contrary, to be	*hithappekh*	
contrasting	*mithappekh*	
controller	*shaliṭ*	*mutasalliṭ*
corporeal	*gashmi, ba'al geshem*	*dhū jism*
corporeality	*gashmut*	*jismāniyya*
correct	*yashar*	*ṣawāb*
correct, to be	*amar emet, yashar*	*aṣāba*
correctness	*yosher*	*ṣawāb*
count	*mana*	*'addada*
counterpart	*dimyon*	*naẓīr*
course	*mahalakh*	*maslak*
cover	*kissa*	
craft (v.)	*tzaraf*	
craftsman	*tzoref*	
create	*ḥiddesh*	*aḥdatha*
created, to be	*hitḥaddesh/nitḥaddesh*	*ḥadatha*
creation	*ḥiddush*	*ḥudūth*
creator	*bore'*	
cut	*nivdal*	*mabtūr*
cycle	*sibuv*	
dancer	*mekharker*	
darkness	*ḥoshekh*	*ẓulma*
dead	*met*	*mayt, bi-mā'it*
deceive		*aghāra*
decline	*ḥissaron*	*tanaqquṣ*
decrease	*ḥissaron*	*nuqṣān*
deemed fit	*kashar*	
definition	*geder*	*ḥadd*
definitively	*'al ha-hagbala*	
delay	*mittun*	
delight	*simḥa*	*faraḥ*
delighted	*sas, samaḥ*	*sarra*
demonstrate	*gazar*	
demonstration	*mofet*	*burhān*
dense	*'av*	

dense, to become	*hitqashsha*	*iktanaza*
deny (a proposition)	*hikhḥish*	*ankara*
deny (something of something)	*shalal*	*nafā*
depend upon	*nitla*	
dependence	*hittalut*	
dependent	*nitla, taluy*	*mu'allaq*
descent	*yerida*	
describe	*te'er, sipper*	*na'ata*
description	*to'ar*	
desire	*teshuqa*	*'ishq*
desire (v.)	*ḥashaq, hishtoqeq*	*tashawwaqa, 'ashiqa*
determination	*'amida*	*wuqūf*
determine	*'amad*	
deviate	*'avar*	
dialectic	*nitztzuaḥ*	
difference	*hefresh, hevdel, ḥiluf*	*firq, ikhtilāf*
different	*mitḥallef*	*mukhtalif, bi-makhālif*
dignified	*nissa'*	
direct	*kivven*	
directed		*mustāq*
directed, to be	*bi-mekhuvvan, halakh*	
directing	*molikh*	*sawwāq*
direction	*tzad*	
director	*manhig*	
disadvantage	*ḥissaron*	
discard	*salleq*	*raf'*
discrete	*neḥlaq*	
discussion	*dibbur, ma'amar, zikaron*	*kalām, qawl*
dispension	*riḥuq*	*barā'*
dispersed	*mefuzzar, nifrad*	*mutafarriq*
dissociation	*perud*	
distilled	*mezuqqaq*	
distinct, to be	*nifrad*	*farada*
distinguished	*muqaf, nifrad, nivdal*	*mubāyin*
distinguished, to be	*yatza'*	*kharaja*
divide	*ḥilleq*	*qassama*
divided	*neḥlaq*	
divine	*elohi*	*ilāhi*
divine [substances]	*elohiyot*	
divinity	*elohut*	*ilahiyya*
divisible	*mitḥalleq*	*munqasim*
do	*'asa*	*fa'ala*
doubt	*safeq*	
drawn away	*raḥaq*	
duration	*ḥeled*	
earlier, to be	*qadam*	*taqaddama*
earth	*eretz*	*arḍ*
ease	*qalut*	
easy	*qal, naqel*	
effort	*'amal*	
element	*yesod*	*'unṣur, rukn*
elevation	*tosefet*	*ziyāda*

embodied	*mugsham*	
eminence	*gedula*	*sharaf*
employ	*ista'mala*	
empty	*req*	
encompass	*yuḥad*	
encounter (v.)	*nafal*	
end	*takhlit, kavvana, mekhuvvan*	*gharaḍ, maqṣūd*
ending	*takhlit*	*inqiḍā'*
enquire into	*hutzrakh*	*iḥtāja*
enquiry	*baqqasha, ḥaqira*	*ṭalab, baḥth*
ensouled	*ba'al nefesh, mitnashshem*	*mutanaffas*
episodic	*nikhnas*	
equal	*shave*	
error	*ṭa'ut*	*khaṭa'*
escape	*baraḥ, nimlaṭ*	*haraba*
essence	*'atzmut, nefesh*	*dhāt, nafs*
establish	*'amad*	
eternal	*nitzḥi*	*azlīy*
eternally	*ha-ḥeled kullo*	*al-dahr kulluhu*
everlasting	*nish'ar, matmid, temidi, temidi ha-hisha'arut*	*dā'im, dā'im al-baqā', abadīy*
everlastingness	*hisha'arut*, temidut	*baqā', dawām*
evil	*ra'*	
evoke [sound]	*hishmi'a*	
excel in finding	*heṭiv limtzo'*	
excellence	*ma'ala*	*faḍīla*
excellence, utmost	*be-takhlit / 'al takhlit ha-ma'ala*	*fī / 'alā ghāyat al-faḍīla*
excluded	*yotze'*	*khārij*
exercise	*hit'asseq*	*ista'mala*
exhibit	*her'a*	
exist	*nimtza'*	*wujida*
existence	*metzi'ut*	*wujūd*
existent, existing [thing]	*nimtza'*	*mawjūd*
expand	*hitpashsheṭ*	*intashara*
expect	*qivva*	*tawaqqa'a*
explain (v.)	*be'er*	*bayyana*
explanation	*be'ur*	
explore	*ḥippes*	
extend	*hotzi'*	
extension	*hitraḥvut*	*ittisā'*
exterior	*ḥitzon*	
external	*yotze', ḥutz*	*khārij*
extreme point	*qatze*	*ṭaraf*
eye	*'ayin*	*'ayn*
fall short	*qatzar*	*naqaṣa*
falling	*nofel*	*wāqi'*
false	*kozev*	
fancy (v.)	*hit'avva*	*tashawwaqa*
far	*raḥoq*	*ba'īd*
fashioned	*mugbal*	*majbūl*
fatigue (v.)	*hel'a*	
ferment	*hirtiaḥ*	*ghallā*

few	*qetzaṭ*	*baʿḍ*
fewer	*meʿaṭ*	*aqall*
find	*matzaʾ*	*wajada*
fine	*naʾe*	
finish	*killa*	
fire	*esh*	*nār*
first	*rishon, rosh, teḥila*	*awwal*
first cause	*ha-sibba ha-rishona, ha-ʿilla ha-rishona*	*al-sabab al-awwal, al-ʿilla al-ūlā*
first divine intellect	*ha-sekhel ha-elohi ha-rishon*	
first form	*ha-tzura ha-rishona*	
first heaven	*ha-raqiʿa ha-rishon*	*al-samāʾ al-ūlā*
first mover	*ha-meniʿa ha-rishon*	*al-muḥarrik al-awwal*
first principle	*ha-hatḥala ha-rishona*	*al-mabdaʾ al-awwal*
first substance	*ʿetzem rishon*	
fitting, more	*yoter raʾuy*	*awlā*
fixed star	*kokhav qayyam*	*kawkab thābit*
flow	*ratz*	*jarā*
follow	*nimshakh aḥar*	*talā, tabʿia*
follow [logically]	*hitḥayyev*	*wajaba, lazima*
follows necessarily	*raʾuy be-hekhreaḥ, yitḥayyev be-hekhreaḥ*	*yajibu ḍurūratan*
foreign	*nokhri*	*gharīb*
foretell	*nibba*	*anbaʾa*
form	*tzura*	*ṣūra*
form (v.)	*tziyyer*	
form, with	*metzuyyar*	
found, to be	*nimtzaʾ*	*wujida*
foundation	*ʿiqqar, shat*	*asās*
founded	*nivna*	*mabnīy*
fountainhead	*mabuʿa*	*yanbūʿ*
free, to be	*nimlaṭ*	
freemen	*ha-nikhbadim min ha-anashim*	
function	*maʿase*	
fundament	*shoresh*	
gained	*niqna*	*muktasab*
general	*kolel*	*ʿāmī*
generally	*bi-khlal*	*bi-l-jumla*
genus	*sug*	*jins*
geometricians	*ḥakhmei ha-tishboret*	
geometry	*tishboret, ḥokhmat ha-tishboret*	
give	*natan*	
give up	*natan, hiniaḥ*	*alghā*
giver [of law]	*meniaḥ*	
go over	*ʿavar*	*taṣaffaḥa*
God	*ha-el*	*alla*
god, secondary	*ha-elohim ha-sheniyim*	*al-ilaha al-thawānī*
going out [from potentiality to actuality]	*yetziʾa [min ha-koaḥ el ha-poʿal]*	
good	*ṭov*	*khayr, ḥasan*

governance	*hanhaga*	
group	*kat*	*farīq*
grow [something]	*hitzmiaḥ*	*anbata*
growth	*gidul, tzemiḥa*	*nushū'*
guide	*holikh*	
halt	*'amida*	
hand	*yad*	
happen	*hissig, hitḥayyev*	*laḥiqa*
happen [randomly]	*qara*	
hardness	*qoshi*	
have the same form	*na'ot ba-tzura*	*muwāfiq fī al-ṣūra*
have to	*hitḥayyev*	*wajaba*
having	*qinyan*	
head	*rosh*	
hear	*shama'*	
hearing	*shema'*	
heaven	*shamayim, raqi'a*	*samā'*
heavy	*kaved*	*thaqīl*
here	*ka'n*	
high pitched	*ḥad*	
higher	*'elyon*	*a'lā*
hinder	*mana'*	*mana'a*
hold	*nasa'*	
hope	*tiqva*	*rajā'*
hot	*ḥom*	*ḥarr*
how	*eikh*	*kayfa*
hypothesis	*hanaḥa*	
Idea (Platonic)	*tzura*	*ṣūra*
idle	*baṭel*	*mut'aṭṭal, 'uṭl*
idleness	*baṭṭala*	*baṭṭāla*
ignorance	*sikhlut*	*jahl*
imagination	*dimyon*	*takhayyul*
imagine	*dimma, tziyyer ba-maḥshava*	
immaterial	*lo' yit'arev bo ha-ḥomer, lo' yit'arev bo ha-yesod, lo' yit'arev bo ha-hiyuli, yit'arev bo davar min ha-hiyuli, she-ha-hiyuli lo' yit'arev bo*	*lā tashūbuhu al-hayūlā, lā yashūbuhu shay' min al-hayūlā*
immeasurable	*be-lo' shi'ur*	*bi-lā mudda*
immediately	*pit'om*	
impairment	*ri'u'a*	
impede	*hi'iq*	*'āqa*
impel	*ratza*	*raghiba*
implanted	*taqu'a*	
impossible	*nimna'*	*mumtani'*
impossible (v.)	*nimna'*	*imtana'a*
imprinted	*neḥtam*	*inṭabaqa*
improperly	*she-lo' ka-shura*	
incline	*naṭa*	*ḥanna*
inclined sphere	*ha-galgal ha-noṭe*	*al-falak al-mā'il*
include	*kalal*	

included	*nikhnas*	*dākhil*
incorporeal	*lo yitʿarev bo davar min ha-gashmut*	*lā yashūbuhu shayʾ min al-jismāniyya*
increase	*gidul, tosefet*	*numuww*
indicate	*hora*	*dalla*
indication	*reʾaya*	
individual	*praṭi*	
indivisible particles	*ḥalaqim asher loʾ yitḥalqu*	*ajzāʾ allatī lā tatajazzaʾu*
induce	*kivven*	
inferior	*paḥut*	*khasīs*
infinite	*ein takhlit lo*	*lā nihāya lahu*
inherit	*yarash*	
in itself	*be-ʿeino, nafsho, be-nafsho*	*bi-ʿaynihi, nafsuhu, fī nafsuhu*
inspiration	*hazkara*	*ilhām*
instant	*regaʿ, heref ʿayin*	*dufʿa, ṭarfat ʿayn*
instantly	*pitʾom*	*dufʿatān*
intellect	*sekhel*	*ʿaql*
intellect, divine	*sekhel elohi*	*ʿaql ilāhi*
intellectual world	*ha-ʿolam ha-sikhli*	
intelligible world	*ha-ʿolam ha-muskal*	
intelligible, object of intellect	*muskal*	*maʿqūl*
intelligize	*hiskil*	*ʿaqala*
intelligizer	*maskil*	*ʿāqil*
intend	*ratza*	
intention	*kavvana*	*qaṣd*
intermixed	*mitmazzeg*	
interrupt	*hifsiq*	*qaṭaʿa*
interruption	*hefseq*	*inqiṭāʿ*
interval	*merḥaq*	
invalidated, to be	*baṭal*	
invent	*himtziʾ*	
investigate	*ḥaqar*	*baḥatha*
involved	*mesubbakh*	
issue	*ʿinyan*	*amr*
joy	*sason, ḥedva, simḥa*	*surūr*
judge	*shafaṭ*	*ḥakama*
judgement	*mishpaṭ*	*ḥukm*
keep	*heḥeziq*	
keep away	*raḥaq*	
keep in mind	*sam be-daʿat, ʿamad ba-maḥshava*	*khaṭara bi-bāl, qāma fī wahm*
keep something away	*hirḥiq*	
kill	*hemit*	*amāta*
kind	*min*	*ṣinf*
know	*yadaʿ*	*raʾā, ʿalima, taʿarrafa*
knowledge	*yediʿa, ḥokhma, madaʿ*	*maʿrifa, ʿilm*
known [thing]	*yaduʿa*	*maʿlūm*
known, well-	*mefursam*	
lacking	*ḥaser*	*nāqiṣ*
laid down [law]	*munaḥ*	

last	*aḥaron*	*aqṣā*
lasting	*hisha'arut*	*baqā'*
lasting, continuously	*daveq ha-hisha'arut*	*muttaṣil al-baqā'*
latent	*ṭamun*	*kāmin*
law	*nimus*	*nāmūs*
leader	*rosh,reshit*	*ra'īs*
learn	*lamad*	
least	*paḥut*	*aql*
leave	*'azav, hiniaḥ*	*taraka, wada'a*
leisure	*penāi*	*farāgh*
lengthy	*arokh*	
less	*paḥot*	
less, to be	*ḥasar*	
let	*baḥar*	*ṣāra*
let go	*hittir*	
life	*ḥayyim*	*ḥayā*
light	*ḍaw'*	*or*
light [weight]	*qal*	*khafīf*
like	*dimyon*	*mathal, naẓīr, ashbah,*
likeness	*hiddamut/hitdamut*	
limit	*geder, takhlit*	*ḥadd*
limit (v.)	*higbil*	*ḥaddada*
limited	*ba'al takhlit*	*mutanāh*
line	*qav*	*khaṭṭ*
linked	*meḥubbar*	*maqrūn*
liquid	*niggar*	*sayyāl*
little bit	*me'aṭ*	
live	*ḥay*	
living	*ḥay*	*ḥayy*
living things	*adonei ha-ḥayyim*	*ḥayā*
logic	*higayon*	*manṭiq*
logical exercise		*al-riyāḍa bi-l-manṭiq*
logos	*yaḥas*	*nasib*
love	*ahava*	*maḥabba*
love (v.)	*ahav*	*ḥabba*
low-pitched	*kaved*	
magnitude	*godel, guf*	*iẓam, juththa*
maintain	*savar*	*ra'ā*
make	*'asa, sam*	
make known	*sipper*	*khabbara*
make proper	*yiḥḥed*	*khaṣṣa*
making	*'asiyya*	*'amal*
man	*ish*	
manifold	*rav*	*kathīr*
manner	*'inyan, derekh*	*ḥāl, amr*
many	*rav*	*kathīr, shattā*
marvel	*tema*	*'ajab*
mathematical [sciences]	*limudiyot*	
mathematical extension	*merḥaq limudi*	*bu'd ta'līmī*
mathematical number	*mispar limudi*	
matter	*ḥomer, hiyuli, yesod*	*mādda, hayūlā, 'unṣur*
mean	*ratza*	*ṣarraḥa, 'anā*
meaning	*'inyan*	*ma'anā*

medicine, art of	*melekhet ha-refu'a*	*ṣinā'at al-ṭibb*
memory	*zikaron*	*dhikr*
mention	*zakhar, hizkir*	*dhakara*
metaphorically	*'al tzad ha-harḥava*	
meticulous, to be	*hiflig*	*daqqaqa*
middle	*emtza'*	
military unit	*kat*	
mineral	*maḥtzav*	
mingle	*'erev*	*khalaṭa*
missing	*ḥasar*	
mix	*hit'arev*	*ikhtalaṭa*
mixed	*nimzag, me'orav*	*mukhtaliṭ*
mixture	*'eruv*	
model	*dimyon*	
modification	*ḥiddush, miqre, 'inyan*	*ḥādath, ḥāl*
moisture	*laḥut*	*ruṭūba*
moment	*'et*	*waqt*
motion	*tenu'a*	*ḥaraka*
motion in place	*tenu'a meqomit*	*ḥaraka mustaqīma*
move [i.e. cause motion]	*hini'a*	*ḥarraka*
moved, to be	*hitno'e'a*	*taḥarraka*
mover	*meni'a*	*muḥarrik*
mover, efficient	*meni'a po'el*	
mover, proximate	*meni'a qarov*	*muḥarrik qarīb*
moving [i.e. causing motion]	*hana'a*	*taḥrīk*
moving power	*koaḥ meni'a*	*quwwa muḥarrika*
multiple	*rav*	*kathīr*
multiplicity	*kefel*	*taḍā'uf*
must	*ra'uy*	*yanbaghī, yajibu*
must necessarily	*ra'uy be-hekhreaḥ, yitḥayyev be-hekhreaḥ*	*yajibu ḍurūratan*
naked, to be	*'arum*	*ta'arrā*
name	*shem*	
name (v.)	*qara'*	
nation	*umma*	
natural	*ṭiv'i*	*ṭabī'ī*
natural [scientists]	*ṭiv'iyim*	
natural [treatises]	*ṭiv'iyot*	
natural science	*ha-ḥokhma ha-ṭiv'it*	*al-'ilm al-ṭabī'ī*
natural scientist	*ba'al ṭeva'im*	
natural treatise	*ma'amar ba-ṭiv'iyot*	
nature	*ṭeva'*	*ṭabī'a, ṭab'*
necessarily	*be-hekhreaḥ, min ha-meḥuyyav she-, ra'uy be-hekhreaḥ*	*ḍurūratan, min al-wājib an, bi-l-wājib*
necessary	*hekhreḥi, meḥuyyav*	*ḍurūrī*
necessitate	*ḥiyyev*	*awjaba*
necessity	*hekhreaḥ*	*ḍurūra*
necessity, demonstrative	*hekhreaḥ mofti*	
need	*tzorekh*	*ḥāja*
need (v.)	*hitzṭarekh*	*iḥtāja*
needed, to be	*hitzrikh*	
neglect	*'azav*	

nobility	*kavod*	*sharaf, ḥamd*
noble	*nadiv, ba'al ma'ala*	*karīm, afḍal*
notion	*'inyan*	
number	*mispar, kamma*	*'adad, kam*
observation	*ma she-yira'e la-'ayin*	
obstruct	*mana'*	*mana'a*
obtaining	*haga'a*	*taḥṣīl*
occupied	*mit'asseq*	
occur	*hitḥaddesh/nitḥaddesh, qara*	*ḥadatha*
one	*eḥad*	*wāḥid*
one and the same	*be-'eino*	*bi-'aynihi*
oneness	*aḥdut*	
opine	*savar*	
opinion	*de'a, da'at, sevara'*	
oppose	*nagad*	
opposed, to be	*nivdal*	
opposing	*mitnagged*	
opposition	*hitnagdut*	*muqābala*
order	*sedder, yosher*	*tartīb, niẓām*
ordered	*mesuddar, meyushshar*	
ordered motion	*tenu'a mesudderet*	
organ	*ever*	*uḍw*
organization	*yosher*	*niẓām*
originate	*bara'*	*ansha'a*
other	*zulat*	*ghayr*
otherwise	*ḥiluf*	*khilāf*
ought	*ra'uy*	*yanbaghī, yajibu*
outrageous	*mekho'ar*	
outset	*hatḥala, teḥila*	
outside	*ḥutz*	*khārij*
part	*ḥeleq*	*juz'*
participate	*hishtattef*	
particular	*nifrad*	*mufrad*
pass	*yatza', 'avar*	
passion	*teshuqa*	*'ishq*
path	*derekh*	*sabīl*
pay attention	*hebiṭ*	
peculiar	*meyuḥad*	*khāṣṣ*
people	*anashim, bri'a*	*nās, qawm, ahl*
per se	*nifrad*	
perceive	*hikir*	
perdurance	*temidut*	*dawām*
perdure	*hitmid*	*dāma*
perduring	*matmid ha-hisha'arut*	*dā'im al-baqā'*
perfect	*shalem*	*tāmm*
perfect (v.)	*hishlim*	*kamala*
perfection	*shelemut*	*kamāl*
periphery	*takhlit*	*nihāya*
perish	*nifsad, kala*	*fasada*
perishable, capable of perishing	*meqabbel/yeqabbel ha-hefsed*	*qābil/yaqbalu li-l-fasād*

persist	*hitqayyem*	*thabata*
persisting	*ʿomed, matmid, qayyam*	*dāʾim*
persuasion	*sippuq*	
persuasive	*maspiq*	*muqniʿ*
Physics	*sefer ha-ḥokhma ha-ṭivʿit, ha-shemaʿ ha-ṭivʿi*	*kitāb al-ʿilm al-ṭabīʿī*
pilot	*manhig*	
piloting	*hanhaga*	
place	*makom*	*makān, mawḍiʿ*
place (v.)	*heʿemid*	
placed	*munaḥ*	
planet	*kokhav navokh*	*kawkab mutaḥayyir*
plant	*tzemaḥ, tzomeaḥ*	*nabāt*
play [an instrument]	*hikka*	
pleasant	*ʿarev*	*ladhīdh*
pleasantness	*ʿarevut*	*ladhdha*
pleasure	*hanaʾa*	*ladhdha*
plurality	*ribbui*	*kathra*
point	*nequdda*	
pole	*qoṭev*	
political administration	*hadrakhat ha-medina*	*siyāsat al-madīna*
posit	*hiniaḥ, hesim*	*waḍaʿa, jaʿala*
position	*matzav*	
positioning	*hanaḥa*	
possess	*baʿal*	
possibility	*efsharut*	*imkān*
possible (v.)	*efshar (haya efshar)*	*yumkin (amkana)*
posterior	*mitʾaḥer*	
potentially, in potentiality	*ba-koaḥ*	*bi-l-quwwa*
poverty	*ʿaniyyut*	
precede	*qadam*	*taqaddama*
preceding	*qodem*	*awlā*
precision	*diqduq*	
predicate	*nasaʾ*	*iḥtamala*
predicated, to be	*hunnaḥ*	
premise	*haqdama*	*muqaddama*
preoccupied, to be	*hitʿasseq, ṭared*	*istaʿmala, mutashāghil*
prescribe	*hiqdim, hora, teʾer, tzivva*	*taqaddama, faraḍa*
preserve	*shamar*	
presume	*ḥashav*	*ẓanna*
pretend	*hitraʾa*	
prevent	*manaʿ*	*manaʿa*
principle	*hatḥala*	*mabdaʾ*
prior	*qodem*	*qabla, mutaqaddim, aqdam*
prior, to be	*qadam*	*taqaddama*
priority	*qedima*	
privation	*heʿader*	*ʿadam*
problem	*safeq*	
proceed	*halakh*	*salaka*
procession	*himashkhut*	
proper	*mitdamme, meḥuyyav, naʾot*	*mushākil, mulāʾim*
property	*segula*	*khāṣṣiya*
proposition	*shoresh*	*aṣl*
proprietary	*meyuḥad*	

proximate	*qarov*	*qarīb*
pursue	*sam megamato*	*qafā atharahu*
put	*sam*	*ja'ala*
putrescence	*'ippush*	*'afan*
puzzled, to be	*lehipale'*	*ta'ajjub*
puzzlement	*pele'*	*'ajab*
quality	*'inyan, eikhut*	*ḥāl, kayfa*
quantity	*shi'ur, kamma, kammut*	*miqdār*
question	*she'ela*	
quick	*memaher*	
quick, to be	*miher*	
raise a problem	*sippeq*	
rank	*madrega*	*martaba*
rarefied	*herekh*	*raqqa*
reach	*haga'a*	*mablagh*
ready	*mukhan*	*mutahayyi'*
realm	*sha'ar*	*bāb*
reason	*heqesh*	*muqāyasa*
recall	*hizkir*	*adhkara*
receive	*qibbel*	*qabila*
receiver [explication of susceptibility]	*meqabbel*	*qābil*
recent	*qerovat ha-zeman*	*qarībat al-'ahd*
rectilinear	*'al ha-yosher*	*mustaqīm*
rectitude	*yosher, derekh ha-yashar*	*niẓām*
refer	*hora*	
refuse	*me'en*	
refutation	*setira*	
refute	*satar*	
regulation	*hanhaga*	
reject	*daḥa*	
relate	*hityaḥes*	
relate accurately	*sipper*	*iqtaṣṣa*
relation	*yaḥas, hitztarfut*	*nisba*
relationship	*semikhut*	*iḍāfa*
remain	*'amad, nish'ar*	*labitha, baqiya*
remaining	*hisha'arut*	*baqā'*
remember	*zakhar*	
remoteness	*roḥaq*	
removed, to be	*sullaq, histalleq, sar*	*nufiya, rufi'a*
render	*sam*	
report	*hizkir*	
reprehensibility	*dofi*	
repugnant	*nim'as*	
resemblance	*hiddamut/hitdamut*	*mushākala*
resemble	*hiddama, dama*	*ashabbaha*
respect	*heqesh, panim*	*muqāyasa, wajh*
rest	*menuḥa*	*sukūn, rāḥa, futūr*
rest (v.)	*naḥ*	
result (v.)	*higi'a*	*balagha*
retreat	*hitgalgel*	
return	*shav, hithappekh, ḥazar*	

revolve	*savav, sav*	
richness	*'osher*	
rid	*'azav, hipil*	*taraka*
right	*nitztzav*	
rising	*mitnase'*	
root	*shoresh*	
rotation	*sibuv*	
royalty	*melukha*	
ruler	*molekh*	*mālik*
rush	*hishtaddel*	*bādara*
safeguarded	*baṭuaḥ*	
sage	*ḥakham*	*'ālim*
same	*dome*	*mithl*
satiated	*hitmale'*	
say	*hodi'a*	
say decisively	*gazar*	
science	*ḥokhma, sevara'*	*'ilm*
scornful	*nivzi*	
sculpture	*tzelem*	
section	*qoṭer*	
see	*ra'a*	*baṣura*
seed	*zera', gar'in*	*bizra*
seeing	*'iyyun*	*'iyān*
seek	*biqqesh*	*ṭalaba*
seeking dominance	*mitgabber*	
seem	*nir'a*	*badā*
seen, to be	*hera'ut*	
segment	*ḥatikha*	*qiṭ'*
self-sufficiency	*sippuq*	*iktifā'*
semblance	*dimyon*	
semen	*zera', shikhvat zera'*	*bizra, minān*
sense, sensing	*ḥush*	*ḥāssa, ḥiss*
sensible, sensory object	*muḥash, murgash*	*maḥsūs*
separate	*nifrad*	*mufrad, munfarid*
separate (v.)	*hifrid*	*afrada*
separated, to be	*nifrad*	*infarada*
separately	*be-yiḥud*	*mufradān*
seperate off	*pereq*	
set	*sam, husam*	*ju'ila*
set apart	*hivdil*	
set out	*kivven, konen*	*qaṣada*
shape	*temuna, tzura*	*shakl*
share	*ḥeleq*	*ḥaẓẓ*
share (v.)	*hishtatef*	*ishtaraka*
sharp	*ḥad*	*ḥādd*
sharpness	*ḥiddud*	
shed	*hifshiṭ*	*lafaẓa*
short	*qatzar*	
should	*ra'uy*	*yanbaghī, yajibu*
should necessarily	*ra'uy be-hekhreaḥ*	*yajibu ḍurūratan*
side	*tzad*	
sight	*mar'e*	

signification	*re'aya*	*dalāla*
similar	*dome*	*ashbah*
simple	*pashuṭ*	*basīṭ*
simpliciter	*muḥlaṭ*	
skill	*'orma*	*ḥidhq*
sleep	*shena*	*nawm*
slight	*qaṭan*	
small	*qaṭan*	*ṣaghīr*
softness	*sefogut*	
some	*qetzaṭ*	*ba'ḍ*
sometimes	*pe'amim*	*rubbamā, qad*
soul	*nefesh*	*nafs*
soul that is in the earth	*ha-nefesh asher ba-aretz*	*al-nafs allatī fī al-arḍ*
sound	*qol*	*ṣawt*
species	*min*	*naw'*
specific	*praṭi*	
specifically	*be-yiḥud*	
sphere	*galgal*	*falak*
spongy	*sefogi*	
stable	*qayyam*	*thābit*
stable, to be	*hitqayyem*	*thabata*
stand	*'amad*	*qāma*
star	*kokhav*	*kawkab*
start	*hatḥala*	*ibtidā'*
start (v.)	*hitḥil*	
state	*'inyan*	*ḥāl*
state (v.)	*zakhar, sipper*	*adhkara, waṣafa*
statement	*ma'amar*	*qawl*
statement about natural things	*ma'amar ba-ṭiv'iyot*	
stationary	*naḥ*	*sākin*
stop	*'amad, nifsaq*	*sakana, inqaṭa'a*
straight	*yashar*	*mustaqīm*
strength	*koaḥ*	
strife	*nitztzaḥon*	*ghalaba*
strive	*hishtaddel, halakh*	*ḥarraḍa*
strong	*ḥazaq*	*qawiyy*
subject	*nafal*	
subsist	*'amad*	
subsisting	*'omed*	*qā'im*
substance	*'etzem*	*jawhar*
substantiality	*'atzmut*	*dhāt*
substrate	*munaḥ*	
substratum	*nose'*	*mawḍū'*
succeed	*nimshakh aḥar*	
succeed one another	*ba' ze be-'eqev ze*	*ta'āqaba*
succession	*meshekh*	
suffice	*hispiq*	
sufficient	*muflag, maspiq*	*bāligh*
suitable	*mezumman*	*musta'idd*
superior	*nikhbad, na'ale*	*sharīf, faḍīl*
suppose	*hiniaḥ, hetzi'a, dimma*	*waḍa'a, waṣafa*
surface	*sheṭaḥ*	*saṭḥ*
surfeited	*nimna'*	*shabi'a*
surpass	*'avar ha-shi'ur*	

susceptible, to be	*qibbel*	*qabila*
swimmer	*shaṭ*	
take	*laqaḥ*	
talk	*dibbur*	*kalām*
term	*shem*	*ism*
testify	*hi'id*	*shahida*
that for the sake of which	*ha-davar asher ba'avuro, ha-davar asher biglalo*	*al-shay' alladhī min ajlihi*
theologian	*medabber ba-devarim ha-elohiyim*	
theology	*ḥokhma elohit*	
theorize	*'iyyen*	*naẓara*
thing	*davar, 'inyan*	*shay', amr*
think	*ḥashav, hiskil, dimma, savar*	*fakkara, tawahhama*
this-something in itself	*ramuz elav be-nafsho*	
thought	*maḥshava, maḥshav, sevara', dimyon*	*ẓann, ra'y, wahm*
tie	*qashar*	
time	*zeman, 'et*	*zaman, waqt*
time period	*midda*	*mudda*
tired, to become	*yaga'*	*istat'aba*
tiredness	*yegi'a*	*ta'ab*
toil	*yegi'a*	
touch	*mishshesh*	*tamāssa*
transform	*hithappekh*	
transition	*he'tteq*	*naqla*
translate	*he'etiq*	
transparent	*bahir*	
transposed	*ne'etaq*	*intaqala*
transposition	*he'tteq*	*intiqāl*
truth	*emet*	*ḥaqq*
turn	*sovev*	*adāra*
turn into	*shav*	
type	*min*	*ḍarb*
ultimate	*aḥaron, ba-takhlit ha-aḥaron*	*aqṣā, fī al-ghāya al-quṣwā*
underlie	*hunnaḥ*	
underlying	*munaḥ, nose', taḥat*	
understand	*hevin*	*fahima*
understanding	*havana*	*fahm*
undetermined	*bilti mugbal*	
undoubtedly	*be-lo' safeq*	*lā maḥālata*
union	*hit'aḥdut*	*ittiḥād*
uniqueness	*yiḥud*	
united	*mit'aḥed*	*muttaḥidān*
universal	*kelali*	*kullīy*
unlimited	*ein takhlit lo, beli takhlit, be-lo' takhlit*	*lā nihāya lahu, bi-ghayr nihāya, bi-lā nihāya*
unmoved mover	*meni'a bilti mitno'e'a*	*muḥarrik ghayr mutaḥarrik, muḥarrik lā yataḥarraku*
utility	*to'elet*	
utterance	*milla*	*lafẓa*

vain	*req*	
variance	*ḥiluf*	
variation	*hitḥalfut*	*ikhtilāf*
vary	*hitḥallef*	*ikhtalafa*
varying	*mitḥallef*	*mukhtalif*
venerable	*nikhbad*	*sharīf*
veneration	*ma'ala*	*sharaf*
vice versa, to be	*hitḥallef*	
vision	*re'ut*	*baṣar*
volition	*ratzon*	
want	*ratza*	
water	*mayyim*	*mā'*
way	*derekh, ofen*	*naḥw*
weak	*ḥalush*	*ḍa'īf*
weakness	*ḥulsha*	
wear	*billa*	*ablā*
weariness	*rifyon*	*istirkhā'*
weight	*koved*	
wise	*ḥakham*	
wither	*baṭal*	*baṭala*
withhold	*hitrashshel*	*bakhula*
within one's power	*yakhol*	*qadara*
without	*yotze'*	*khārij*
wonder	*pele'*	*'ajab*
word	*milla, dibbur*	*lafẓa*
work	*ma'ase*	*'amal*
work (v.)	*'asa*	*'amala*
world	*'olam, ka'n*	*'ālam*
yearn	*nimshakh*	
zodiac	*galgal ha-mazalot*	

Hebrew-Arabic-English Index

The following Index is relatively selective and is limited to terms that have bearings on the text. All references are to page and line numbers of Landauer's original Hebrew edition, which are noted in the body of the translation and are retained in the recently published critical edition of the text, in which the surviving Arabic parts mirror the Hebrew.

Entries are arranged according to the Hebrew alphabet and ordered according to the principles of a Hebrew dictionary. Verbs appear under their respective roots (listed in parentheses) according to the order of their form, while other parts of speech appear independently in the alphabetical sequence. Expressions and constructs appear as indented sub-entries.

If a given term occurs more than once in a line, the number of instances is indicated in superscript. Cases in which there is a translation error or a textual problem are indicated by a circumflex. References in **bold** signify occurrences for which both the Arabic and the Hebrew are available. Otherwise, only the Hebrew survives.

Due to translation constraints, when a literal translation is impossible and an alternate expression is chosen within the semantic field, this is not always noted in the Index so as to not burden the reader further. In many cases, translations that deviate from an accepted meaning of a term are explained in the notes.

ever – *uḍw* – organ **1,5**; 29,2^{2}.3

adonei ha-ḥayyim – *ḥayā* – living things 21,23

(*'-h-v*)

ahav – *ḥabba* – to love 25,27; **28,18**

ahava – *maḥabba* – love (n.) 12,9; **14,31**; 17,32; 18,1.4^{2}.13; **28,15.16**; 32,12.16

ahuv – object of love 33,22

(*'-v-y*)

hit'avva – *tashawwaqa* – to fancy **16,24**.25; 26,5.9; 31,19 – to have appetite 18,6^{2}.7.8.**11**; 31,26.27

avir – *hawā'* – air **2,19.21**; **4,8**; **10,25**; 34,18^{2} – *hāwiyya*^ – abyss **14,19**

uman – *ṣāniʿ* – artisan 8,8; **30,5**

umanut – *ṣanʿ* – artistry **8,12.14** – *ṣināʿa* – art 6,3.4; 7,23.25; 30,5.**6**; 34,22

umanut maʿasit – *ṣināʿa ʿamaliyya* – productive art **30,4**

or – *ḍaw'* – light **9,28.29**; **10,25**

eḥad – *wāḥid*, *aḥad* – one *passim*

aḥdut – oneness 35,11.12

aḥaron – *aqṣā* – ultimate **17,17**.26 – last 4,11; 33,25

eikh – *kayfa* – how 4,26; 11,13^{2}; 12,30.**23**; **14,23**; **22,22**; 29,3; 33,16

eikhut – *kayfa* – quality 8,32; 9,5.11.22.**27**

ish – man 30,22

enoshi – human 5,7

anashim – *nās* – people **2,13.27**; 3,19; 5,7; 11,7^{2}; 14,18; 25,15.17; 28,17; **30,26**.30; 31,12.14.24; 32,3.9^{2}; 33,11 – *qawm* 8,22 – *ahl* 17,29

(*ha-*)*el* – *alla* – God 14,31; 17,25; **21,8.12.24.25**.27; 28,33; **29,6**.21.**23**; 30,16.**25**.21.26; 31,8; 33,19.29.32

elohut – *ilahiyya* – divinity **27,31**

elohi – *ilāhi* 20,32^{2}; **24,32**; 26,14.16.19.20

geshem elohi – divine body 26,14

ḥokhma elohit – theology 14,19

medabber ba-devarim ha-elohiyim – theologian 34,16

sekhel elohi – *al-ʿaql al-ilāhi* – divine intellect 20,8.**32**; 28,26; 29,10.12.14.15.20

ha-sekhel ha-elohi ha-rishon – first divine intellect 20,25

elohiyot – divine [substances] 18,21

ha-elohim ha-sheniyim – *al-ilaha al-thawānī* – secondary god 8,20
umma – nation 17,8.11
emtza' – middle 24,7.8; 33,29
  emtza'i – medial 33,27
emet – *ḥaqq* – truth **14,28**; **17,25**; 21,31; 26,20
  be-takhlit ha-emet – *'alā ghāyat al-ḥaqīqa* – most truly 20,13^2
  be-emet – *bi-l-ḥaqīqa* – truly 5,10; **8,27**; 11,6.10; **16,24.29**; 17,4.**10**.24; 35,9
  lefi ha-emet – *'alā al-ḥaqīqa* – truly **16,30**; 17,8; 18,28; 31,20.28
  amar emet – *aṣāba* – to be correct **22,12**
amitut – accurateness 15,15
('-n-s)
  anas – to coerce 5,13
ones – coercion 32,17
ofen – way 11,14^2.26; 13,15.18
efshar (haya efshar) – *yumkin (amkana)*; *yajūz (jāza)* – to be possible, can *passim*
efsharut – *imkān* – possibility 5,12; 18,22.23.**24**.30; 19,1; **19,8**
arokh – lengthy 15,14
eretz – *arḍ* – earth **2,19^2.21.30.32**; **3,3**; **14,26**.27; 31,3; 33,4.27.28
  ha-nefesh asher ba-aretz – *al-nafs allatī fī al-arḍ* – the soul that is in the earth **8,19**
esh – *nār* – fire **2,19^2.21.32**; 7,9

be'ur – *taṣrīḥ* – assertion **10,13** – explanation 13,25; 22,3
(b-'-r)
  be'er – *bayyana* – to explain **3,32**; **4,3**; 5,26; 6,1; 9,10.**24**; 11,12; 13,14.25.27; 16,10.11; 18,9; 22,8; 23,16; 25,20.21.26; 27,7; 32,19; 34,28
  hitba'er – *bāna* – to be explained **2,9**; 11,16.20; **13,10**; 16,6; 17,14; 30,10; 33,1– *tabayyana* **22,3.5**; **29,23**
biglal
  ha-davar asher biglalo – that for the sake of which 30,13
(b-d-l)
  nivdal – to be opposed 16,1
  hivdil – to set apart 33,3
bohu – chaos 4,16; 34,17
bahir – transparent 29,17^2
bore' – creator 5,12.14.15.16.20
beḥira – choice 17,32
(b-ḥ-r)
  baḥar – *ṣāra* – to let **3,30** – *ikhtāra* – to choose **16,23**.24.25; **17,16**
baṭuaḥ – safeguarded 33,24
(b-ṭ-l)
  baṭal – *baṭala* – to wither **2,3**; 17,21 – to be invalidated 22,9
baṭel – *mu'aṭṭal* – idle **13,30**; 26,30; 34,20 – *'uṭl* – idle **24,32**
baṭṭala – *baṭṭāla* – idleness **19,23**
(b-y-n)
  hevin – *fahima* – to understand **8,16.21.22**; 15,29; 17,8; 18,1; 23,25; 29,11^2.13.18 – to comprehend 29,14 – to become aware 29,31.32^2
  huvan – to be understood 23,28
(b-l-y)
  billa – *ablā* – to wear **11,22**
ba'al – *ṣāḥib* – author **7,28**; 9,14; 12,16 – to possess 27,21
  ba'al geshem – *dhū jism* – corporeal **25,18**; 33,22; 33,31
  ba'al hadrakha – governor 17,20
  ba'al ṭeva'im – natural scientist 14,20; 34,17
  ba'al ma'ala – *afḍal* – noble **30,25**
  ba'al nefesh – *mutanaffas* – ensouled **21,14**; 28,32
  ba'al takhlit – *mutanāh* – limited **22**,7.8.9.**11.17**.28
  ba'al ḥayyim – *ḥayawān* – animal **2,30**; **3,3**; 5,20.22; **7,28**; **8,2.3**; **16,18**; 21,29; 26,17.18; 27,18; 30,31; 35,11
(b-q-sh)
  biqqesh – *ṭalaba* – to enquire into **2,6.25^2**; 6,32; **11,22**; **16,3**; 34,17; to seek **11,10.18**; 16,26^2; **21,3**; 31,20.22 – to consider as 31,9
  buqqash – *ṭuliba* – to be enquired into **2,11.31**
baqasha – *ṭalab* – enquiry **1,3.4**; **2,7**; **9,31.32**; **10,9^2**; **11,21**
(b-r-')
  bara' – *ansha'a* – to originate **8,1**
(b-r-ḥ)
  baraḥ – *haraba* – to escape 6,27; 7,6; **27,28**
bri'a – people 26,15
(b-r-r)
  hitbarer – to be assured 11,18

(*g-b-l*)
higbil – *ḥaddada* – to limit **23,4**
gadol – *akbar* – bigger **8,10** – *ashaddu* – bigger **29,5**
gidul – *nushū'* – growth **3,26** – *numuww* – increase **4,10**
godel – *'iẓam* – magnitude **22**,7.8.**16.22.31**; 26,6; 34,23^2
gedula – *sharaf* – eminence 27,10.**24.26**.29; **28,12**
geder – *ḥadd* – definition **4,7**; 7,22; **25,1**.17.**19**; 32,14 – limit **12,17**
guf – *badan* – body **1,5.6.8**; 7,4.**29**^{2}; **10,26**^{2}.**27**; **19,18**; 28,23; 29,1.12.13; **30,6**; 33,7.8; 35,4 – *juththa* – body **8,1** – magnitude **8,15**
(*g-z-r*)
gazar – to demonstrate 23,18 – to [say] decisively 24,28
(*g-l-g-l*)
hitgalgel – to retreat 6,22^2
galgal – *falak* – sphere *passim*
galgal ha-mazalot – zodiac 24,1.2.6.7
ha-galgal ha-noṭe – *al-falak al-mā'il* – the inclined sphere **8,20**; **11,1**; 24,2
gemar – *inqiḍā'* – completion **22,25**
genai – absurdity 12,28.29; 27,33; 34,6
gerem
gerem shememi – *jism samāwī* – celestial body **4,11**; 33,23
gar'in – seed 21,30
geshem – *jism* – body *passim*
ba'al geshem – *dhū jism* – corporeal **25,18**; 33,22.31
geshem elohi – divine body 26,14
geshem shememi – *jism samāwī* – celestial body **2,29**; **3,5**^{2}; 4,17.18; 15,13; **18,25**; 19,1.**3**; 26,12; 31,2; 33,3.9.26; 34,14
gashmut – *jismāniyya* – corporeality **22,22**
lo yit'arev bo davar min ha-gashmut – *lā yashūbuhu shay' min al-jismāniyya* – incorporeal **3,8**
gashmi – corporeal 34,15

dibba – *shanā'a* – absurdity **28,3**.10
dibbur – *kalām* – discussion **3,17.32**; **22,33** – talk **8,22** – word 9,13 – account 15,28
derekh ha-dibbur – according to language 14,9
daveq – adherent 18,12 – contiguous 34,23; 35,16
daveq ha-hisha'arut – *muttaṣil al-baqā'* – continuously everlasting **17,22**
devequt – *ittiṣāl* – continuity **13,15.17**; **27,15**.16.17
davar – *shay'*, *amr* – thing *passim*
ha-davar asher biglalo – that for the sake of which 30,13
ha-davar asher ba'avuro – *al-shay' alladhī min ajlihi* – that for the sake of which 9,2; **17,16**
dome – *ashbahu* – similar **1,11.20**; 12,16 – like **1,16**; **2,4** – *naẓīr* – like **4,3**; 6,1; 9,15.16; 31,6 – *mithl* – like **8,2** – the same **10,4** – similar 12,16; 18,24 – resembling 20,32
(*d-ḥ-y*)
daḥa – to reject 34,29
deḥiya – rejection 34,29
dam ha-niddot – *dam al-ṭamth* – blood of the menses **14,26**
(*d-m-y*)
dama – to resemble 31,17
dimma – *tawahhama* – to consider **3,13**; to imagine 5,21; 17,23; 21,14; to suppose 21,29.31; to think 24,14; 26,17
dumma – *tuwuhhima* – to be imagined **12,24** – to be thought **22,22** – to be supposed 21,28
ma she-yedumme – *al-mutakhayyil* – that which is thought of **17,1**
hiddama – *tashabbaha* – to resemble **18,15**
dimyon – *takhayyul* – imagination **16,32**; **17,1** – *mathal* – like **7,28**; **8,24**^{2}; **19,14**; 12,20 – *naẓīr* – counterpart **8,5** – model 7,21.22.24.25.26; 13,30; 34,21^2 – semblance 4,20 – thought 7,1
de'a – opinion 34,2
da'at – opinion 32,4
sam be-da'at – *khaṭara bi-bāl* – to keep in mind 8,8
dofi – reprehensibility 27,33
diqduq – precision 15,15
derekh – *naḥw* – way **1,9**; 6,7 – *sabīl* – path **19,17** – sense 5,1 – manner 11,31.33; 14,9; 18,13; 25,9; 28,29; 30,14
derekh ha-yashar – rectitude 18,4.6

be-derekh / *ke-derekh* – *bi-manzila*; *ka-* – as, like, the same as, etc. *passim*
'al derekh – *'alā naḥw* – in a way **1,3.8**; 4,32; *'alā ṭarīq* – in a sense **9,24.30**; **11,2^{2}.3** – *'alā an* – as **21,11** – *'alā sabīl* – as 26,13.**28** – *bi-manzila* – in a manner 5,27.31; 8,29; 11,11.**31**; 27,23; 30,28

hevdel – difference 25,17; 29,14; 30,19.20
havana – *fahm* – understanding 18,2; **19,19**; 23,25; 30,10
higayon
ḥokhmat^ ha-higayon – *al-riyāḍa bi-l-manṭiq* – logical exercise **2,14**
hagbala
'al ha-hagbala – definitively 23,29
haga'a – *taḥṣīl* – obtaining **2,12** – *mablagh* – reach **19,24**; 23,2; 25,29; 31,5 – amount 35,3
hiddamut/hitdamut – *mushākala* – resemblance **3,31**; 26,18 – likeness 33,26
hadrakha – *siyāsa* – administration **17,18**.20.23.24; 18,13^{2}; 21,15.17.19; 25,27.28; 31,15
ba'al hadrakha – administrator 17,20
hadrakhat ha-medina – *siyāsat al-madīna* – political administration **17,29**; **25,25**
hove – *kā'in* – a thing that comes-to-be – 5,3; 6,6; **12,10**
(*h-v-y*)
hithavva – to come-to-be 4,16.17; 5,3.8.27; 6,6; 9,20
haviya – *kawn* – coming-to-be *passim*
meqabbel/yeqabbel ha-haviya – *qābil/yaqbalu al-kawn* – to receive coming-to-be 4,30; **10,19**; 15,18; 16,2; **18,20**; 33,7; 34,1
hazkara – *idhkār* – recall **2,24**
ilhām – inspiration **8,18**
hiyuli – *hayūlā* – matter *passim*
(lo') yit'arev bo davar min ha-hiyuli – *(lā) yashūbuhu shay' min al-hayūlā* – (im)material **14,7**; **16,14**.20
(lo') yit'arev bo ha-hiyuli – *(lā) tashūbuhu al-hayūlā* – (im)material 17,22; 20,6.**20**; **22,31**.32.33; 29,20; 30,8; 33,21; 34,5.19; 35,9
she-ha-hiyuli lo' yit'arev bo – immaterial 23,5
(*h-y-y*)
haya – *kāna* – to be *passim* – *ṣāra* – to be **8,3.13.21**; **15,26.27**; **19,26**; **26,31**; **27,9** – *takhallafa^* – to remain **12,10**
hekhreaḥ – *ḍurūra* – necessity **19,12/14**; **19,15** – coercion 15,6
be-hekhreaḥ – *ḍurūratan* – necessarily 12,12; 15,27; **19,10**.11; 23,7; 33,27 – *bi-l-wājib* – necessarily **15,27**
hekhreaḥ mofti – demonstrative necessity 13,17
yitḥayyev be-hekhreaḥ – *yajibu ḍurūratan* – follows necessarily **15,21**; **16,14** – must necessarily 18,29; **23,8.10**; 24,15; 34,1
ra'uy be-hekhreaḥ – *yajibu ḍurūratan* – should necessarily **2,25**; **15,23** – must necessarily **4,3** – follows necessarily **13,25** – necessarily 7,13; 33,18
hekhreḥi – *ḍurūrī* – necessary **13,17**; **24,30**; 27,18
huledet – *tawallud* – to be begotten **8,24**
(*h-l-k*)
halakh – *salaka* – to proceed **8,10**; 11,30.33; 25,9; 28,29; 30,1; 35, 17 – to strive 31,20.22 – to be directed 24,31 – to apply 30,15 – to be carried out 31,11
holikh – to guide 17,20
himashkhut – procession 24,28
hana'a – *ladhdha* – pleasure **19,21.22**
hanhaga – governance 17,19; 25,28; 26,3; 30,25.30; 31,11.16; 35,17 – piloting 6,9 – regulation 31,1 – reflection^ 12,3
hanaḥa – assumption 12,14 – hypothesis 15,28 – positioning 24,11
hana'a – *taḥrīk* – moving [= causing motion] **13,26.27^{2}**; **16,9**; 19,8; 22,10; 26,29; **29,5**; 32,20.22.23; 33,22.23
hester – concealment 6,26
he'ader – *'adam* – privation 4,33; 5,2; 6,7; **9,25.26.27.29**; **10,6**; **11,3**; **19,23**; 32,6.27
he'tteq – *naqla* – transition **4,10**; 27,24 – *intiqāl* – transposition **20,27**
hipukh – *taḍādd* – contrariety **4,13**

(*h-f-k*)
hithappekh - to transform 6,15.26 - to return 30,2.3 - to be contrary 34,4
hefekh - *ḍidd* - contrary *passim*
hefsed - *fasād* - perishing *passim*
meqabbel/yeqabbel ha-hefsed - *qābil/ yaqbalu li-l-fasād* - capable of perishing, perishable *passim*
hefseq - *inqiṭāʿ* - interruption **15,20**; **16,9**; 35,10
hipaʿalut - *infiʿāl* - affection **2,4**; 9,11
hefresh - *firq* - difference **2,9**
hitztarfut - relation 8,31; 9,5.11
haqdama - *muqaddama* - premise 17,8; **29,9**
heqesh - *qiyās* - analogy 6,20; **9,28**; 29,15.16 - *muqāyasa* - comparison **9,31**; 12,14; 17,14; 26,7 - respect 11,15; **15,16**; 20,10^2.11 - reason 21,12; **23,7** - argument 14,16; 15,11 - account 29,34
hera'ut - to be seen 6,27
harḥava
ʿal tzad ha-harḥava - metaphorically 26,15
harkava - *tarkīb* - composition - **1,6**^{2}; 7,15; **8,12**; **17,15**; **29,7** - compositeness **17,6**
heref ʿayin - *ṭurfat ʿayn* - instant **19,21**
hisha'arut - *baqā'* - lasting **15,24**^{2} - remaining 7,16.17; 15,25; **19,15** - everlastingness **21,25**.27; perduring 31,1
daveq ha-hisha'arut - *muttaṣil al-baqā'* - continuously lasting **17,22**
matmid ha-hisha'arut - *dā'im al-baqā'* - perduring **2,28.29**; 6,12
temidi ha-hisha'arut - *dā'im al-baqā'* - everlasting **15,21**; 21,19
hasaga - apprehension 6,24; 28,25; 29,9.15.30; 30,17
hishtannut - *istiḥāla* - alteration **4,9**; **11,23**
hit'aḥdut - *ittiḥād* - union 1,5
hatḥala - *mabda'* - principle *passim* - *ibtidā'* - beginning **11,4**; start **16,31**.**32** - *awwal* - beginning **21,20** - outset 21,29
ha-hatḥala ha-rishona - *al-mabda' al-awwal* - first principle 8,28; **10,16**; **11,25**.**27**; 12,13; **13,34**; **16,20**; **23,4.6**; **26,27**; 29,19.24; 31,28; 32,9.10; 34,7.12; 35,13
hitḥallfut - *ikhtilāf* - variation **15,17.20.21**^{2}**.26.27**; **19,5** - *istiḥāla* - alteration **13,2**
hittalut - dependence 26,10; 34,14
hitnagdut - *muqābala* - opposition **4,13**
hitraḥvut - *ittisāʿ* - extension **29,6**

(*z-h-r*)
nizhar - *tawaqqā* - to be cautious **10,16**
zulat - *ghayr* - other *passim*
(*z-k-r*)
zakhar - *dhakara* - to mention **4,11**; 5,26; 12,11; 24,24.28 - *adhkara* - to state **4,7** - to remember 11,17; 13,16
nizkar - to be mentioned 11,18
hizkir - *adhkara* - to recall **2,24** - to mention 8,29 - to report 23,28
huzkar - *ulhima* - to be inspired **8,18.22**
zikaron - *dhikr* - memory 19,26; **28,6** - discussion 13,11
(*z-l-z-l*)
zilzel - *aghāra* - to deceive^ 8,7
zeman - *zamān* - time *passim*
qerovat ha-zeman - *qarībat al-ʿahd* - recent **2,17**
zeraʿ - *bizra* - seed **8,2.4**; 14,27.28; **22,3**^{2} - semen 4,25; 5,6.7^2.8 - *minān* - semen **8,4**^{2}
shikhvat zeraʿ - *minān* - semen **8,2**

ḥibbur - *ta'līf* - combination 1,7^2
(*ḥ-b-r*)
ḥibber - to connect 5,17; 33,18.25.33 - to compose 35,14
hitḥabber - to bring together^ 32,12 - to be combined 35,6 - to associate 35,15
ḥad - *ḥādd* - sharp **28,27**; 29,9 - high pitched 28,32
ḥiddud - sharpness 29,12
ḥedva - *surūr* - joy **19,20**
ḥiddush - *ḥādith* - accident **12,25** - *ḥadath* - accident **3,25**.**26** - modification **10,13**; **12,21**; 21,5 - *ʿaraḍ* - accident **3,17**^{2} - *ḥudūth* - creation 9,20; 12,8.**18**.19.**32**; **13,6**^{2}.7.8^2; 31,18; being made of 31,22.29; 34,18
(*ḥ-d-sh*)
ḥiddesh - *aḥdatha* - to create **8,6**; **12,25**; 34,25.26

hitḥaddesh/nitḥaddesh – *ḥadatha* – to be created *passim* – to occur **2,3**; 19,2; 21,5; 33,5
(*ḥ-v-b*)
ḥiyyev – *awjaba* – to necessitate **12,27**²; 13,1; **23,11**; 25,23; 33,13 – to affirm 12,19; 15,11; 32,23 – to allow 31,10
hitḥayyev –*wajaba* – to have to, to follow [logically] *passim* – *lazima* – to follow [logically] *passim* – to happen **10,16**
yitḥayyev be-hekhreaḥ – *yajibu ḍurūratan* – follows necessarily **15,21**; **16,14** – must necessarily 18,29; **23,8.10**; 24,15; 34,1
ḥutz – *khārij* – outside **10,1.4**; 19,13; **20,18.19** – external 9,7²; **21,11**; **27,4**; 27,32 – besides 15,5; 25,2.**22**; 34,12 – beyond 23,16 – apart 34,19
mi-ḥutz – *min khārij* – external **21,2**; **27,11**
ḥush – *ḥāssa* – sense, sensing **2,17**; 6,11.12.20; 15,29; 20,4.22; **21,10**; 29,28; 34,9.10².12 – *ḥiss* – sense, sensing **2,28**; **15,28**; **19,23**; **20,17**; **23,7**
ḥosheq – *ʿāshiq* – desirer **16,19**; **26,29**; **28,18**
(*ḥ-z-q*)
heḥeziq – to keep 11,17
ḥazaq – *qawiyy* – strong **11,4**; **12,29**; 15,8; 19,31; **24,30**; 28,25; 29,26^
(*ḥ-z-r*)
ḥazar – to return 11,18
ḥay (n.) – *ḥayawān* – animal **1,8**; **8,5.6.7.10**; **18,2**; 30,28; 31,3.18; 35,5.6 – *ḥayy* – living **21,13**
(*ḥ-y-y*)
ḥay (v.) – to live 17,24; 21,18
liḥyot – living 17,3
ḥayyim – *ḥayā* – life 18,12; 21,18.**19².20**. **21².22³.23.24.25²**.27; **25,1**; 26,3.22².**32**
adonei ha-ḥayyim – *ḥayā* – living things **21,23**
ḥitzon – exterior 20,15
ḥakham – wise 5,13; 5,14 – *ʿālim* – sage **26,25**
ḥakhamei ha-tishboret – geometricians 29,16
ḥokhma – *ʿilm* – science **3,24**; 23,15²; 34,8² – knowledge **17,26.27**; **19,17.21**; **26,25**
ha-ḥokhma ha-elohit – theology 14,19
ḥokhmat ha-higayon – *al-riyāḍa bi-l-manṭiq*^ – logical exercise **2,14**
ha-ḥokhma ha-ṭivʿit – *al-ʿilm al-ṭabīʿī* – natural science **3,23.25**
sefer ha-ḥokhma ha-ṭivʿit – *kitāb al-ʿilm al-ṭabīʿī* – *Physics* **3,32**; 5,26
ḥokhmat ha-kokhavim – *ʿilm al-nujūm* – astronomy **23,15**.22.25
ḥokhmat ha-tishboret – geometry 23,28
ḥeled – duration 12,30
ha-ḥeled kullo – *al-dahr kulluhu* – eternally **11,23**; **12,24**; **19,16**; **21,26**; 35,10
ḥiluf – *ikhtilāf* – difference **3,12**; 15,8; 18,21; 23,18.20.22 – *khilāf* – otherwise **19,14** – variance 18,26
ḥalush – *ḍaʿīf* – weak **14,3**; 18,30; 28,23.24; **29,7**
(*ḥ-l-f*)
hitḥallef – *ikhtalafa* – to be different **10,28**; 15,8; **22,22** – to vary **15,19** – to alter 12,31; 27,24 – to be vice versa 16,21
(*ḥ-l-q*)
ḥalaq – *ʿānada* – to confront **21,10**
neḥlaq – to be divided 20,9.21
ḥilleq – *qassama* – to divide **3,19.20**; 6,12; **11,32**; 28,24; 32,7
hitḥalleq – to be divided 31,21; 33,12; 35,9
ḥeleq – *juzʾ* – part **1,6.7**; **3,19**; 4,19.21; 12,1.**17**; 29,3²; 30,9; 31,13.17; 32,12; 35,9 – *ḥaẓẓ* – share **1,16**
ḥalaqim asher lo yitḥalqu – *ajzāʾ allatī lā tatajazzaʾu* – indivisible particles **14,22.30**
ḥulsha – weakness 6,8.26; 28,22; 32,27
ḥom – *ḥarr* – hot **9,26**; 34,3.9.10
ḥomer – *ʿunṣur* – matter **8,7**; 25,17; 32,29 – *mādda* – matter **14,24**; **25,16** – *hayūlā* – matter **25,18**
loʾ yitʿarev bo ha-ḥomer – immaterial 23,18
(*ḥ-s-r*)
ḥasar – to be missing 21,4 – to be less 24,16
ḥaser – *nāqiṣ* – lacking 28,4

ḥissaron - *tanaqquṣ* - decline **3,26**; 31,6
- *nuqṣān* - decrease **4,10**; 19,6
- disadvantage 23,21

(*ḥ-p-s*)
ḥippes - to explore 22,31; 23,31

ḥaqira - *baḥth* - investigation, enquiry *passim*

(*ḥ-q-r*)
ḥaqar - *baḥatha* - to investigate, to enquire *passim* - *naẓara* - to enquire **11,29**^

(*ḥ-sh-b*)
ḥashav - *tawahhama* - to think **3,18.19**; 5,14; 9,6^{2}; 13,19; 20,21; 24,12; 26,19; 32,14.18.24.25; 33,15; 34,25 - to consider **3,15**; **20,31**
- *darā* - to be aware **8,17**
- *ẓanna* - to presume **3,22** - to imagine 21,13; 29,13

neḥshav - to be thought 7,1
davar she-ḥoshvim bo - *maẓnūn* - thing that is thought of **17,1**

ḥeshbon - arithmetic 23,24

ḥashuq - *ma'shūq* - desired, object of desire **16,16.17.18.19.20.21.22^{2}.28**; 17,22.24; 18,3.4.5.**14**; 25,29; 26,5.**29**; 33,22

ḥoshekh - *ẓulma* - darkness **9,28**; **10,25**; **14,19**; 16,4

(*ḥ-sh-q*)
ḥashaq - *tashawwaqa* - to desire **17,18**
- *'ashiqa* - to desire **18,15.16**

ḥesheq - *'ishq* - desire **16,28**; 18,3; **25,25**; 31,19

ḥatikha - *qiṭ'* - segment **13,19**

(*ḥ-t-m*)
neḥtam - *inṭabaqa* - to be imprinted **20,18**; 34,10

ṭeva' - *ṭabī'a*, *ṭab'* - nature *passim*
ba'al ṭeva'im - natural scientist 14,20; 34,17

ṭiv'i - *ṭabī'ī* - natural *passim*
ṭiv'iyyim - natural [scientists] 4,27
ha-ḥokhma ha-ṭiv'it - *al-'ilm al-ṭabī'ī* - natural science **3,23.25**
sefer ha-ḥokhma ha-ṭiv'it - *kitāb al-'ilm al-ṭabī'ī* - *Physics* **3,32**; 5,26
ma'amarim ṭiv'iyyim - natural treatises 12,11
ṭiv'iyot - natural [treatises] 25,20
ma'amar ba-ṭiv'iyyot - natural treatise 22,8 - statement about natural things 33,1
ha-shema' ha-ṭiv'i - *Physics* 13,17

(*ṭ-v-b*)
heṭiv le'ayyen^ - *am'ana* - to continue **2,23**
heṭiv limtzo' - to excel in finding 32,10

ṭov - *khayr* - good **16,30^{2}**; **30,21**; *ḥasan* - good **16,24**.25; 24,33; 27,20; 30,19.22.23; 31,12; 32,7^{2}.9.10.12.18.25; 35,18 - best 20,1^{2}
yoter ṭov - *afḍal* - better **8,13**; 31,8 - best 19,13; 23,31
qibbutz min ha-ṭovim - aristocracy - 26,14

ṭamun - *kāmin* - latent **8,26.27**

ṭa'ut - *khaṭa'* - error **14,22**
'al ha-ṭa'ut - wrongly 35,18

(*ṭ-'-y*)
ṭa'a - to err 31,30

ṭared - *mutashāghil* - preoccupied **19,18**

ya'ut - appropriate 8,29; 26,31; 27,23

yegi'a - *ta'ab* - tiredness **27,17**; **28,15** - toil 29,11

(*y-g-'*)
yaga' - *istat'aba* - to become tired **22,26**; 27,16^{2}
yigge'a - *at'aba* - to tire **27,15**; 28,16

yad - hand 29,2
mashakh yado - to abstain 12,32

(*y-d-y*)
hoda - *aqarra* - to acknowledge **14,29** - to admit 22,10; 29,19

yadu'a - *ma'lūm* - known [thing] **28,20**; 29,28.32

yedi'a - *'ilm* - knowledge 12,13; **21,1**.15.17; 28,29; 29,7.28; 30,7; 34,8.9.11^{2} - *ta'arruf* - to know **23,14** - *ma'rifa* - knowledge **29,8**

(*y-d-'*)
yada' - *'alima* - to know 6,21; **8,2.25**; 29,13.**24**; 34,11 - *ra'ā* - to know **21,14**
noda' - *'ulima* - to be known **3,28**; 23,1 - *'urifa* - to be known **4,7**
hodi'a - to say 26,16

yotze' - *khārij* - excluded **3,8** - external **10,29** - without **19,29**

(*y-ḥ-d*)
yiḥed - *khaṣṣa* - to make proper **8,3**

yuḥad – to encompass 26,14
yiḥud – *uniqueness* 35,7
be-yiḥud – *mufradān* – separately 5,30; 7,1; **11,29** – specifically 12,12; 31,20
(*y-ḥ-s*)
yuḥas – to be ascribed 6,7; 26,21
hityaḥes – *jānasa* – to have affinity **3,30** – to relate 12,7; 30,29
yaḥas – *nasib* – *logos* 5,9; **8,3.5.6.11.14.15.18.23** – *nisba* – relation 12,7; 14,6; **19,29**; 30,29 – *munāsaba* – analogy **9,24.31**; 11,15
(*y-k-l*)
yakhol – *qadara* – to be within one's power **12,26.27** – *qādir* – capable 7,25; **13,31**^{2} – can 31,10
yekholet – *qudra* – ability **17,25**
(*y-l-d*)
nolad – to be begotten 7,19.20 – to be born 34,16
holid – *walada* – to beget 7,19.20; **10,5.8**; **21,11** – to birth **14,19** – *antaja* – to conclude **29,8**
hityalled – *tawallada* – to be begotten 5,5; 7,21.**29**^{2}**.30**; **8,1.3**^{2}**.5.12.24**^{2}; **10,21.23**; 32,30
yesod – *'unṣur* – element **2,31**; 5,19; 9,2.3^{2}.4^{3}.5^{2}.6^{2}.9^{2}.10.11^{2}.12^{2}.14.15.17.18.22.23.30^{2}.31; 10,1.2.3.**23.28**; 14,28; 17,8; 33,2.12 – matter 6,13.17^{2}.23^{2}.24.25.26.29; **9,25.26.28**; **10,22.23.24.26.28**^{2}**.29.30**; **11,2**.11^{6}; **25,16**; 30,1.4^{2} – *rukn* – element **2,5.7.20.21**
lo' yit'arev bo ha-yesod – immaterial 29,33
(*y-s-f*)
hosif – to add 12,29
husaf – to be added 24,23
hittosef – to be added 24,13.14
yafe – *ḥasan* – beautiful **17,19**; 19,31
yofi – *ḥusn* – beauty 17,17; 21,28.30
(*y-tz-'*)
yatza' – *kharaja* – to be brought out **3,4**; 13,10; **29,8**; 31,21; to be distinguished **22,25;** to be excluded 3,1; to pass 30,2
yatza' el ha-po'al – *kharaja ilā al-fi'l* – to be brought into actuality **8,7**; **14,14**; **22,5**; **27,17**; 28,14
hotzi' – to bring out 5,13 – to extend 5,30; 23,2
yetzi'a [*min ha-koaḥ el ha-po'al*] – going out [from potentiality to actuality] 4,22.23^{2}.24; 13,32
(*y-tz-'*)
hetzi'a – *waṣafa* – to suppose 9,14.**24**
(*y-r-y*)
hora – *dalla* – to indicate **1,17.19**; **3,12**; **8,17**; 26,11 – to refer 6,16; 17,6.10; 18,27.28.29 – to prescribe 18,13; 22,34
yerida – descent 23,20
(*y-r-sh*)
yarash – to inherit 26,20
(*y-sh-r*)
yashar – to be correct 29,3
yosher – *niẓām* – order 12,1; 15,12^{3}.13; 17,19.20.**25.28**; **18,11**; **21,12**; 30,17.18.**21**.23^{2}.24.26; 31,1.8.9; 34,13; 35,10 – rectitude 18,8.**16**; 35,11 – organization **1,8** – *ṣawāb* – correctness **3,15**; 5,12; 9,4; **10,13**; 26,11; 28,29
'al ha-yosher – *mustaqīm* – rectilinear 13,15
yashar (adj.) – *mustaqīm* – straight **1,10.22**^{2}**.23.24** – *ṣawāb* – correct **2,22**; 31,8
derekh ha-yashar – rectitude 18,4.6
yittakhen – can 5,5.6

ka'n – here 17,30; 33,18; 34,22 – the world 25,3^{2}.4; 29,22
kavod – *sharaf* – nobility **19,24**; 27,29 – *ḥamd* – nobility **26,28**
kaved – *thaqīl* – heavy **11,32**; **25,22** – low-pitched 28,33
koved – weight 11,33
kozev – false 17,9
kokhav – *kawkab* – star **22,11.12.17.27**^{2}**.29**; 23,12.17.26; 24,9.17.20.31^{2}; 25,7; 31,1; 33,4
ḥokhmat ha-kokhavim – *'ilm al-nujūm* – astronomy **23,15**.22.25
kokhav navokh – *kawkab mutaḥayyir* – planet **15,30**; **18,19**; 23,16.27; 24,3.14.16; 33,5
kokhav qayyam – *kawkab thābit* – fixed star **18,15.19**; 24,1.5.18
kolel – *'āmīy* – general **2,14.15.16.19.20**^{3}**.23**; **14,22**; 31,2.6; 34,30 – common 4,22

(*k-v-n*)
kivven - *qaṣada* - to set out **1,4**; **2,6.7.8.24**; 7,24; **10,31**; 11,17; 16,26²; **23,14**; 30,10; 34,30 - *za'ama* - to claim **3,9** - to induce 26,7 - to direct 29,11
konen - *qaṣada* - to set out **1,3**; 11,31
kavvana - *qaṣd* - intention **2,8**; 8,28; **9,32**; **10,8.9**; 28,23 - *gharaḍ* - aim **3,17**; **8,21²**; 9,2.3; 11,17.26.31; 26,4; 28,14; 30,30; 31,23².24; 35,10 - end **8,16** - *maqṣūd* - a thing aimed at **22,20**
koaḥ - *quwwa* - potentiality *passim* - power **14,28**; **22,7.12².14.17.28**; **23,14**; 26,17; **29,6** - capacity **19,17** - strength 11,32
ba-koaḥ - *bi-l-quwwa* - potentially, in potentiality *passim*
koaḥ meni'a - *quwwa muḥarrika* - moving power **22,27**; **23,18**
(*k-ḥ-sh*)
hikhḥish - *ankara* - to deny **29,6**
(*k-l-y*)
kala - to perish 7,16
killa - to finish 33,29
killayon - perishing 35,10
(*k-l-l*)
kalal - to include 9,15; 18,22; 30,32; 35,16
nikhlal - to be common 7,22
kelal - *jumla* - entirety **1,8**; sum **8,23** - *aṣlān* - at all *passim*
bi-khlal - *bi-l-jumla* - generally, in sum *passim*
bi-khlalo - *bi-asrihi* - in general **3,23** - as a whole **8,16** - completely 4,18; 6,19 - entirely 7,17 - collectively 29,2
kelali - *kullīy* - universal **2,16**; 7,19; 11,5.6.7.9².12.14; 28,30
kamma - *kamm* - number **2,10.11**; **4,6**; 23,27² - quantity 11,9²
kammut - quantity 8,32; 9,5.11.21; 23,24.25
(*k-s-y*)
kissa - to cover 6,29
kefel - *taḍā'uf* - multiplicity **17,15**
ka-shura
she-lo' ka-shura - improperly 30,31
(*k-sh-r*)
kashar - to be deemed fit 27,8
kat - *farīq* - group **2,22** - military unit 26,1.2; 30,22
(*l-'-y*)
hel'a - to fatigue 27,15.16
(*l-b-sh*)
lavash - *lābasa* - to be in contact **20,15**.17 - to assume 6,20
lehipale' - *ta'ajjub* - to be puzzled **16,15**; 29,18
laḥut - *ruṭūba* - moisture **10,21**
(*l-m-d*)
lamad - to learn 23,30; 33,23
limudi
merḥaq limudi - *bu'd ta'līmī* - mathematical extension **3,20.22**
mispar limudi - mathematical number 35,13
limudiyot - mathematical [sciences] 23,23
(*l-q-ḥ*)
laqaḥ - to take 5,21; 26,13

ma'amar - *qawl* - statement, discussion, argument, etc. *passim*
ma'amarim ṭiv'iyyim - natural treatises 12,11
ma'amar ba-ṭiv'iyyot - natural treatise 22,8 - statement about natural things 33,1
(*m-'-n*)
me'en - to refuse 6,19
mevo'ar - *bayyin* - clear *passim*
mevulbal - *muḍṭarib* - confused **14,31**; 15,9; 18,30
mabu'a - *yanbū'* - fountainhead **26,32**
mugbal - *majbūl* - fashioned **3,30**
bilti mugbal - undetermined 31,2
megama
sam megamato - *qafā atharahu* - to pursue 17,31.32; **18,11**
megunne - absurd 16,4; 31,10; 32,11.16.24; 33,14²
mugsham - embodied 6,4²
medabber ba-devarim he-elohiyyim - theologian 34,16
midda - *mudda* - time period 17,21; **19,16.19**; 30,1
medina - *madīna* - **1,7**; **18,8**; 31,22
hadrakhat ha-medinot - *siyāsat al-mudun* - political administration **17,29**; 25,25
hanhagat ha-medina - city's governance 30,25; 31,11
anshei ha-medina - *ahl al-madīna* - people of the city **17,29**; 31,12

mada‘ – knowledge 29,32
madrega – *martaba* – rank **8,19**; **18,17**; 23,20^{2}.21; 24,11; 30,20.23; 31,16
mehavve – agent of coming-to-be 33,33
mahalakh – *maslak* – course **8,10**
(*m-h-r*)
miher – to be quick 29,13.14
meḥuddash – *ḥadutha* – to be created 9,21; **12,23^{2}**
muḥlaṭ – absolute 14,16 – *simpliciter* 27,30
ba-muḥlaṭ – *‘alā al-iṭlāq* – absolutely **9,30** – *muṭlaqān* – absolutely **19,14**
‘al derekh muḥlaṭ – in an absolute manner 11,11
muḥash – *maḥsūs* – sensible, sensory object *passim*
mukhan – *mutahayyi’* – ready **8,6**
molid – *muwālid* – begetting 7,23^{2}; **8,27**
molikh – *sawwāq* – directing **8,16**
molekh – *mālik* – ruler **29,25^{2}**; 31,17
munaḥ – underlying 4,16.17^{2} – placed 4,33 – hypothetical 15,28 – laid down 21,13 – substrate 29,22
mone‘a – *māni‘* – hinderer, preventer **2,24**; 7,15; **12,24.28.29**.31; **19,20**; 30,9; 32,23
mofet – *burhān* – demonstration **11,24^{2}**; 25,23
hekhreaḥ mofti – demonstrative necessity 13,17
motzi’ – *mukhrij* – bringer [to actuality] 14,1.**17**
muqaf – distinguished 30,20
(*m-v-r*)
humar – *tabaddala* – to alternate **2,3**
moshel – *qā’id* – commander **18,8**
(*m-v-t*)
hemit – *amāta* – to kill **26,31**
(*m-z-g*)
nimzag – to be mixed 31,8
mezuyyaf – ‘bastard’ 6,21
mezumman – *musta‘idd* – suitable 8,6
mezuqqaq – distilled 35,9
meḥubbar – *maqrūn* – linked **12,17**
meḥuyyav – proper 29,15 – necessary 34,14
min ha-meḥuyyav she- – *min al-wājib an* – necessarily **27,15**
maḥtzav – mineral 5,29
maḥshav – thought 17,26.27; 20,5
maḥshavi – *wahmī* – according to thought **10,5**
maḥshava – *wahm* – thought **1,25**; **2,12**; 5,16; 7,3.4.26; 29,12.29; 30,9; 35,8 – *ẓann* – thought **16,32**; **17,1**
‘amad ba-maḥshava – *qāma fī wahm* – to keep in mind **10,31**; 11,5
tziyyer ba-maḥshava – to imagine 29,12
meyuḥad – *khāṣṣ* – peculiar 23,15.22; 24,7.9.**32**; 26,9.10 – proprietary 6,15
meyushshar – ordered 30,27; 31,2.17
mayyim – *mā’* – water **2,19.21**; **4,8^{2}**; 34,15^{2} – B (letter)^ 11,8 – BA^ (letter combination) 11,8
min – *naw‘* – species **7,30**; **8,6^{2}**; **13,2**; 25,14.15; 26,16.18 – *ṣinf* – kind **4,6**; 17,2; 18,3^{2}; 34,26 – *ḍarb* – type **4,13**
mekho’ar – outrageous 32,30
mekhuvvan – *maqṣūd* – aimed at **8,17**; end **19,13**
bi-mekhuvvan – directed 30,29
mukhraḥ – coerced 15,8; 19,12
mekharker – dancer 29,1
(*m-l-’*)
hitmalle’ – to be satiated 18,5
melākha – art 14,26; 24,30; 30,8^{2}; 31,24
melākhuti – artificial 7,2.8; 10,5
melekhet ha-refu’a – *ṣinā‘at al-ṭibb* – art of medicine **30,6**
milla – *lafẓa* – word **1,17^{2}.19^{2}.20.24** – utterance **12,15.16**.19
melukha – royalty 31,16
(*m-l-ṭ*)
nimlaṭ – to be free 32,8; to escape 34,3
lo’ nimlaṭ mi- – *lā yakhlū min* – cannot avoid **3,24.33**; 4,14.29.31; 7,3^{2}; 12,8.17; 14,5; **19,21**; **27,1**; 28,3; 29,4
memaher – quick 29,13; 29,14
manhig – pilot 6,8 – director 23,17
menuḥa – *sukūn* – rest **13,4.5**.7.10; 16,6.**7.8.9**; 29,21 – *rāḥa* – rest **22,16** – *futūr* – resting **13,2**
(*m-n-y*)
mana – *‘addada* – to count **4,6**; 13,32
nimna – to be counted 6,18
meniaḥ – giver [of law] 21,14.18.19
meni‘a – *muḥarrik* – mover *passim*
meni‘a bilti mitno‘e‘a – *muḥarrik ghayr mutaḥarrik* – unmoved mover

16,14 - *muḥarrik lā yataḥarraku* - unmoved mover **16,15**
koaḥ meni'a - *quwwa muḥarrika* - moving power **22,27**; **23,18**
meni'a po'el - efficient mover - 7,10
meni'a qarov - *muḥarrik qarīb* - proximate mover **10,4.9**
ha-meni'a ha-rishon - *al-muḥarrik al-awwal* - first mover **10,9**; 13,25; **17,15**.22; **25,18.19**
sibba meni'a - *sabab muḥarrik* - moving cause **10,1.7** - *'illa muḥarrika* - moving cause **10,31**
'illa meni'a - *'illa muḥarrika* - moving cause **15,17**; **24,27**; 25,5^{2}.21; 34,24
(*m-n-'*)
mana' - *mana'a* - to hinder, obstruct, prevent *passim* - to avoid 25,9
nimna' - *imtana'a* - to be impossible **3,6**; 10,2 - *shabi'a* - to be surfeited **28,16**^{2}
mesubbakh - involved 7,8
mesuddar - ordered 21,15; 30,27; 31,17
tenu'a mesudderet - ordered motion 15,10
maspiq - *muqni'* - persuasive **7,27** - sufficient 13,25; 22,3; 34,29
mispar - *'adad* - number *passim*
mispar limudi - mathematical number 35,13
me'aṭ - *aqall* - fewer **2,33** - a little bit 11,18; 12,3; 19,17; 23,25; 30,32; 31,3
me'iq - impediment 6,6.9^{2}; 19,31
ma'ala - *faḍīla* - excellence **17,17**; 18,4; **19,24**; 27,10.25.27; 29,14; 33,24; 34,28 - *sharaf* - veneration **26,28**
ba'al ma'ala - *afḍal* - noble **30,25**
be-takhlit / 'al takhlit ha-ma'ala - *fī / 'alā ghāyat al-faḍīla* - utmost best, utmost excellence *passim*
me'orav - *mukhtaliṭ* - mixed **19,18**
ma'ase - *'amal* - work **8,15**; **30,5** - function 35,4
umanut ma'asit - *ṣinā'a 'amaliyya* - productive art **30,4**
mefuzzar - *mutafarriq* - dispersed **1,7**
mefursam - well-known 4,25
muflag - *bāligh* - sufficient **2,25**; **3,32**; 11,21
mufshaṭ - abstracted 7,6 - bare 20,20
(*m-tz-'*)
matza' - *wajada* - to find *passim*
heiṭiv limtzo' - to excel in finding 32,10
nimtza' - *wujida* - to exist, to be *passim* - to be found - 15,29; **17,29**.30; 20,4; **27,17**
himtzi' - to invent 21,18 - *awjaba* - to necessitate^ 23,7
matzav - position 4,18
mitzvah - command 25,28; 31,11.13
metzuyyar - with form 6,17; 20,26; 32,6
metzi'ut - *wujūd* - existence *passim*
meqabbel - *qābil* - receiver, [explication of susceptibility] **2,29**; 4,29; 5,1.12.16.21.27.31.32; 6,13^{2}; **9,29**; 15,18; 16,2; 33,2.7; 34,1
maqom - *makān, mawḍi'* - place *passim*
tenu'a meqomit - *ḥaraka mustaqīma* - motion in place **13,15**; 15,3
miqre - *'araḍ* - **1,20.25**; **2,2**^{2}; **10,16**; **12,5**; **13,13**; **21,10**; 23,23 - modification 21,5
be-miqre - *bi-l-'araḍ* - accidentally 15,5; **23,9.11**; 30,32; 31,4
mar'e - *lawn* - colour **4,3**; 9,27; 28,25 - sight 19,31; 27,12; 29,9
murgash - *maḥsūs* - sensible 2,28
merḥaq - interval 24,11
merḥaq limudi - *bu'd ta'līmī* - mathematical extension **3,20.22**
murkav - *murakkab* - composed, composite **2,31**; 6,14.31.33; 7,12; 9,13.17^{2}.18^{2}; **10,24.25.28**; **16,11**; 31,25; 34,13.18
masig - happens 23,24
(*m-sh-k*)
nimshakh - to yearn 31,20; 33,26.30 - to be attached 20,21
nimshakh aḥar - *talā* - to follow **1,12** - *tab'ia* - to follow **2,17**; 13,11; 18,8; 23,21; 25,11.26; 26,10; **28,2**.15 - to succeed 13,3; 34,28
himshikh - *ittaba'a* - to continue **9,24**
meshekh - succession 12,1
maskil - *'āqil* - intelligizer **27,10**
muskal - *ma'qūl* - intelligible, object of intellect *passim*
ha-'olam ha-muskal - the intelligible world 29,11
meshullal - abstract 12,6
mishpaṭ - *ḥukm* - judgement 24,29.**30**

(*m-sh-sh*)
mishshesh – *tamāssa* – to touch **1,6**; 19,2; 20,15.16
mishtoqeq^ – *mustāq* – to be directed **8,21**
mishtane – *mutaghayyir* – changing **3,13.29.33**; 4,20.31; 19,10^{2}
– *mustaḥīl* – altering **19,4**
meshuttaf – common 24,6.10; 31,9
met – *mayt* – dead **7,29.30**; 21,17.18
– *bi-mā'it* – dead **22,6**
mit'aḥed – *muttaḥidān* – united **1,5**; 6,25; 11,35
mit'aḥer – posterior 34,27
mitgabber – seeking dominance 31,27
mitdabbeq – *muttaṣil* – continuous **13,19.20.21**; 15,4; **21,26**; 34,26
mitdamme – *mushākil* – proper **4,1**
mithavve – that which comes-to-be 4,34; 5,3.15.20; 33,2
mithappekh – contrasting 26,4; 32,28; 34,2.5.9^{2}
mittun – delay 29,10
mitḥallef – *mukhtalif* – different **3,6^{2}.7^{2}**; 5,18; **10,18^{2}**; 16,27; 18,26; **19,17**; **21,21** – varying 5,9; **15,17^{2}**; **16,1**.2; **18,24**; 26,2.3; 33,10
– *bi-makhālif* – different **16,29**
mitḥalleq – *munqasim* – divisible **22,6**
mitmazzeg – intermixed 20,16
matmid – *abadīy* – everlasting **3,2**; 4,30; 16,9; 21,27; 33,10^{2} – *dā'im*
– everlasting **15,20**; **21,24.26**
– persisting **10,18**; **12,4**; **22,16**
matmid ha-hisha'arut – *dā'im al-baqā'*
– perduring **2,28.29**; 6,12
mitnagged – opposing 14,5; 34,3.30
mitno'e'a – *mutaḥarriq* – moved *passim*
meni'a bilti mitno'e'a – *muḥarrik ghayr mutaḥarrik* – unmoved mover **16,14** – *muḥarrik lā yataḥarraku*
– unmoved mover **16,15**
mitnase' – rising 31,26
mitnashshem – ensouled 22,11
mit'asseq – occupied 18,13

na'e – fine 27,20
ne'ehav – loved 18,3
na'ot – *mulā'im* – proper **8,7** – according 24,13
na'ot ba-tzura – *muwāfiq fī al-ṣūra*
– to have the same form **10,31**; **11,3**
yoter na'ot – *awlā* – better **27,28**
nibba' – *anba'a* – to foretell **8,22**
nivdal – *mabtūr* – cut **13,19**
mubāyin – distinguished 6,25; **22,4**; 29,34
navokh
kokhav navokh – *kawkab mutaḥayyir*
– planet **15,30**; **18,19**; 23,16.27; 24,3.14.16; 33,5
nivzi – scornful 31,10
nivḥar – *mukhtār* – chosen **17,19**
(*n-b-ṭ*)
hebiṭ – to pay attention 1,8
nivna – *mabnīy* – founded **3,7**
(*n-g-d*)
nagad – to oppose 34,2
neged
ke-neged – *naẓīr* – as **9,26^{2}.27^{2}.28^{2}**
(*n-g-'*)
higi'a – *balagha* – to result **14,28**
niggar – *sayyāl* – liquid **3,29**
nidbaq – continuous 23,24
nidda
dam ha-niddot – *dam al-ṭamth*
– blood of the menses **14,26**
nadiv – *karīm* – noble **8,18**
(*n-h-g*)
hinhig – to reflect^ 12,3
nehevva – [a thing that] comes-to be 31,31
noda' – known 32,9; 33,11
(*n-v-ḥ*)
naḥ – *askara* – to be intoxicating^ **10,21** – to rest 29,22
hiniaḥ – *waḍa'a* – to suppose, to assume, to posit *passim* – *alghā*
– to give up **3,22** – to leave 23,1; 24,30
hunnaḥ – to be predicated 12,8 – to underlie 17,4 – to be considered 27,29
noṭe – inclining 14,5; 24,8
ha-galgal ha-noṭe – *al-falak al-mā'il*
– the inclined sphere **8,20**; **11,1**; 24,2
(*n-v-'*)
hini'a – *ḥarraka* – to move [i.e. cause motion] *passim*
hitno'e'a – *taḥarraka* – to be moved *passim*
nofel – *wāqi'* – falling **2,28**
nose' – *mawḍū'* – substratum **4,4** – underlying 9,28.29 – carrying 23,17
naḥ – *sākin* – stationary **13,30**; 33,28
neḥlaq – discrete 23,25; 34,26

(*n-ṭ-y*)
naṭa - *ḥanna* - to incline 14,4; 18,28; **26,28**; 34,20
neṭiyya - inclination 24,2²
nimus - *nāmūs* - law **17,18**.18.19.20.**21**.23.**25**.31; 18,12; **21,12.13²**.14.15.18.**19**; **25,25**.26.29; 26,16
nikhbad - *faḍīl* - superior **13,24**; **27,19**; 33,19.32 - best 15,24; **19,22**.30; 20,1.**2.3**.12²; **21,23²**; 27,30; 31,31 - *sharīf* - venerable **3,24**; **8,19**; **21,21**; 26,22; **27,12**.32; 29,26 - superior **14,23**
ha-nikhbadim min ha-anashim - freemen 30,30
(*n-k-y*)
hikka - to play [an instrument] 28,31.32
nikhlal - containing 26,8
nikhnas - *dākhil* - included **25,1** - episodic 35,15.16
(*n-k-r*)
hikir - to perceive 27,13
nokhri - *gharīb* - foreign **21,11**
nim'as - repugnant 32,12; 33,14.15
nimna' - *mumtani'* - impossible **3,6**; **4,11**
nimtza' - *mawjūd* - existent, existing [thing] *passim*
ne'edar - privated 6,21
na'ale - *faḍīl* - best **21,20** - superior **27,11**.33; 34,12 - beyond 28,30
ne'etaq - *muntaqil* - transposable **19,5**
(*n-f-l*)
nafal - to be applied 6,1; 18,30 - to be subject 6,11; to encounter 29,10
hipil - *awqa'a* - to apply **1,17.19.20.21.23.24** - to rid 16,5
nifrad - *mufrad* - particular **2,13.14.15.18.23**; 6,31²; 7,9.19; 11,6².10.12 - distinct **3,9².12.16**; 35,7 - apart **16,12²**; 13,29 - alone 21,10 - separate **22,24** - per se 17,5 - distinguished 30,20 - dispersed 34,24 - *munfarid* - separate **10,24**
nefesh - *nafs* - soul 5,22; 7,6.16; **10,15**; 15,10; **22,14**; **23,11**; 29,1.30; 30,16; 35,4 - *nafs* - essence **28,18.19**
nafsho, be-nefesh - *fī nafsuhu* - in itself **10,22** - *nafsuhu* - itself 7,22; 12,22; 16,28; **28,18**; 32,20; 33,20 - *bi-'aynihi* - itself **21,22** - in itself 7,25; 12,6 - of the essence 18,23 - self 28,16.17.18
ba'al nefesh - *mutanaffis* - ensouled **21,14**; 28,32
ramuz elav be-nafsho - this-something in itself 6,15.17.18.24.27.29.30
ha-nefesh asher ba-aretz - *al-nafs allatī fī al-arḍ* - the soul that is in the earth **8,19**
nitztzav - right 29,31
nitztzuaḥ - dialectic 12,9
nitztzaḥon - *ghalaba* - strife **14,31**; 32,17
nitzḥi - *azalīy* - eternal *passim*
nequdda - point 9,20; 15,14
naqi - clean 35,9
naqel - easy 28,24
niqna - *muktasab* - gained **19,21**
(*n-q-f*)
hiqqif - *ḥawā* - to contain **3,10.11**; 15,30; 28,34
(*n-q-sh*)
hiqqish - *qāsa* - to compare **29,6** - *qāyasa* - to compare **14,16**
nir'e - visible 23,26; 27,4.6.16
(*n-s-'*)
nasa' - *ḥamala* - to carry **4,5²**; **11,32²**; 28,23.24 - to hold 20,19 - *iḥtamala* - to be predicated **10,26**
nissa'- to be predicated 17,3
nissa' (adj.) - dignified 15,25
nish'ar - *bāqī* - remaining (the rest; the other) **2,1.20**; 12,3; 13,16; **18,11.19**; **19,9** - everlasting 34,28
(*n-s-g*)
hissig - *adraka* - to apprehend 6,20²; **28,21**.25; 29,14 - *laḥiqa* - to happen **28,13** - to achieve 11,26.31; 21,4; 26,8 - to arrive at 34,6
hissig be-shelemut - *fāza* - to completely attain **25,1**
hussag - to be apprehended 6,11².28; 29,30 - to be attained 30,7
nishma' - heard [thing] 27,6
nitla - *mu'allaq* - dependent **22,13**
(*n-t-n*)
natan - to give 5,20; 34,25 - to give up 27,32
(*n-t-r*)
hittir - to let go 12,30

(*s-b-b*)
sav – to revolve 24,1.2
savav – to revolve 15,13
sovev – *adāra* – to turn **22,15**; 24,16.17.18.20.21.22.23; 33,28
sibba – *sabab*, *'illa* – cause *passim*
sibba meni'a – *sabab muḥarrik* – moving cause **10,1**.7 – *'illa muḥarrika* – moving cause **10,31**
sibba po'elet – efficient cause 33,4
ha-sibba ha-rishona – *al-sabab al-awwal* – first cause **10,31** – *al-'illa al-ūlā* – first cause 11,5.**25**; **16,31**; **17,27**; 18,1.**14**; **22,14**; 26,29; 33,25
ha-sibba asher ba'avura – *al-sabab allatī lahu* – cause for the sake of which **13,4**; 32,19
sibuv – cycle 15,3.13.14; 33,28 – rotation 24,18; 29,15; 33,28
'al ha-sibuv – *mustadīr* – circular **13,15**.20.**21**; 16,6
(*s-b-r*)
savar – *ra'ā* – to maintain **27,34** – to think 11,27 – to opine 14,18.20
sevara' – *'ilm* – science **3,28** – *ra'y* – thought **19,24** – opinion 14,18.20
segula – *khāṣṣiya* – property 6,16; **15,26**[2]
(*s-d-r*)
sidder – to arrange 26,6; 32,30
sedder – *tartīb* – order *passim*
sug – *jins* – genus *passim*
(*s-v-r*)
sar – *zāla* – to cease **11,22**; **12,22**; **21,17** – to be removed 4,26
(*s-k-l*)
sakhal – to be ignorant 28,31
sikhlut – *jahl* – ignorance **10,6**[2]; **19,23**; **29,8**; 34,11
(*s-k-m*)
hiskim – *ittafaqa* – to agree **2,27**; 22,9; 24,12; 31,29; 33,20 – to bring into accord 33,16.18
(*s-l-q*)
sullaq – *nufiya* – to be removed **27,22**
histalleq – *rufi'a* – to be removed 6,22; **30,4**
salleq – *raf'* – discard **7,28**
semikhut – *iḍāfa* – relationship **1,16**
(*s-m-k*)
nismakh – to rely 6,21
sefogi – spongy 34,3
sefogut – softness 32,28; 33,19
sippuq – *iktifā'* – self-sufficiency **28,5** – persuasion 26,15
(*s-p-q*)
sippeq – to raise a problem 4,25
hispiq – to suffice 4,15; 32,29; 34,24
safeq – doubt 23,1; 33,24; 34,30 – problem 4,25
be-lo' safeq – *lā maḥāla* – undoubtedly **10,3**; 12,6.21; 14,12.13; **22,16**; 23,14; 25,13; **26,32**; 30,17; 31,5; 32,1
(*s-p-r*)
lo' yisapper me-rov – *la yuḥṣā* – beyond measure **19,20**
sipper – *khabbara* – to make known **13,4**; 15,1.4 – *waṣafa* – to state **4,6**; 29,22 – *iqtaṣṣa* – to relate accurately **3,18** – to describe 26,22; 30,27
stira – refutation 32,4; 34,4.22 – contradiction 19,1
(*s-t-r*)
satar – *nāqaḍa* – to contradict 12,15 – to refute 33,31

'av – dense 34,3
'avur
ha-davar asher ba'avuro – *al-shay' alladhī min ajlihi* – that for the sake of which 9,2; **17,16**
ha-sibba asher ba'avura – *al-sabab allatī lahu* – cause for the sake of which **13,4**; 32,19
(*'-b-r*)
'avar – *taṣaffaḥa* – to go over **28,2.6**.21; **29,7** – to pass 18,2; 31,13 – to deviate 33,11
(*'-v-d*)
hi'id – *shahida* – to testify **2,6**; **15,28**; **23,7**; 26,13
'olam – *'ālam* – world *passim*
ha-'olam ha-muskal – the intelligible world 29,11
ha-'olam ha-sikhli – the intellectual world 30,11
'omed – *qā'im* – subsisting 12,6; **16,12**[2] – persisting 5,2
(*'-v-q*)
hi'iq – *'āqa* – to impede 6,6.9; **12,26**; 19,31; 20,4
'ivvaron – blindness 15,29

(ʿ-z-b)
ʿ*azav* – *taraka* – to rid **16,3** – to leave **28,2** – *wadaʿa* – to leave **28,21** – to neglect 32,10
ʿ*iyyun* – *naẓar* – theorizing **2,21**; **8,9**; 17,20; 26,24 – ʿ*iyān* – seeing **1,25**
(ʿ-y-n)
ʿ*iyyen* – *naẓara* – to theorize 7,14; **26,23**; 27,1; 30,19
*heṭiv le*ʿ*ayyen* – *am*ʿ*ana* – to continue^ **2,23**
ʿ*ayin* – ʿ*ayn* – eye 6,28; **28,27**
*be-*ʿ*eino* – *bi-*ʿ*aynihi* – itself, one and the same *passim*
heref ʿ*ayin* – *ṭirfati* ʿ*ayn* – instant **19,21**
*ma she-yira'e la-*ʿ*ayin* – observation 24,14.16
ʿ*illa* – ʿ*illa* – cause *passim*
ʿ*illa meni*ʿ*a* – ʿ*illa muḥarrika* – moving cause **15,17**; **24,27**; 25,5^{2}.21; 34,24
*ha-*ʿ*illa ha-rishona* – *al-*ʿ*illa al-ūlā* – first cause **15,22.23**; 18,9.**10**; 21,1; **22,14**; **23,8**; **25,13**; **26,21**; 33,26.30; 34,4.6
ʿ*elyon* – *a*ʿ*lā* – higher **8,19**
(ʿ-m-d)
ʿ*amad* – *sakana* – to stop **13,18** – *qāma* – to stand **2,12** – to be constituted **11,24** – *labitha* – to remain 28,8 – to subsist 7,10.26; 17,21.23 – to establish 18,9; 34,13 – to rely 12,12 – to determine 31,11 – to be content 31,29
ʿ*amad ba-maḥshava* – *qāma fī wahm* – to keep in mind **10,31**; 11,5
*he*ʿ*emid* – to place 14,30
ʿ*amida* – *qiwām* – constitution 4,19; **12,1**; **19,16**; 20,6; **29,25**; 31,25 – *wuqūf* – determination **23,14**; 32,16; 34,24^{2} – halt 13,16
ʿ*amal* – effort 28,13; 28,15
ʿ*aniyyut* – poverty 6,19
ʿ*inyan* – *ḥāl* – state **2,28**; **3,6.15**; 5,9; **8,13**^{3}; **10,18**^{2}**.19.26**; **11,23**; **12,25**.32; 15,6^{2}.15.**16**^{2}**.17.18.19**.25; 16,30; 19,13; 20,7.8.14; **21,21**; 30,28^{2}; 31,1.19.21; 33,10 – quality **1,11.15**; **2,3.8**; **4,9**; 9,20; 18,24; 23,25 – manner 5,18; 7,2^{2}.4; 11,35; 16,25.26; **19,10**.11; **22,29**; **23,7**^{2}; 24,14.32; 25,9.10; 26,5.**19**.23; 27,22; **28,17**; 31,12.13 – accident **2,1** – modification **10,14**; 27,17 – *amr* – issue, manner [sometimes not translated, but implied] **2,22.31**; **3,22**; **8,10**; **10,11**; 12,3; 13,10.11; 15,2; 16,9.**30**; 17,18.20; 18,3; 23,1.**11**.23; 25,25.26; 27,20; 31,15 – thing **2,33**; **3,7**; 5,4; 6,18; 14,4^{2}.10^{2}.11; 21,28; 26,6.19; 27,18; 35,7 – *ma*ʿ*anā* – meaning **1,5**; 19,1; 30,15 – attribute 11,28.**29**; 13,17 – notion 12,14; 13,12 – command 14,31; 18,9; 25,30
(ʿ-s-q)
*hit*ʿ*asseq* – *ista*ʿ*mala* – to be preoccupied **2,13**; to exercise **26,25**
ʿ*ippush* – ʿ*afan* – putrescence **7,30**
ʿ*atzla*^ – *tahayyub* – apprehensiveness **10,13**
ʿ*etzem* – *jawhar* – substance *passim*
ʿ*etzem rishon* – first substance 17,9; 26,12.19
ʿ*atzmut* – *dhāt* – essence, substantiality *passim*
ʿ*eqev*
*ba' ze be-*ʿ*eqev ze* – *ta*ʿ*āqaba* – to succeed on another **2,3**
ʿ*iqqar* – foundation 12,1
(ʿ-r-b)
ʿ*erev* – *khalaṭa* – to mingle **14,30**
*hit*ʿ*arev* – *ikhtalaṭa* – to be mixed 17,3; **20,24**
*lo yit*ʿ*arev bo davar min ha-gashmut* – *lā yashūbuhu shay' min al-jismāniyya* – incorporeal **3,8**
*(lo') yit*ʿ*arev bo davar min ha-hiyuli* – *(lā) yashūbuhu shay' min al-hayūlā* – (im)material **14,7**; **16,14**.20
*(lo') yit*ʿ*arev bo ha-hiyuli* – *(lā) tashūbuhu al-hayūlā* – (im)material 17,22; 20,6.**20**; **22,31**.32.33; 29,20; 30,8; 33,21; 34,5.19; 35,9
*she-ha-hiyuli lo' yit*ʿ*arev bo* – immaterial 23,5
*lo' yit*ʿ*arev bo ha-ḥomer* – immaterial 23,18

lo' yit'arev bo ha-yesod – immaterial 29,33
'arev – *ladhīdh* – pleasant **16,23**; **19,22.23.25.26**; 20,1
'arevut – *ladhdha* – pleasantness **19,28**; **20,32**; 21,3.6
'eruv – mixture 16,4; 32,13
'arum – *ta'arrā* – to be naked **2,1**; 6,19.32
'orma – *ḥidhq* – skill **8,8.9**
(*'-s-y*)
'asa – *fa'ala* – to act, to do **8,17.21**^{2}; 13,26; 14,9.19; **19,30**; 21,4; **26,24**.26.**27**.30.31; 27,1.6; 29,16; 30,30; 31,4.12; 33,9.20; 35,15 – *'amala* – to work **8,8.9.11**^{2}**.15.16** – to make 5,22; 7,12.24.25^{2}.26 – *ista'mala* – to employ **12,18**.19; 32,28
'asiyya – *'amal* – making **8,8**; 12,17
'osher – richness 29,6
'et – *waqt* – moment, time *passim* – *amr* – time^ **19,18**
(*'-t-q*)
ne'etaq – *intaqala* – to be transposed **20,23**
he'etiq – to translate 29,14

po'el – *fā'il* – active **26,24**; 33,17 – agent 7,18
meni'a po'el – efficient mover 7,10
sibba po'elet – efficient cause 33,4
'illa po'elet – *'illa fā'ila* – efficient
paḥut – *khasīs* – inferior 13,24; 14,10; **27,14.20.23**.25.**26**.27^{2}; 31,15 – *aqall* – least **2,34**
paḥot – less 31,16
pele' – *'ajab* – puzzlement **1,17**; **8,16**; **12,5**; **18,10**; 20,30; 29,17 – admiration **8,8** – wonder **21,8.9**^{2}
(*p-l-g*)
hiflig – *daqqaqa* – to be meticulous **8,9**
penai – *farāgh* – leisure **19,18**
panim – *wajh* – respect **3,14**; **4,12**.27.28; 7,5; 9,1; 10,7.8
mi-bifnim – from within 19,2
(*p-s-d*)
nifsad – *fasada* – to perish **3,4**; 4,16.17; 5,32; 12,2.**6.10**; 32,17
(*p-s-q*)
nifsaq – *inqaṭa'a* – to stop **13,16**; 33,9
hifsiq – *qaṭa'a* – to interrupt **20,4**
(*p-'-l*)
hitpa'el – to be acted upon 31,4; 33,7
pe'ula – *fi'l* – action, activity *passim*
po'al – *fi'l* – actuality, activity *passim*
ba-po'al – *bi-l-fi'l* – actually, in actuality *passim*
yatza' el ha-po'al – *kharaja ilā al-fi'l* – to be brought into actuality **8,7**; **14,14**; **22,5**; **27,17**; 28,14
pa'am...u-fa'am – *marra... wa-marra* – sometimes... and sometimes *passim*
pe'amim – *rubbamā, qad* – sometimes *passim*
perud – dissociation 32,28; 34,3
(*p-r-d*)
nifrad – *farada* – to be distinct **3,10** – *infarada* – to be separated **10,24.25**
hifrid – *afrada* – to separate **1,24.25**; **11,29**
peraṭi – individual 11,6^{2}; 27,20 – specific 22,33
peruq – separating off 5,17
(*p-r-q*)
pereq – to separate off 5,17
pashuṭ – *basīṭ* – simple **2,32**; 9,13.16.17.18; **17,2**.4.5.7.8^{2}.10.**13**.14.23; **21,10**; 34,18
(*p-sh-ṭ*)
hifshiṭ – *lafaẓa* – to shed **4,5**
hitpashsheṭ – *intashara* – to expand **2,34**
pit'om – *duf'atan* – instantly **28,21**; 28,27 – immediately 33,25

tzad – *jiha, sabīl* – [signifying adverbial language] *passim* – direction 4,13.14 – side 14,4.5; 18,28^{2}
tzivvui – command 30,26; 31,13
(*tz-v-y*)
tzivva – to command 25,30; 26,6 – to prescribe 30,25
hitzṭavva – to be commanded 31,12
tzomeaḥ – *nabāt* – plant **1,6**; 31,18
tzura – *ṣūra* – form *passim* – Idea **3,20.22**; 7,7^{2}.8.20.24.**27**; **13,29**; **22,34**.34; 23,3; 33,32^{2}; 34,20.21 – shape 26,16^{2}
ha-tzura ha-rishona – first form 25,18; 32,8
tzoref – craftsman 5,16.22.24.28.29^{2}
tziyyur – conception 32,12; 34,26
(*tz-y-r*)
tziyyer – to form 7,18; 32,30 – to conceive 32,10.12; 33,9.10.12

tzuyyar - to assume a form 6,29 - to be conceived 20,5; 23,29
tziyyer ba-maḥshava - to imagine 29,12
tzelem - sculpture 6,24; 7,12
(*tz-m-ḥ*)
hitzmiaḥ - *anbata* - to grow [something] **14,26**
tzemaḥ - *nabāt* - plant **2,30**; **3,3**; 5,19.22; **8,2.3.4^2.5**; **14,27**.28; 21,29; 30,28; 31,3.7; 35,6
tzemiḥa - growth 31,5
tzarikh - *iḥtāja* - need **8,24**; 12,12; **28,27**; 32,1.30
(*tz-r-k*)
hitzrikh - to be needed 32,22
hutzrakh - *iḥtāja* - to enquire into **8,25**
hitzṭarekh - *iḥtāja* - to need **3,24**; 4,15^2; 5,11.17.18; 7,24; 9,8; **14,1**; **15,19.20**; **21,2**; 22,16; **28,6**; 29,7; 33,33; 34,24 - *udṭurra* - to be compelled **14,29**
tzorekh - *ḥāja* - need 7,20.21; **16,3**; 29,8.**9**; 31,5
haya tzorekh bo - *iḥtāja fīhi* - to be needed **3,23**
(*tz-r-p*)
tzaraf - to conjoin 5,17 - to craft 5,23.24
tzoraf - to be crafted 5,24

qibbutz - association 31,24; 32,28; 34,2
qibbutz min ha-ṭovim - aristocracy 26,12
(*q-b-l*)
qibbel - *qabila* - to receive, to admit [sometimes explicates susceptibility] *passim*
(*q-b-tz*)
qibbetz - to bring together 33,17
hitqabbetz - *ijtamaʿa* - to be collected **2,13** - to be combined 13,8 - to become associated 33,20
qedima - priority 33,24; 34,8
(*q-d-m*)
qadam - *taqaddama* - to be prior **1,12.13**; 9,10; 14,16.24; 15,11.12 - to precede, to be earlier 11,21; **13,5**.6; 16,1; 21,26; **22,26**; 27,7
hiqdim - *taqaddama* - to prescribe **23,4**
qodem - *qabla* - prior - **3,21**; 9,8; **11,34**; 13,30; 14,31; before 7,11.12^2.17; 12,16; **13,1**; 25,23; 26,23; 27,21; 33,1 - *awwal* - early **2,31**
qav - *khaṭṭ* - line **1,10**; 9,20
qodem - *mutaqaddim* - prior **1,12**; 9,9 - *aqdam* - prior **14,23** - *awlā* - preceding **25,24**
yoter qodem - *aqdam* - before **12,10**.19; 14,13; 22,1.2.3; 23,13^2 - prior 6,30; 9,9.13^2.14; 14,16.18.20.**29** - early 14,11
(*q-v-y*)
qivva - *tawaqqaʿa* - to expect **19,26**
qol - *ṣawt* - sound **4,2^2**; 20,1; 27,5.13.16; 28,32.33
(*q-w-m*)
qiyyem - *thabbata* - to affirm **1,21**; **12,18**
hitqayyem - *thabata* - to be stable **2,2**; 6,27 - to persist **15,19**; 33,29
(*q-w-tz*)
niqwatz - *inqabaḍa* - to contract **2,33**
qoṭev - pole 24,7.8.9.10
qaṭan - *ṣaghīr* - small **8,1** - *yasīr* - brief **19,19** - slight 4,20
qoṭer - section 30,9
qayyam - *thābit* - stable **2,2** - persisting 12,20.32 - extending^ 25,24
kokhav qayyam - *kawkab thābit* - fixed star **18,15**; 24,1.5.18
qal (adj.) - *khafīf* - light 25,22 - easy 29,14
qalut - ease 29,15^2
be-qalut - easily 11,31; 28,22.33
(*q-l-l*)
qal - to be easy 11,32; 13,11
(*q-n-y*)
qana - *istafāda* - to acquire 18,6.**16.17**; **27,26.28**; **28,11**
qeniyya - *istifāda* - acquiring **22,27**; **28,6**
qinyan - having 9,11
qatze - *ṭaraf* - extreme point **22,21**
(*q-tz-r*)
qatzar - *naqaṣa* - to fall short **17,30**
qatzar - short 6,28; 15,14
qetzaṭ - *baʿḍ* - some, a few *passim*
qetzaṭam qeṭzat - *baʿḍuhum baʿḍān* - each other *passim*
qor - *bard* - cold **9,26**; 34,3.9.10
(*q-r-ʾ*)
qaraʾ - *sammā* - to call **4,8**; to name 26,17
niqraʾ - *qīla lahu* - to be called **4,9.10**; 6,8; 10,2

(*q-r-b*)
qarav – *qariba* – to be close **17,28.29**; 18,1.6.**14**
qurva – closeness 6,23; 33,9
qarov – *qarīb* – proximate, close **4,1**; 6,23; **10,32**^{2}; **11,3.4**; 12,7; **16,22**; **18,16.17**; 25,30; 26,26
meni'a qarov – *muḥarrik qarīb* – proximate mover **10,4.9**
qerovat ha-zeman – *qarībat al-ʿahd* – recent **2,17**
(*q-r-y*)
qara – to happen [in the sense of randomness] 5,4; 16,27 – to occur 6,8; 14,3; 25,10
(*q-sh-y*)
hiqsha – *aghfala* – to neglect^ **7,28**
hitqasha – *iktanaza* – to become dense **3,1**
qoshi – hardness 32,28; 33,19
(*q-sh-r*)
qashar – to tie 21,16

ra'uy – *yanbaghī*, *yajibu* – must, ought, should *passim*
ra'uy bo – *akhlaqa bihi-* – to be appropriate for it **9,24.31**
yoter ra'uy – *awlā* – more fitting **1,14**.5; **2,14.17**; 6,7.29; 9,16; more so 12,7; rather 15,1; 16,5 – *bi-l-ḥarī* – all the more so **13,13**
ra'uy be-hekhreaḥ – *yajibu ḍurūratan* – should necessarily **2,25**; **15,23** – must necessarily **4,3** – follows necessarily **13,25** – necessarily 7,13; 33,18
re'ut – *baṣar* – vision **2,28**; 19,30; 27,4.12.16.**28**; 28,24.25.**27**; 29,9.12
(*r-'-y*)
ra'a – *ra'ā* – to see 5,10; 7,8.**29**^{2}.**30**^{2}; **8,22**; **15,29**; **16,22**; **26,29**; 27,4.6; 29,10.21; 31,23; to think **8,19.20**; 15,27; 22,30; to perceive 16,25^2.26.27.**28**; 18,6; 19,30; **21,2** – *baṣura* – to see **27,29**; **28,28**
nir'a – *badā* – to seem 6,9.18.27; **16,29** – *ru'iya* – to be apparent **22,23** – to be seen 6,19
ma she-yira'e la-ʿayin – observation 24,14.16
her'a – to exhibit 6,19
hitra'a – to pretend 6,21
re'aya – *dalāla* – signification **12,17** – indication 31,18
rosh – *awwal* – first **1,7** – *ra'īs* – leader **26,1**; 31,24 – head 29,2 – chief 31,14^2
reshit – *awwal* – beginning **2,8** – leader 35,18
rishon – *awwal* – first *passim*
ha-hatḥala ha-rishona – *al-mabda' al-awwal* – first principle **10,16**; **11,25.27**; 12,13; **13,34**; **16,20**; **23,4.6.27**; 29,19.24; 31,28; 32,9.10; 34,7.12; 35,13
ha-ʿilla ha-rishona – *al-ʿilla al-ūlā* – first cause **15,22.23**; 18,9.**10**; 21,1; **22,14**; **23,8**; **25,13**; **26,21**; 33,26.30; 34,4.6
ha-meni'a ha-rishon – *al-muḥarrik al-awwal* – first mover **10,9**; 13,25; **17,15**.22; **25,18.19**
ha-sibba ha-rishona – *al-sabab al-awwal* – first cause **10,31** – *al-ʿilla al-ūlā* – first cause 11,5.**25**; **16,31**; **17,27**; 18,1.**14**; **22,14**; 26,29; 33,25
ʿetzem rishon – first substance 17,9; 26,12.19
ha-tzura ha-rishona – first form 25,18; 32,8
ha-raqi'a ha-rishon – *al-samā' al-ūlā* – first heaven **18,15**
ha-sekhel ha-elohi ha-rishon – first divine intellect 20,25
rav – *kathīr* – many, multiple, manifold *passim* – *shattā* – many **1,3**
rov – *akthar* – most **3,30**; 7,8; **19,18**; 27,22; 30,32; 31,4 – more **21,9**
lo' yisapper me-rov – *la yuḥṣā* – beyond measure **19,20**
ribbui – *kathra* – plurality 5,10^2.11.12.13.16.20^2.23; 17,5; **22,32**; 32,4; 35,1^2.3.7.18 – great number **7,28** – large amount **20,24** – abundance **21,9** – number **23,14** – many **25,16**; 31,26 – multifold **29,6**
regaʿ – *dufʿa* – instant **20,27**; **28,7**
(*r-g-sh*)
hirgish – to become aware 29,30^2
redifa – adherence 17,31
(*r-v-tz*)
ratz – *jarā* – to flow **3,29**
roḥav – breadth 24,2^2

raḥoq - *ba'īd* - far 6,17; **10,32**; **11,1**^{2}.**4**; 19,6.9
riḥuq - *barā'* - dispension **28,10**
(*r-ḥ-q*)
raḥaq - *ba'uda* - to be far **17,29**; 29,15 - to keep away 7,7; 9,10; 25,9 - to be drawn away 20,21
hirḥiq - to keep something away 13,32
roḥaq - remoteness 6,26; 33,10
req - empty 20,5; 26,31 - vain 25,9
(*r-k-b*)
hirkiv - to compound 5,17
hurkav - to be combined 24,15
hitrakkev - *tarakkaba* - to be composed **17,13**
(*r-k-k*)
herekh - *raqqa* - to be rarefied **2,33**
ramuz elav be-nafsho - a this-something in itself 6,15.17.18.24.27.29.30
remez - allusion 26,14
remiza elav - being a 'this-something' 6,16
ra' - evil 32,7^{2}.25.26.27
ri'u'a - impairment 6,6.8
re'iya - community 25,26.30; 30,26
rifyon - *istirkhā'* - weariness **27,17**
raqi'a - *samā'* - heaven 18,18
ha-raqi'a ha-rishon - *al-samā' al-ūlā* - first heaven **18,15**
ratz - *jārī'* - flowing **3,29**
ratzon - volition 17,32
(*r-tz-y*)
ratza - *'anā* - to mean **10,23**^{2}; **13,31**; 18,7.26 - *raghiba* - to impel **12,26** - *ṣarraḥa* - to mean **14,29** - to want 29,11; 31,21 - to intend 12,19
hitratza - to accede 32,26
(*r-sh-l*)
hitrashshel - *bakhula* - to withold 24,32
(*r-t-ḥ*)
hirtiaḥ - *ghallā* - to ferment 10,21

(*sh-'-l*)
sha'al - to ask 28,7
nish'al - to be asked 5,14; 9,14
she'ela - question 8,29; 9,2; 28,7
(*sh-'-r*)
nish'ar - *baqiya* - to remain 7,14; **11,23**; **20,18.19**; 32,19
(*sh-d-l*)
hishtaddel - *ḥarraḍa* - to strive **18,15**; 23,15 - *bādara* - to rush **19,25**
(*sh-v-b*)
shav - *ṣāra* - to come **19,26** - to return 15,14; 24,17 - to turn into 34,5
shave - equal 29,31; 32,3.4; 33,24; 34,7
(*sh-v-q*)
hishtoqeq - to desire 6,18
(*s-v-s*)
sas - to be delighted 19,31
seḥoq
qarov le-seḥoq - *muḥāl* - virtually absurd 26,26
shaṭ - swimmer 30,28
sheṭaḥ - *saṭḥ* - surface **9,28**; 20,15; 35,14^{2}
(*s-y-m*)
sam - *ja'ala* - to posit *passim* - to put 15,10; **20,29**; 31,27; 32,7 - to consider **4,11**; 17,30; 27,30 - to render 33,30; 35,11.15 - to set 7,24; 35,12 - to ascribe 31,29 - to appoint 31,14 - to make 33,1
sam be-da'at - *khaṭara bi-bāl* - to keep in mind **8,8**
sam kavanato - to aim 31,24
sam megamato - *qafā atharahu* - to pursue 17,31.32; **18,11**
hesim - *ja'ala* - to posit **2,18.19**; 7,7; 34,7^{2}
husam - *ju'ila* - to be posited **3,6**; 11,9; **15,15** - to be set 5,21; **8,6.11.14** - to be considered 27,12.13.**14** - to be articulated 26,15
shikhvat zera' - *minān* - semen **8,2**
shekhuna - adjacency 30,24
(*s-k-l*)
hiskil - *'aqala* - to intelligize *passim* - *fakkara* - to think **8,17**
huskal - *'uqila* - to be intelligized **16,30**^{2}; 20,6.9.12; **28,19**
sekhel - *'aql* - intellect *passim*
ha-sekhel ha-elohi - *al-'aql al-ilāhī* - the divine intellect 20,8.**32**; 28,26; 29,10.12.14.15.20
ha-sekhel ha-elohi ha-rishon - first divine intellect 20,25
shaliṭ - *mutasalliṭ* - controller **27,5**.7
(*sh-l-ṭ*)
hishliṭ - to charge 31,15
(*sh-l-k*)
hishlikh - *iṭṭaraḥa* - to cast **19,19**; 28,23
(*sh-l-l*)
shalal - *nafā* - to deny **1,20**

(*sh-l-m*)
nishlam – to be completed 31,15
hishlim – *kamala* – to perfect 17,20; **28,3.4^2.5.8^2** – to complete 26,5; 33,29 – *atamma* – to accomplish **19,16**
shalem – *tāmm* – perfect 14,3; **28,8**
shelemut – *kamāl* – perfection 14,3; **17,16.17.30**; 21,30; **28,26**.29; 32,11 – completion 25,30
hissig be-shelemut – *fāza* – to completely attain **25,1**
shem – *ism* – term **12,18**; 18,28 – name 6,2; 7,22
(*s-m-ḥ*)
samaḥ – *sarra* – to be delighted **19,29**.31
simḥa – *faraḥ* – delight **19,20**.31; **20,2** – *surūr* – joy **19,29**
shamayim – *samāʾ* – heaven **19,15**
shememi
gerem shememi – *jism samāwī* – celestial body **4,11**; 33,23
geshem shememi – *jism samāwī* – celestial body **2,29**; **3,5^2**; 4,17.18; 15,13; **18,25**; 19,1.**3**; 26,12; 31,2; 33,3.9.26; 34,14
(*sh-m-ʿ*)
shamaʿ – to hear 20,1; 27,4.7; 32,26
hishmiʿa – to evoke [sound] 28,32
shemaʿ – hearing 20,1; 27,4.7.13.16
ha-shemaʿ ha-ṭivʿi – *Physics* 13,17
(*sh-m-r*)
shamar – to preserve 17,20
nishmar – *ḥadhira* – to be careful **10,15**
shinnuy – *taghayyur* – change **3,3.4.8.28.33^2**; **4,6.7.8.9.11^2**.15^2.29; 5,2; **11,23**; **13,2**; **18,25**; 19,2^2.**4**.7; 23,6; 27,24; 33,21; 35,15 – *istiḥāla* – alteration **3,14**; 6,5; **12,27** – *taʾthīr* – affection **22,5**; 32,1
shena – *nawm* – sleep **19,23**; **26,29**; 27,18
shaquʿa be-shena – *ghariqa fī al-nawm* – to be sound asleep **26,28**
(*sh-n-y*)
shinna – *aḥāla* – to alter **12,27**; **13,31**
shunna – *istaḥāla* – to be altered **22,4**
hishtana – *taghayyara* – to be changed **2,29**; 4,18^2.29; 5,19; 6,10; 12,31; **13,5**.18; 19,1; 20,6; **22,5**; 27,24
shiʿur – *miqdār* – quantity **1,11.15**; **2,3.8**; **4,9**; **12,21**.8; 17,10; **22,6^2**; 28,30^2; 30,1
be-loʾ shiʿur – *bi-lā mudda* – immeasurable **28,7**
ʿavar ha-shiʿur – to surpass 18,2
shaʿar – *bāb* – realm **9,27**; 18,30
(*sh-f-ṭ*)
shafaṭ – *ḥakama* – to judge **10,16**; 24,29
(*sh-q-ʿ*)
shaquʿa be-shena – *ghariqa fī al-nawm* – to be sound asleep **26,28**
shoresh – *aṣl* – proposition **12,15**.16 – *ḥāl* **28,2**^– fundament 5,9.11 – root 12,1; 21,31
sason – *surūr* – joy **20,2**
shat – *asās* – foundation **2,5** – *rukn* **2,31** – cause^ 2,7
shittuf – *mushāraka* – [something in] common **3,16.25**
(*sh-t-f*)
hishtattef – *ishtaraka* – to share **3,5**; 31,15; 33,3 – to participate 31,13

taʾava – *shahwa* – appetite **16,31**; 17,31; 18,2.4^2.5.12; 31,19
(*t-ʾ-r*)
teʾer – *naʿata* – to describe **1,16**; 33,8 – *faraḍa* – to prescribe **14,31**
toʾar – *nuʿita* – to be described **1,13.14**; 9,16.18
toʾar – attribute 6,16 – description 9,15; 13,14
tolada – *natīja* – conclusion **29,8**
tosefet – *ziyāda* – elevation **19,24** – increase 19,6
toʿelet – utility 26,16; 31,3.6
hayta toʿelet – *intafaʿa* – to benefit **13,28**
qibbel toʿelet – to benefit 21,31
(*t-ḥ-l*)
hitḥil – to start 6,32; 15,14; 24,18; 26,23
teḥila – *awwalān* – first **1,9.11**; **3,30**; 4,21; 5,19; 8,29.30; 9,3; 11,17.29; 25,29; 26,18 – *awwal* – first **20,6** – beginning 12,1; outset 21,28; 35,7
taḥat – *taḥta* – under **2,28**; **4,4**; 9,10.12.14; 25,14.15; 31,27; 32,8 – underlying 4,16; 17,4; 32,3.4

takhlit - *ghāya* - [as superlative] *passim*
- boundary **3,11**; **22,19** - *inqiḍā'*
- ending **21,20** - *nihāya*
- periphery **8,15** - end 28,14; 31,6; 35,12 - limit 23,3
ba'al takhlit - *mutanāhan* - limited **22,7**.8.9.**11.17.28**
ein takhlit lo - *lā nihāya lahu* - infinite 5,30; 12,30; 14,22; **19,24**; 23,2; 25,11 - unlimited **22,6**.10.**12.13.15.21.26.27**; **25,10**
beli takhlit, be-lo' takhlit - *bi-ghayr nihāya, bi-lā nihāya* - unlimited **22,7**.8.9.**24**
ba-takhlit ha-aḥaron - *fī al-ghāya al-quṣwā* - ultimate **17,17**.25
be-takhlit / 'al takhlit ha-ma'ala - *fī / 'alā ghāyat al-faḍīla* - utmost best, utmost excellence *passim*
(*t-k-n*)
tukkan - *tahayya'a* - can 5,4; **19,20**
tekhef - as soon as 29,10
taluy - *mu'allaq* - dependent 12,3; **19,15**; 26,10.30; 33,10
(*t-l-y*)
nitla - to depend upon 16,3
(*t-m-d*)
hitmid - *dāma* - to perdure 6,19; **22,24.26**
tema - *'ajab* - marvel **29,5**
temuna - *shakl* - shape **1,10.13**; 6,6; 7,14; 29,16
temidut - *dawām* - everlastingness **15,22**.27 - perdurance 15,25; **22,24** - constancy **27,16**
temidi - *dā'im* - everlasting **13,26.27**; **14,30**; 15,13.**15**; 16,2; **19,20**; 21,18.**19.24.25**; 23,6.**12**; **25,1**
temidi ha-hisha'arut - *dā'im al-baqā'* - everlasting **15,21**; 21,19
temimut - *tamām* - completeness **28,26**
tenai - condition 32,24
tenu'a - *ḥaraka* - motion *passim*
tenu'a meqomit - *ḥaraka mustaqīma* - motion in place **13,15**; 15,3
tiqva - *rajā'* - hope **19,26**
taqu'a - implanted 20,22
tishboret - geometry 23,24
ḥakhmei ha-tishboret - geometricians 29,16
ḥokhmat ha-tishboret - geometry 23,28
teshuqa - *'ishq* - passion **16,31**; 17,30.32; 25,26.27

Arabic–Hebrew–English Index

All references are to page and line numbers of Landauer's original Hebrew edition, which are noted in the body of the translation and are retained in the recently published critical edition of the text, in which the surviving Arabic parts mirror the Hebrew.

Entries are listed according to their root and arranged according to the Arabic alphabet. Within the root, verbs are listed first according to their form, followed by other parts of speech. Expressions and constructs appear as indented sub-entries.

If a given term occurs more than once in a line, the number of instances is indicated in superscript. Cases in which there is either a translation error, or a problem of transmission, or some other unclarity are indicated by a circumflex.

(*'-b-d*)
abadīy – *matmid* – everlasting **3,2**
(*'-th-r*)
qafā atharahu – *sam megamato* – to pursue **18,11**
ta'thīr – *shinnuy* – affection **22,5**
(*'-j-l*)
al-shay' alladhī min ajlihi – *ha-davar asher ba'avuro* – that for the sake of which **17,16**
(*'-r-ḍ*)
arḍ – *eretz* – earth **2,19^2.21.30.32; 3,3; 14,26**
al-nafs allatī fī al-arḍ – *ha-nefesh asher ba-aretz* –the soul that is in the earth **8,19**
(*'-z-l*)
azalīy – *nitzḥi* – eternal *passim*
(*'-s-r*)
bi-asrihi – *bi-khlalo* – in general **3,23** – as a whole **8,16**
(*'-s-s*)
asās – *shat* – foundation **2,5**
(*'-ṣ-l*)
aṣl – *shoresh* – proposition **12,15**
aṣlān – *kelal* – at all **3,4.10.13.25.27; 22,21**
(*'-l-f*)
ta'līf – *ḥibbur* – combination **1,7^2**
(*'-l-h*)
alla – *(ha-)el* – God **21,8.12.24.25; 29,6.23; 30,25**
al-ilaha al-thawānī – *ha-elohim ha-sheniyim* – secondary god **8,20**
ilāhi – *elohi* – divine **24,32**
al-'aql al-ilāhi – *sekhel elohi* –divine intellect **20,32**
ilahiyya – *elohut* – divinity **27,31**
(*'-m-r*)
amr – *davar* – thing *passim* – *'et* – time **19,18^** – *'inyan* – issue, manner [sometimes not translated, but implied] **2,22.31; 3,22; 8,10; 10,11; 16,30; 23,11** – thing **2,33; 3,7**
(*'-n-s*)
nās – *anashim* – people **2,13.27; 30,26**
(*'-h-l*)
ahl – *anashim* – people **17,29**
(*'-w-l*)
awwal – *rishon* – first *passim* – *hatḥala* – beginning **21,20** – *rosh* – first **1,7** – *reshit* – beginning **2,8** – *teḥila* – first **20,6** – *qodem* – early **2,31**
al-sabab al-awwal – *ha-sibba ha-rishona* – first cause **10,31**
al-samā' al-ūlā – *ha-raqi'a ha-rishon* – first heaven **18,15**
al-'illa al-ūlā – *ha-'illa ha-rishona* – first cause **15,22.23; 18,10; 22,14; 23,8; 25,13; 26,21** – *ha-sibba ha-rishona* – first cause **11,25; 16,31; 17,27; 18,14; 22,14**
al-mabda' al-awwal – *ha-hatḥala ha-rishona* – first principle **10,16; 11,25.27; 13,34; 16,20; 23,4.6; 26,27**

al-muḥarrik al-awwal – *ha-meni'a ha-rishon* – first mover **10,9; 17,15; 25,18.19**
awwalān – *teḥila* – first **1,9.11; 3,30**
awlā – *yoter ra'uy* – more fitting **1,14; 2,14.17** - *qodem* – preceding **25,24** – *yoter na'ot* – better **27,28**
(*b-t-r*)
mabtūr – *nivdal* – cut **13,19**
(*b-ḥ-th*)
baḥatha – *ḥaqar* – to investigate, to enquire **10,14.31; 11,29.30; 27,1**
baḥth – *ḥaqira* – investigation, enquiry **2,9.10^{2}.24**
(*b-kh-l*)
bakhula – *hitrashshel* – to withhold **24,32**
(*b-d-'*)
mabda'– *hatḥala* – principle *passim*
al-mabda' al-awwal – *ha-hatḥala ha-rishona* – first principle **10,16; 11,25.27; 13,34; 16,20; 23,4.6; 26,27**
ibtidā' – *hatḥala* – beginning **11,4** – start **16,31.32**
(*b-d-r*)
bādara – *hishtaddel* – to rush **19,25**
(*b-d-l*)
tabaddala – *humar* – to alternate **2,3**
(*b-d-n*)
badan – *guf* – body **1,5.6.8; 7,29^{2}; 10,26^{2}.27; 19,18; 30,6**
(*b-d-w*)
badā – *nir'a* – to seem **16,29**
(*b-r-'*)
barā' – *riḥuq* – dispensing **28,10**
(*b-r-d*)
bard – *qor* – cold **9,26**
(*b-r-h-n*)
burhān – *mofet* – demonstration **11,24^{2}**
(*b-z-r*)
bizra – *zera'* – seed **8,2.4; 22,3^{2}**
(*b-s-ṭ*)
basīṭ – *pashuṭ* – simple **2,32; 17,2.13; 21,10**
(*b-ṣ-r*)
baṣura – *ra'a* – to see **27,29; 28,28**
baṣar – *re'ut* – vision **2,28; 27,28; 28,27**
(*b-ṭ-l*)
baṭala – *baṭal* – to wither **2,3**
baṭṭāla – *baṭṭala* – idleness **19,23**
(*b-'-d*)
ba'uda – *raḥaq* – to be far **17,29**
ba'īd – *raḥoq* – far **10,32; 11,1^{2}.4**
bu'd ta'līmī – *merḥaq limudi* – mathematical extension **3,20.22**
(*b-'-ḍ*)
ba'ḍ – *qetzaṭ* – some, a few *passim*
ba'ḍuhum ba'ḍān – *qetzaṭam qeṭzat* – each other *passim*
(*b-gh-y*)
yanbaghī – *ra'uy* – must, ought, should **1,14.20; 13,30; 15,15; 20,31**
(*b-q-y*)
baqiya – *nish'ar* – to remain **11,23; 20,18.19**
bāqī – *nish'ar* – remaining (the rest; the other) **2,1.20; 18,11.19; 19,9**
baqā' – *hisha'arut* – lasting **15,24^{2}** – remaining **19,15** – everlastingness **21,25**
muttaṣil al-baqā'– *daveq ha-hisha'arut* – continuously lasting **17,22**
dā'im al-baqā' – *matmid ha-hisha'arut* – perduring **2,28.29** – *temidi ha-hisha'arut* – everlasting **15,21**
(*b-l-gh*)
balagha – *higi'a* – to result **14,28**
bāligh – *muflag* – sufficient **2,25; 3,32**
mablagh – *haga'a* – reach **19,24**
(*b-l-w*)
ablā – *billa* – to wear **11,22**
(*b-n-y*)
mabnīy – *nivna* – founded **3,7**
(*b-w-b*)
bāb – *sha'ar* – realm **9,27**
(*b-w-l*)
khaṭara bi-bāl – *sam be-da'at* – to keep in mind **8,8**
(*b-y-n*)
bāna – *hitba'er* – to be explained **2,9; 13,10**
bayyana – *be'er* – to explain **3,32; 4,3; 9,24**
tabayyana – *hitba'er* – to be explained **22,3.5; 29,23**
bayyin – *mevo'ar* – clear **2,31; 10,11; 21,9; 22,33; 23,26; 29,9**
mubāyin – *nivdal* – distinguished **22,4**
(*t-b-'*)
tabi'a – *nimshakh aḥar* – to follow **2,17; 28,2**
ittaba'a – *himshikh* – to continue **9,24**
(*t-ḥ-t*)
taḥta – *taḥat* – under **2,28; 4,4**
(*t-r-k*)
taraka – *'azav* – to rid **16,3** – to leave **28,2**

(*t-ʿ-b*)
atʿaba - *yiggeʿa* - to tire **27,15**
istatʿaba - *yagaʿ* - to become tired **22,26**
taʿab - *yegiʿa* - tiredness **27,17**; **28,15**
(*t-l-w*)
talā - *nimshakh aḥar* - to follow **1,12**
(*t-m-m*)
atamma - *hishlim* - to accomplish **19,16**
tāmm - *shalem* - perfect **28,8**
tamām - *temimut* - completeness **28,26**
(*th-b-t*)
thabata - *hitqayyem* - to be stable **2,2**; to persist **15,19**
thabbata - *qiyyem* - to affirm **1,21**; **12,18**
thābit - *qayyam* - stable **2,2**
kawkab thābit - *kokhav qayyam* - fixed star **18,15**
(*th-q-l*)
thaqīl - *kaved* - heavy **11,32**; **25,22**
(*j-b-l*)
majbūl - *mugbal* - fashioned **3,30**
(*j-th-th*)
juththa - *guf* - body **8,1**; magnitude **8,15**
(*j-r-y*)
jarā - *ratz* - to flow **3,29**
jārī - *ratz* - flowing **3,29**
(*j-z-ʾ*)
juzʾ - *ḥeleq* - part **1,6.7**; **3,19**; **12,17**
ajzāʾ allatī lā tatajazzaʾu - *ḥalaqim asher lo yitḥalqu* - indivisible particles **14,22.30**
(*j-s-m*)
jism - *geshem* - body *passim*
dhū jism - *baʿal geshem* - corporeal **25,18**
jism samāwī - *geshem shememi* - celestial body **2,29**; **3,5**[2]; **18,25**; **19,3** - *gerem shememi* - celestial body **4,11**
jismāniyya - *gashmut* - corporeality **22,22**
lā yashūbuhu shayʾ min al-jismāniyya - *loʾ yitʿarev bo davar min ha-gashmut* - incorporeal **3,8**
(*j-ʿ-l*)
jaʿala - *sam* - to posit *passim* - to put **20,29** - to consider **4,11** - *hesim* - to posit **2,18.19**
juʿila - *husam* - to be posited **3,6**; **15,15** - to be set **8,6.11.14** - to be considered **27,14**
(*j-m-ʿ*)
ijtamaʿa - *hitqabbetz* - to be collected **2,13**
(*j-m-l*)
jumla - *kelal* - entirety **1,8**; sum **8,23**
bi-l-jumla - *bi-khlal* - generally **22,24**
(*j-n-s*)
jānasa - *hityaḥes* - to have affinity **3,30**
jins - *sug* - genus **1,17**; **2,1.4.5.10.12**; **7,29**
(*j-h-l*)
jahl - *sikhlut* - ignorance **10,6**[2]; **19,23**; **29,8**
(*j-w-z*)
yajūz (*jāza*) - *efshar* (*haya efshar*) - to be possible, can **10,1.2.3.11**
(j-*w-h-r*)
jawhar - *ʿetzem* - substance *passim*
(*ḥ-b-b*)
ḥabba - *ahav* - to love **28,18**
maḥabba - *ahava* - love **14,31**; **28,15.16**
(*ḥ-d-th*)
ḥadatha - *hitḥaddesh*/*nitḥaddesh* - to be created **3,27**; **7,28**; **8,7.20**[2]**.25**; **11,2**; **12,25**[3]; **13,4.5** - to occur **2,3**
ḥadutha - *meḥuddash* - to be created **12,23**[2]
ḥadath - *ḥiddush* - accident **3,25.26** - modification **10,13**; **12,21**
aḥdatha - *ḥiddesh* - to create **8,6**; **12,25**
ḥādith - *ḥiddush* - accident **12,25**
ḥudūth - *ḥiddush* - creation **12,18.32**; **13,6**[2]
(*ḥ-d-d*)
ḥaddada - *higbil* - to limit **23,4**
ḥadd - *geder* - definition **4,7**; **25,1.19** - limit **12,17**
ḥādd - *ḥad* - sharp **28,27**
(*ḥ-dh-r*)
ḥadhira - *nishmar* - to be careful **10,15**
(*ḥ-dh-q*)
ḥidhq - *ʿorma* - skill **8,8.9**
(*ḥ-r-r*)
ḥarr - *ḥom* - hot **9,26**
(*ḥ-r-ḍ*)
ḥarraḍa - *hishtadel* - to strive **18,15**
(*ḥ-r-k*)
ḥarraka - *hiniʿa* - to move [i.e. cause motion] *passim*
taḥarraka - *hitnoʿeʿa* -to be moved *passim*

muḥarrik – *meni'a* – mover **10,8; 11,3; 12,23; 13,22.26; 16,13; 23,8.9.13**
al-muḥarrik al-awwal – *ha-meni'a ha-rishon* – first mover **10,9; 17,15; 25,18.19**
muḥarrik ghayr mutaḥarrik – *meni'a bilti mitno'e'a* – unmoved mover **16,14**
muḥarrik lā yataḥarraku – *meni'a bilti mitno'e'a* – unmoved mover **16,15**
muḥarrik qarīb – *meni'a qarov* – proximate mover **10,4.9**
sabab muḥarrik – *sibba meni'a* – moving cause **10,1.7**
'illa muḥarrika – *sibba meni'a* – moving cause **10,31** – *'illa meni'a* – moving cause **15,17; 24,27**
quwwa muḥarrika – *koaḥ meni'a* – moving power **22,27; 23,18**
taḥrīk – *hana'a* – moving [= causing motion] **13,26.27^{2}; 16,9; 29,5**
ḥaraka – *tenu'a* – motion *passim*
ḥaraka mustaqīma – *tenu'a meqomit* – motion in place **13,15**
mutaḥarriq – *mitno'e'a* – moved *passim*
muḥarrik ghayr mutaḥarrik – *meni'a bilti mitno'e'a* – unmoved mover **16,14**
muḥarrik lā yataḥarraku – *meni'a bilti mitno'e'a* – unmoved mover **16,15**
(*ḥ-s-s*)
ḥiss – *ḥush* – sense, sensing **2,28; 15,28; 19,23; 20,17; 23,7**
ḥāssa – *ḥush* – sense, sensing **2,17; 21,10**
maḥsūs – *muḥash* – sensible, sensory object *passim* – *murgash* – sensible **2,28**
(*ḥ-s-n*)
ḥasan – *ṭov* – good **16,24** – *yafe* – beautiful **17,19**
ḥusn – *yofi* – beauty **17,17**
(*ḥ-ṣ-l*)
taḥṣīl – *haga'a* – obtaining **2,12**
(*ḥ-ṣ-w*)
la yuḥṣā – *lo' yisapper me-rov* – beyond measure **19,20**
(*ḥ-ẓ-ẓ*)
ḥaẓẓ – *ḥeleq* – share **1,16**
(*ḥ-q-q*)
ḥaqq – *emet* – truth **14,28; 17,25**
bi-l-ḥaqīqa – *be-emet* – truly **8,27; 16,24.29; 17,10**
'alā al-ḥaqīqa – *lefi ha-emet* – truly **16,30**
(*ḥ-k-m*)
ḥakama – *shafaṭ* – to judge **10,16**
ḥukm – *mishpaṭ* – judgement **24,30**
(*ḥ-m-d*)
ḥamd – *kavod* – nobility **26,28**
(*ḥ-m-l*)
ḥamala – *nasa'* – to carry **4,5^{2}; 11,32^{2}**
iḥtamala – *nasa'* – to be predicated **10,26**
(*ḥ-n-n*)
ḥanna – *naṭa* – to incline **26,28**
(*ḥ-w-j*)
iḥtāja – *hitzṭarekh* – to need **3,24; 14,1; 15,19.20; 21,2; 28,6** – *hutzrakh* – to enquire into **8,25** – *tzarikh* – need **8,24; 28,27**
iḥtāja fīhi – *haya tzorekh bo* – to be needed **3,23**
ḥāja – *tzorekh* – need **16,3; 29,9**
(*ḥ-w-l*)
aḥāla – *shinna* – to alter **12,27; 13,31**
istaḥāla – *shunna* – to be altered **22,4**
ḥāl – *'inyan* – state **2,28; 3,6.15; 8,13^{3}; 10,18^{2}.19.26; 11,23; 12,25; 15,16^{2}.17.18.19; 21,21** – manner **19,10; 22,29; 23,7^{2}; 26,19; 28,17** – quality **1,11.15; 2,3.8; 4,9** – accident **2,1** – modification **10,14** – *shoresh* **28,2^**
istiḥāla – *hishtanut* – alteration **4,9; 11,23** – *shinnuy* – alteration **3,14; 12,27** – *hitḥalfut* – alteration **13,2**
mustaḥīl – *mishtane* – altering **19,4**
lā maḥāla – *be-lo' safeq* – undoubtedly **10,3; 22,16; 26,32**
(*ḥ-w-y*)
ḥawā – *hiqqif* – to contain **3,10.11**
(*ḥ-y-r*)
kawkab mutaḥayyir – *kokhav navokh* – planet **15,30; 18,19**
(*ḥ-y-y*)
ḥayy – *ḥay* – living **21,13**
ḥayā – *ḥayyim* – life **21,19^{2}.20,21^{2}.22^{3}.23.24.25^{2}; 25,1; 26,32** – *adonei ha-ḥayyim* – living things **21,23**
ḥayawān – *ḥay* – animal **1,8; 8,5.6.7.10; 18,2** – *ba'al ḥayyim* – animal **2,30; 3,3; 7,28; 8,2.3; 16,18**

(*kh-b-r*)
khabbara – *sipper* – to make known **13,4**
(*kh-r-j*)
kharaja – *yatza'* – to be brought out **3,4**; **29,8** – to be distinguished **22,25**
kharaja ilā al-fi'l – *yatza' el ha-po'al* – to be brought into actuality **8,7**; **14,14**; **22,5**; **27,17**
khārij – *ḥutz* – outside **10,1.4**; **20,18.19** – external **21,11**; **27,4** – besides **25,22** – *yotze'* – excluded **3,8** – external **10,29** – without **19,29**
min khārij – *mi-ḥutz* – external **21,2**; **27,11**
mukhrij – *motzi'* – bringer [to actuality] **14,17**
(*kh-s-s*)
khasīs – *paḥut* – inferior **27,14.20.23.26**
(*kh-ṣ-ṣ*)
khaṣṣa – *yiḥḥed* – to make proper **8,3**
khāṣṣ – *meyuḥad* – peculiar **24,32**
khāṣṣiya – *segula* – property **15,26**²
(*kh-ṭ-'*)
khaṭa' – *ṭa'ut* – error **14,22**
(*kh-ṭ-r*)
khaṭara bi-bāl – *sam be-da'at* – to keep in mind **8,8**
(*kh-ṭ-ṭ*)
khaṭṭ – *qav* – line **1,10**
(*kh-f-f*)
khafīf – *qal* – light **25,22**
(*kh-l-ṭ*)
khalaṭa – *'erev* – to mingle **14,30**
ikhtalaṭa – *hit'arev* – to be mixed **20,24**
mukhtaliṭ – *me'orav* – mixed **19,18**
(*kh-l-f*)
takhallafa^ – *haya* – to remain **12,10**
ikhtalafa – *hitḥallef* – to be different **10,28**; **22,22** – to vary **15,19**
khilāf – *ḥiluf* – otherwise **19,14**
bi-makhālif – *mitḥallef* – different **16,29**
mukhtalif – *mitḥallef* – different **3,6**².**7**²; **10,18**²; **19,17**; **21,21** – varying **15,17**²; **16,1**; **18,24**
ikhtilāf – *hitḥalfut* – variation **15,17.20.21**².**26.27**; **19,5** – *ḥiluf* – difference **3,12**
(*kh-l-q*)
akhlaqa bihi- – *ra'uy bo* – to be appropriate for it **9,24.31**
(*kh-l-y*)
lā yakhlū min – *lo' nimlaṭ mi-* – cannot avoid **3,24.33**; **19,21**; **27,1**
(*kh-y-r*)
ikhtāra – *baḥar* – to choose **16,23**; **17,16**
khayr – *ṭov* – good **16,30**²; **30,21**
mukhtār – *nivḥar* – chosen **17,19**
(*kh-y-l*)
takhayyul – *dimyon* – imagination **16,32**; **17,1**
al-mutakhayyil – *ma she-yedumme* – that which is thought of **17,1**
(*d-kh-l*)
dākhil – *nikhnas* – included **25,1**
(*d-r-k*)
adraka – *hissig* – to apprehend **28,21**
(*d-r-y*)
darā – *ḥashav* – to be aware **8,17**
(*d-f-'*)
duf'a – *rega'* – instant **20,27**; **28,7**
duf'atan – *pit'om* – instantly **28,21**
(*d-q-q*)
daqqaqa – *hiflig* – to be meticulous **8,9**
(*d-l-l*)
dalla – *hora* – to indicate **1,17.19**; **3,12**; **8,17**
dalāla – *re'aya* – signification **12,17**
(*d-m*)
dam al-ṭamth – *dam ha-niddot* – blood of the menses **14,26**
(*d-h-r*)
al-dahr kulluhu – *ha-ḥeled kullo* – eternally **11,23**; **12,24**; **19,16**; **21,26**
(*d-w-r*)
adara – *sovev* – to turn **22,15**
mustadīr – *'al ha-sibuv* – circular **13,15.21**
(*d-w-m*)
dāma – *hitmid* – to perdure **22,24.26**
dā'im – *temidi* – everlasting **13,26.27**; **14,30**; **15,15**; **19,20**; **21,19.24.25**; **23,12**; **25,1** – *matmid* – everlasting **15,20**; **21,24.26** – persisting **10,18**; **12,4**; **22,16**
dā'im al-baqā' – *temidi ha-hisha'arut* – everlasting **15,21** – *matmid ha-hisha'arut* – perduring **2,28.29**
dawām – *temidut* – everlastingness **15,22** – perdurance **22,24** – constancy **27,16**
(*dh-k-r*)
dhakara – *zakhar* – to mention **4,11**
adhkara – *hizkir* – to recall **2,24** – *zakhar* – to state **4,7**

dhikr – *zikaron* – memory **28,6**
idhkār – *hazkara* – recall **2,24**
(*dh-w*)
dhāt – *'atzmut* – essence, substantiality *passim*
(*r-'-s*)
ra'īs – *rosh* – leader **26,1**
(*r-'-y*)
ra'ā – *ra'a* – to see **7,29².30²; 8,22; 15,29; 16,22; 26,29** – to think **8,19.20** – to perceive **16,28; 21,2** – *yada'* – to know **21,14** – *savar* – to maintain **27,34**
ru'iya – *nir'a* – to be apparent **22,23**
ra'y – *sevara'* – thought **19,24**
(*r-b-b*)
rubbamā – *pe'amim* – sometimes **10,22².27²**
(*r-t-b*)
tartīb – *sedder* – order **17,25.27; 18,12; 21,12; 30,21**
martaba – *madrega* – rank **8,19; 18,17**
(*r-j-w*)
rajā' – *tiqva* – hope **19,26**
(*r-kh-w*)
istirkhā' – *rifyon* – weariness **27,17**
(*r-ṭ-b*)
ruṭūba – *laḥut* – moisture **10,21**
(*r-gh-b*)
raghiba – *ratza* – to impel **12,26**
(*r-f-'*)
rufi'a – *histalleq* – to be removed **30,4**
raf' – *salleq* – discard **7,28**
(*r-q-q*)
raqqa – *herekh* – to be rarefied **2,33**
(*r-k-b*)
tarakkaba – *hitrakkev* – to be composed **17,13**
tarkīb – *harkava* – composition – **1,6²; 7,15; 8,12; 17,15; 29,7** – compositeness **17,6**
murakkab – *murkav* – composed, composite **2,31; 10,24.25.28; 16,11**
(*r-k-n*)
rukn – *yesod* – element **2,5.7.20.21** – *shat* – foundation **2,31**
(*r-w-ḥ*)
rāḥa – *menuḥa* – rest **22,16**
(*r-w-ḍ*)
al-riyāḍa bi-l-manṭiq – *ḥokhmat^ ha-higayon* – logical exercise **2,14**
(*z-'-m*)
za'ama – *kivven* – to claim **3,9**
(*z-m-n*)
zamān – *zeman* – time *passim*
(*z-w-l*)
zāla – *sar* – to cease **11,22; 12,22; 21,17**
(*z-y-d*)
ziyāda – *tosefet* – elevation **19,24**
(*s-b-b*)
sabab – *sibba* – cause **9,32; 12,29; 13,4; 15,15.24; 17,25; 21,12; 25,16; 27,12.12.14**
al-sabab al-awwal – *ha-sibba ha-rishona* – first cause **10,31**
al-sabab allatī lahu – *ha-sibba asher ba'avura* – cause for the sake of which **13,4**
sabab muḥarrik – *sibba meni'a* – moving cause **10,1.7**
(*s-b-l*)
sabīl – *derekh* – path **19,17**– *tzad* – [signifying adverbial language] **28,20**
'alā sabīl – *'al derekh* – as **26,28**
(*s-r-r*)
sarra – *samaḥ* – to be delighted **19,29**
surūr – *ḥedva* – joy **19,20** – *simḥa* – joy **19,29** – *sason* – joy **20,2**
(*s-ṭ-ḥ*)
saṭḥ – *sheṭaḥ* – surface **9,28**
(*s-'-d*)
musta'idd – *mezumman* – suitable **8,6**
(*s-k-r*)
askara – *naḥ* – to be intoxicating **10,21^**
(*s-k-n*)
sakana – *'amad* – to stop **13,18**
sākin – *naḥ* – stationary **13,30**
sukūn – *menuḥa* – rest **13,4.5; 16,7.9**
(*s-l-ṭ*)
mutasalliṭ – *shaliṭ* – controller **27,5**
(*s-l-k*)
salaka – *halakh* – to proceed **8,10**
maslak – *mahalakh* – course **8,10**
(*s-m-w*)
sammā – *qara'* – to call **4,8**
ism – *shem* – term **12,18**
samā' – *shamayim* – heaven **19,15**
al-samā' al-ūlā – *ha-raqi'a ha-rishon* – first heaven **18,15**
jism samāwī – *geshem shememi* – celestial body **2,29; 3,5²; 18,25; 19,3** – *gerem shememi* – celestial body **4,11**

(*s-w-s*)
siyāsa – *hadrakha* – administration **17,18**
siyāsat al-madīna – *hadrakhat ha-medina* – political administration **17,29**; **25,25**
(*s-w-q*)
sawwāq – *molikh* – directing **8,16**
mustāq – *mishtoqeq*^ – to be directed **8,21**
(*s-y-l*)
sayyāl – *niggar* – liquid **3,29**
(*sh-b-ʿ*)
shabiʿa – *nimnaʿ* – to be surfeited **28,16**[2]
(*sh-b-h*)
tashabbaha – *hiddama* – to resemble **18,15**
ashbahu – *dome* – similar **1,11.20** – like **1,16**; **2,4**
(*sh-t-t*)
shattā – *rav* – many **1,3**
(*sh-d-d*)
ashaddu – *gadol* – bigger **29,5**
(*sh-r-f*)
sharaf – *gedula* – eminence **27,24.26**; **28,12** – *kavod* – nobility **19,24** – *maʿala* – veneration **26,28**
sharīf – *nikhbad* – venerable **3,24**; **8,19**; **21,21**; **27,12** – superior **14,23**
(*sh-r-k*)
ishtaraka – *hishtattef* – to share **3,5**
mushāraka – *shittuf* – [something in] common **3,16.25**
(*sh-gh-l*)
mutashāghil – *ṭared* – preoccupied **19,18**
(*sh-k-l*)
shakl – *temuna* – shape **1,10.13**
mushākil – *mitdamme* – proper **4,1**
mushākala – *hiddamut* – resemblance **3,31**
(*sh-n-ʿ*)
shanāʿa – *dibba* – absurdity **28,3**
(*sh-h-d*)
shahida – *hiʿid* – to testify **2,6**; **15,28**; **23,7**
(*sh-h-w*)
shahwa – *taʾava* – appetite **16,31**
(*sh-w-b*)
(lā) tashūbuhu al-hayūlā – *(loʾ) yitʿarev bo ha-hiyuli* – (im)material **20,20**; **22,31**
(lā) yashūbuhu shayʾ min al-hayūlā – *(loʾ) yitʿarev bo davar min ha-hiyuli* – (im)material **14,7**; **16,14**
lā yashūbuhu shayʾ min al-jismāniyya – *loʾ yitʿarev bo davar min ha-gashmut* – incorporeal **3,8**
(*sh-w-q*)
tashawwaqa – *hitʾavva* – to fancy **16,24** – to have appetite **18,11** – *ḥashaq* – to desire **17,18**
(*sh-y-ʾ*)
shayʾ – *davar* – thing *passim*
al-shayʾ alladhī min ajlihi – *ha-davar asher baʿavuro* – that for the sake of which **17,16**
(lā) yashūbuhu shayʾ min al-hayūlā – *(loʾ) yitʿarev bo davar min ha-hiyuli* – (im)material **14,7**; **16,14**
lā yashūbuhu shayʾ min al-jismāniyya – *loʾ yitʿarev bo davar min ha-gashmut* – incorporeal **3,8**
(*ṣ-ḥ-b*)
ṣāḥib – *baʿal* – author **7,28**
(*ṣ-r-ḥ*)
ṣarraḥa – *ratza* – to mean **14,29**
taṣrīḥ – *beʾur* – assertion **10,13**
(*ṣ-gh-r*)
ṣaghīr – *qaṭan* – small **8,1**
(*ṣ-f-ḥ*)
taṣaffaḥa – *ʿavar* – to go over **28,2.6**; **29,7**
(*ṣ-n-ʿ*)
ṣanʿ – *umanut* – artistry **8,12.14**
ṣāniʿ – *uman* – artisan **30,5**
ṣināʿa – *umanut* – art **30,6**
ṣināʿat al-ṭibb – *melekhet ha-refuʾa* – art of medicine **30,6**
ṣināʿa ʿamaliyya – *umanut maʿasit* – productive art **30,4**
(*ṣ-n-f*)
ṣinf – *min* – kind **4,6**
(*ṣ-w-b*)
aṣāba– *amar emet* – to be correct **22,12**
ṣawāb – *yashar* – correct **2,22** – *yosher* – correctness **3,15**; **10,13**
(*ṣ-w-t*)
ṣawt – *qol* – sound **4,2**[2]
(*ṣ-w-r*)
ṣūra – *tzura* – form *passim* – Idea **3,20.22**; **7,27**; **13,29**; **22,34**
muwāfiq fī al-ṣūra – *naʾot ba-tzura*

– to have the same form **10,31; 11,3**
(*ṣ-y-r*)
ṣāra – *haya* – to be – **8,3.13.21; 15,26.27; 19,26; 26,31; 27,9** – *baḥar* – to let **3,30** – *shav* – to come **19,26**
(*ḍ-d-d*)
ḍidd – *hefekh* – contrary **3,33^2; 4,1^2.4^2.5.12^2**
taḍādd – *hipukh* – contrariety **4,13**
(*ḍ-r-b*)
ḍarb – *min* – type **4,13**
muḍṭarib – *mevulbal* – confused **14,31**
(*ḍ-r-r*)
uḍṭurra – *hitzṭarekh* – to be compelled **14,29**
ḍurūra – *hekhreaḥ* – necessity **19,12.14.15**
ḍurūratan – *be-hekhreaḥ* – necessarily **19,10**
yajibu ḍurūratan – *yitḥayyev be-hekhreaḥ* – follows necessarily **15,21; 16,14** – must necessarily **23,8.10** – *ra'uy be-hekhreaḥ* – should necessarily **2,25; 15,23** – must necessarily **4,3** – follows necessarily **13,25**
ḍurūrī – *hekhreḥi* – necessary **13,17; 24,30**
(*ḍ-ʿ-f*)
ḍaʿīf – *ḥalush* – weak **14,3; 29,7**
taḍāʿuf – *kefel* – multiplicity **17,15**
(*ḍ-w-'*)
ḍaw' – *or* – light **9,28.29; 10,25**
(*ḍ-y-f*)
iḍāfa – *semikhut* – relationship **1,16**
(*ṭ-b-b*)
ṣināʿat al-ṭibb – *melekhet ha-refu'a* – art of medicine **30,6**
(*ṭ-b-ʿ*)
ṭabʿ – *ṭevaʿ* – nature **3,17.29; 28,9**
ṭabīʿa – *ṭevaʿ* – nature *passim*
ṭabīʿī – *ṭivʿi* – natural **10,4; 11,19; 22,13**
al-ʿilm al-ṭabīʿī – *ha-ḥokhma ha-ṭivʿit* – natural science **3,23.25**
kitāb al-ʿilm al-ṭabīʿī – *sefer ha-ḥokhma ha-ṭivʿit* – *Physics* **3,32**
(*ṭ-b-q*)
inṭabaqa – *neḥtam* – to be imprinted **20,18**
(*ṭ-r-ḥ*)
iṭṭaraḥa – *hishlikh* – to cast **19,19**
(*ṭ-r-f*)
ṭaraf – *qatze* – extreme point **22,21**
ṭurfat ʿayn – *heref ʿayin* – instant **19,21**
(*ṭ-r-q*)
ʿalā ṭarīq – *ʿal derekh* – in a sense **9,24.30; 11,2^2.3**
(*ṭ-l-b*)
ṭalaba – *biqqesh* – to enquire into **2,6.25^2; 11,22; 16,3** – to seek **11,10.18; 21,3**
ṭuliba – *buqqash* – to be enquired into **2,11.31**
ṭalab – *baqasha* – enquiry **1,3.4; 2,7; 9,31.32; 10,9^2; 11,21**
(*ṭ-l-q*)
muṭlaqān – *ba-muḥlaṭ* – absolutely **19,14**
ʿalā al-iṭlāq – *ba-muḥlaṭ* – absolutely **9,30**
(*ṭ-m-th*)
dam al-ṭamth – *dam ha-niddot* – blood of the menses **14,26**
(*ẓ-l-m*)
ẓulma – *ḥoshekh* – darkness **9,28; 10,25; 14,19**
(*ẓ-n-n*)
ẓanna – *ḥashav* – to presume **3,22**
ẓann – *maḥshava* – thought **16,32; 17,1**
maẓnūn – *davar she-ḥoshvim bo* – thing that is thought of **17,1**
(*ʿ-j-b*)
ʿajab – *pele'* – puzzlement **1,17; 8,16; 12,5; 18,10** – admiration **8,8**; wonder **21,8.9** – *tema* – marvel **29,5**
taʿajjub – *lehipale'* – to be puzzled **16,15**
(*ʿ-d-d*)
ʿaddada – *mana* – to count **4,6**
ʿadad – *mispar* – number **1,9.13; 2,12.33; 23,18.19; 24,24.25.27^3.28; 25,16.19**
(*ʿ-d-m*)
ʿadam – *heʿader* – privation **9,25.26.27.29; 10,6; 11,3; 19,23**
(*ʿ-r-ḍ*)
ʿaraḍ – *ḥiddush* – accident **3,17^2** – *miqre* – accident **1,20.25; 2,2^2; 10,16; 12,5; 13,13; 21,10**
bi-l-ʿaraḍ – *be-miqre* – accidentally **23,9.11**
(*ʿ-r-f*)
ʿurifa – *nodaʿ* – to be known **4,7**
maʿrifa – *yediʿa* – knowledge **29,8**
taʿarruf – *yediʿa* – to know **23,14**

(ʿ-r-y)
taʿarrā – *ʿarum* – to be naked **2,1**
(ʿ-sh-q)
ʿashiqa – *ḥashaq* – to desire **18,15.16**
ʿāshiq – *ḥosheq* – desirer **16,19**; **26,29**; **28,18**
maʿshūq – *ḥashuq* – desired, object of desire **16,16.17.18.19.20.21.22**^{2}**.28**; **18,14**; **26,29**
ʿishq – *ḥesheq* – desire **16,28**; **25,25** – *teshuqa* – passion **16,31**
(ʿ-ḍ-w)
ʿuḍw – *ever* – organ **1,5**
(ʿ-ṭ-l)
ʿuṭl – *baṭel* – idle **24,32**
mutʿaṭṭal – *baṭel* – idle **13,30**
(ʿ-ẓ-m)
ʿiẓam – *godel* – magnitude **22,7.16.22.31**
(ʿ-f-n)
ʿafan – *ʿippush* – putrescence **7,30**
(ʿ-q-b)
taʿāqaba – *baʾ ze be-ʿeqev ze* – to succeed one another **2,3**
(ʿ-q-l)
ʿaqala – *hiskil* – to intelligize *passim*
ʿuqila – *huskal* – to be intelligized **16,30**^{2}; **28,19**
ʿāqil – *maskil* – intelligizer **27,10**
maʿqūl – *muskal* – intelligible, object of intellect *passim*
ʿaql – *sekhel* – intellect *passim*
al-ʿaql al-ilāhī – *ha-sekhel ha-elohi* – the divine intellect **20,32**
(ʿ-l-q)
muʿallaq – *nitla* – dependent **22,13** – *taluy* – dependent **19,15**
(ʿ-l-l)
ʿilla – *sibba* – cause **1,32**; **11,1.2.4.24.25**; **13,23.24**; **14,29**; **15,22.27**; **30,12** – *ʿilla* – cause **15,16.19.22.23**^{2}**.24.26**^{2}; **22,21**; **27,12**
al-ʿilla al-ūlā – *ha-sibba ha-rishona* – first cause **11,25**; **16,31**; **17,27**; **18,14**; **22,14** – *ha-ʿilla ha-rishona* – first cause **15,22.23**; **18,10**; **22,14**; **23,8**; **25,13**; **26,21**
ʿilla muḥarrika – *sibba meniʿa* – moving cause **10,31** – *ʿilla meniʿa* – moving cause **15,17**; **24,27**
ʿilla fāʿila – *ʿilla poʿelet* – efficient cause **15,20**
(ʿ-l-m)
ʿalima – *yadaʿ* – to know **8,2.25**; **29,24**
ʿulima – *nodaʿ* – to be known **3,28**
ʿālim – *ḥakham* – sage **26,25**
maʿlūm – *yaduʿa* – known [thing] **28,20**
ʿilm – *ḥokhma* – science **3,24** – knowledge **17,26.27**; **19,17.21**; **26,25** – *yediʿa* – knowledge **21,1** – *sevaraʾ* – science **3,28**
al-ʿilm al-ṭabīʿī – *ha-ḥokhma ha-ṭivʿit* – natural science **3,23**; **3,25**
kitāb al-ʿilm al-ṭabīʿī – *sefer ha-ḥokhma ha-ṭivʿit* – *Physics* **3,32**
ʿilm al-nujūm – *ḥokhmat ha-kokhavim* – astronomy **23,15**
ʿālam – *ʿolam* – world **14,19**; **17,25**; **25,13.20**; **29,4**
buʿd taʿlīmī – *merḥaq limudi* – mathematical extension **3,20.22**
(ʿ-l-y)
aʿlā – *ʿelyon* – higher **8,19**
(ʿ-m-l)
ʿamala – *ʿasa* – to work **8,8.9.11**^{2}**.15.16**
istaʿmala – *hitʿasseq* – to be preoccupied **2,13**; to exercise **26,25** – *ʿasa* – to employ **12,18**
ʿamal – *maʿase* – work **8,15**; **30,5** – *ʿasiyya* – making **8,8**
ṣināʿa ʿamaliyya – *umanut maʿasit* – productive art **30,4**
(ʿ-m-m)
ʿāmīy – *kolel* – general **2,14.15.16.19.20**^{3}**.23**; **14,22**
(ʿ-n-d)
ʿānada – *ḥalaq* – to confront **21,10**
(ʿ-n-ṣ-r)
unṣur – *yesod* – element **2,31**; **10,23.28** – matter **9,25.26.28**; **10,22.23.24.26.28**^{2}**.29.30**; **11,2**; **25,16**; **30,4**^{2} – *ḥomer* – matter **8,7**
(ʿ-n-y)
ʿanā – *ratza* – to mean **10,23**^{2}; **13,31**
maʿanā – *ʿinyan* – meaning **1,5**; attribute **11,29**
(ʿ-h-d)
qarībat al-ʿahd – *qerovat ha-zeman* – recent **2,17**
(ʿ-w-q)
ʿāqa – *hiʿiq* – to impede **12,26**
(ʿ-y-n)
ʿayn – *ʿayin* – eye **28,27**
ṭirfati ʿayn – *heref ʿayin* – instant **19,21**

bi-ʿaynihi – *be-ʿeino* – itself, one and the same **1,20.23; 2,2²; 8,10; 9,30; 10,20; 15,18.30; 16,22; 17,13; 27,3; 28,3** – *be-nefesh* – itself **21,22**
ʿiyān – *ʿiyyun* – seeing **1,25**
(*gh-r-b*)
gharīb – *nokhri* – foreign **21,11**
(*gh-r-ḍ*)
gharaḍ – *kavvana* – aim **3,17; 8,21²** – end **8,16**
(*gh-r-q*)
ghariqa fī al-nawm – *shaquʿa be-shena* – to be sound asleep **26,28**
(*gh-f-l*)
aghfala – *hiqsha* – to neglect **7,28^**
(*gh-l-b*)
ghalaba – *nitztzaḥon* – strife **14,31**
(*gh-l-y*)
ghallā – *hirtiaḥ* – to ferment **10,21**
(*gh-w-y*)
ghāya – *takhlit* – [as superlative] **18,16; 20,13.23; 27,24; 28,26** – boundary **3,11; 22,19**
ghāya quṣwā – *takhlit aḥaron* – ultimate **17,17**
fī / ʿalā ghāyat al-faḍīla – *be-takhlit / ʿal takhlit ha-maʿala* – utmost best, utmost excellence **17,19; 19,15; 21,1.2.20.25; 27,9².31; 28,13**
(*gh-y-r*)
aghāra – *zilzel* – to deceive **8,7^**
taghayyara – *hishtanna* – to be changed **2,29; 13,5; 22,5**
ghayr – *zulat* – other *passim*
taghayyur – *shinnuy* – change **3,3.4.8.28.33²; 4,6.7.8.9.11²; 11,23; 13,2; 18,25; 19,4**
mutaghayyir – *mishtanne* – changing **3,13.29.33**
(*f-t-r*)
futūr – *menuḥa* – resting **13,2**
(*f-r-ḥ*)
faraḥ – *simḥa* – delight **19,20; 20,2**
(*f-r-d*)
farada – *nifrad* – to be distinct **3,10**
afrada – *hifrid* – to separate **1,24.25; 11,29**
infarada – *nifrad* – to be separated **10,24.25**
mufrad – *nifrad* – particular **2,13.14.15.18.23** – distinct **3,9².12.16** – apart **16,12²** – separate **22,24**
mufradān – *be-yiḥud* – separately **11,29**
munfarid – *nifrad* – separate **10,24**
(*f-r-ḍ*)
faraḍa – *teʾer* – to prescribe **14,31**
(*f-r-gh*)
farāgh – *penaʾi* – leisure **19,18**
(*f-r-q*)
firq – *hefresh* – difference **2,9**
farīq – *kat* – group **2,22**
mutafarriq – *mefuzzar* – dispersed **1,7**
(*f-s-d*)
fasada – *nifsad* – to perish **3,4; 12,6.10**
fasād – *hefsed* – perishing **4,9; 12,9.11.13; 15,20**
qābil/yaqbalu li-l-fasād – *meqabbel/ yeqabbel ha-hefsed* – capable of perishing, perishable **2,30; 10,19; 11,34.35; 18,20; 22,23**
(*f-ḍ-l*)
afḍal – *yoter ṭov* – better **8,13** – *baʿal maʿala* – noble **30,25**
faḍīl – *nikhbad* – superior **13,24; 27,19** – best **19,22; 20,2.3; 21,23²** – *naʿale* – best **21,20** – superior **27,11**
faḍīla – *maʿala* – excellence **17,17; 19,24**
fī / ʿalā ghāyat al-faḍīla – *be-takhlit / ʿal takhlit ha-maʿala* – utmost best, utmost excellence **17,19; 19,15; 21,1.2.20.25; 27,9².31; 28,13**
(*f-ʿ-l*)
faʿala – *ʿasa* – to act, to do **8,17.21²; 19,30; 26,24.27**
fāʿil – *poʿel* – active **26,24**
ʿilla fāʿila – *ʿilla poʿelet* – efficient cause **15,20**
fiʿl – *poʿal* – actuality, activity *passim* – *peʿula* – action, activity *passim*
bi-l-fiʿl – *ba-poʿal* – actually, in actuality *passim*
kharaja ilā al-fiʿl – *yatzaʾ el ha-poʿal* – to be brought into actuality **8,7; 14,14; 22,5; 27,17**
infiʿāl – *hipaʿalut* – affection **2,4**
(*f-k-r*)
fakkara – *hiskil* – to think **8,17**

(*f-l-k*)
falak – *galgal* – sphere **15,29.30; 16,8; 18,15.19**[2]**; 24,23; 25,25**
al-falak al-mā'il – *ha-galgal ha-noṭe* – the inclined sphere **8,20; 11,1**
(*f-h-m*)
fahima – *hevin* – to understand **8,16.21.22**
fahm – *havana* – understanding **19,19**
(*f-w-z*)
fāza – *hissig be-shelemut* – to completely attain **25,1**
(*f-y-ḍ*)
istafāda – *qana* – to acquire **18,16.17; 27,26.28; 28,11**
istifāda – *qeniyya* – acquiring **22,27; 28,6**
(*q-b-ḍ*)
inqabaḍa – *niqwatz* – to contract **2,33**
(*q-b-l*)
qabila – *qibbel* – to receive, to admit [sometimes explicates susceptibility] **3,3**[2]**.13.28; 4,6; 10,19; 11,23.33.35; 18,20; 22,5.23**[2]**, 28,2.21**
qābil – *meqabbel* – receiver, [explication of susceptibility] **2,29; 9,29**
qābil/yaqbalu al-kawn – *meqabbel/yeqabbel ha-haviya* – to receive coming-to-be **10,19; 18,20**
qābil/yaqbalu li-l-fasād – *meqabbel/yeqabbel ha-hefsed* – capable of perishing, perishable **2,30; 10,19; 11,34.35; 18,20; 22,23**
qabla – *qodem* – prior **3,21; 11,34**; before **13,1**
muqābala – *hitnagdut* – opposition **4,13**
(*q-d-r*)
qadara – *yakhol* – to be within one's power **12,26.27**
qādir – *yakhol* – capable **13,31**[2]
qudra – *yekholet* – ability **17,25**
miqdār – *shi'ur* – quantity **1,11.15; 2,3.8; 4,9; 12,21; 22,6**[2]
(*q-d-m*)
taqaddama – *hiqdim* – to prescribe **23,4** – *qadam* – to be prior **1,12.13** – to precede, to be earlier **13,5; 22,26**
aqdam – *yoter qodem* – before **12,10** – prior **14,29**– *qodem* – prior **14,23**
muqaddama – *haqdama* – premise **29,9**
mutaqaddim – *qodem* – prior **1,12**
(*q-r-b*)
qariba – *qarav* – to be close **17,28.29; 18,14**
qarīb – *qarov* – proximate, close **4,1; 10,32**[2]**; 11,3.4; 16,22; 18,16.17**
muḥarrik qarīb – *meni'a qarov* – proximate mover **10,4.9**
qarībat al-'ahd – *qerovat ha-zeman* – recent **2,17**
(*q-r-r*)
aqarra – *hoda* – to acknowledge **14,29**
(*q-r-n*)
maqrūn – *meḥubbar* – linked **12,17**
(*q-s-m*)
qassama – *ḥilleq* – to divide **3,19.20; 11,32**
munqasim – *mitḥalleq* – divisible **22,6**
(*q-ṣ-d*)
qaṣada – *kivven* – to set out **1,4; 2,6.7.8.24; 10,31; 23,14** – *konen* – to set out **1,3**
maqṣūd – *kavvana* – a thing aimed at **22,20** – *mekhuvvan* – aimed at **8,17**; end **19,13**
qaṣd – *kavvana* – intention **2,8; 9,32; 10,8.9**
(*q-ṣ-ṣ*)
iqtaṣṣa – *sipper* – to relate accurately **3,18**
(*q-ṣ-w*)
aqṣā – *aḥaron* – ultimate **17,17**
ghāya quṣwā – *takhlit aḥaron* – ultimate **17,17**
(*q-ḍ-w*)
inqiḍā' – *gemar* – completion **22,25** – *takhlit* – ending **21,20**
(*q-ṭ-'*)
qaṭa'a – *hifsiq* – to interrupt **20,4**
inqaṭa'a – *nifsaq* – to stop **13,16**
qiṭ' – *ḥatikha* – segment **13,19**
inqiṭā' – *hefseq* – interruption **15,20; 16,9**
(*q-f-w*)
qafā atharahu – *sam megamato* – to pursue **18,11**
(*q-l-l*)
aqall – *me'aṭ* – fewer **2,33** – *paḥut* – least **2,34**
(*q-n-'*)
muqni' – *maspiq* – persuasive **7,27**
(*q-w-d*)
qā'id – *moshel* – commander **18,8**
(*q-w-l*)
qīla lahu – *niqra'* – to be called **4,9.10**

qawl – *ma'amar* – statement, discussion, argument, etc. *passim*
(*q-w-m*)
qāma – *'amad* – to stand **2,12**; to be constituted **11,24**
qāma fī wahm – *'amad ba-maḥshava* – *to keep in mind* **10,31**
qā'im – *'omed* – subsisting **16,12**^{2}
qiwām – *'amida* – constitution **12,1**; **19,16**; **29,25**
qawm – *anashim* – people **8,22**
mustaqīm – *yashar* – straight **1,10.22**^{2}**.23.24** – *'al ha-yosher* – rectilinear **13,15**
ḥaraka mustaqīma – *tenu'a meqomit* – motion in place **13,15**
(*q-w-y*)
qawiyy – *ḥazaq* – strong **11,4**; **12,29**; **24,30**
quwwa – *koaḥ* – potentiality **13,32**; **14,2.16**; **27,8.17** – power **14,28**; **22,7.12**^{2}**.14.17.28**; **23,14**; **29,6** – capacity **19,17**
bi-l-quwwa – *ba-koaḥ* – potentially, in potentiality *passim*
quwwa muḥarrika – *koaḥ meni'a* – moving power **22,27**; **23,18**
(*q-y-s*)
qāsa – *hiqqish* – to compare **29,6**
qāyasa – *hiqqish* – to compare **14,16**
qiyās – *heqesh* – analogy **9,28** – respect **15,16** – reason **23,7**
muqāyasa – *heqesh* – comparison **9,31**
(*k-b-r*)
akbar – *gadol* – bigger **8,10**
(*k-th-r*)
kathīr – *rav* –many, multiple, manifold *passim*
kathra – *ribbui* – plurality **22,32** – great number **7,28**; large amount **20,24**; abundance **21,9**; number **23,14**; many **25,16** – multifold **29,6**
akthar –*rov* –most **3,30**; **19,18** – more **21,9**
(*k-r-m*)
karīm – *nadiv* – noble **8,18**
(*k-s-b*)
muktasab – *niqna* – gained **19,21**
(*k-f-y*)
iktifā' – *sippuq* – self-sufficiency **28,5**
(*k-l-l*)
kullīy – *klali* – universal **2,16**
(*k-l-m*)
kalām – *dibbur* – discussion **3,17.32**; **22,33** – talk **8,22**
(*k-m-l*)
kamala – *hishlim* – to perfect **28,3.4**^{2}**.5.8**^{2}
kamāl – *shelemut* – perfection **17,16.17.30**; **28,26**
(*k-m-m*)
kamm – *kamma* – number **2,10.11**; **4,6**
(*k-m-n*)
kāmin – *ṭamun* – latent **8,26.27**
(*k-n-z*)
iktanaza – *hitqasha* – to become dense **3,1**
(*k-w-k-b*)
kawkab – *kokhav* – star **22,11.12.17.27**^{2}**.29**
kawkab mutaḥayyir – *kokhav navokh* – planet **15,30**; **18,19**
kawkab thābit – *kokhav qayyam* – fixed star **18,15.19**
(*k-w-n*)
kāna – *haya* – to be *passim*
kā'in – *hove* – a thing that comes-to-be **12,10**
kawn – *haviya* – coming-to-be **4,9**; **12,8.10.13**; **15,20**
qābil/yaqbalu al-kawn – *meqabbel/yeqabbel ha-haviya* – to receive coming-to-be **10,19**; **18,20**
makān – *makom* – place **2,4**; **3,4.9.10**^{2}**.11.26**; **4,10**^{3}**.12**^{2}**.13**; **18,25**; **22,18.19**^{2}**.28**
(*k-y-f*)
kayfa – *eikh* –how **12,23**; **14,23**; **22,22** – *eikhut* – quality **9,27**
(*l-'-m*)
mulā'im – *na'ot* – proper **8,7**
(*l-b-th*)
labitha – *'amad* – to remain **28,8**
(*l-b-s*)
lābasa – *lavash* – to be in contact **20,15**
(*l-ḥ-q*)
laḥiqa – *hissig* – to happen **28,13**
(*l-dh-dh*)
ladhdha – *hana'a* – pleasure **19,21.22** – *'arevut* – pleasantness **19,28**; **20,32**
ladhīdh – *'arev* – pleasant **16,23**; **19,22.23.25.26**
(*l-z-m*)
lazima– *hitḥayyev* – to follow [logically] *passim* – to happen **10,16**

(*l-gh-w*)
alghā - *hiniaḥ* - to give up **3,22**
(*l-f-ẓ*)
lafaẓa - *hifshiṭ* - to shed **4,5**
lafẓa - *milla* - word **1,17**²**.19**²**.20.24** - utterance **12,15.16**
(*l-h-m*)
ulhima - *huzkar* - to be inspired **8,18.22**
ilhām - *hazkara* - inspiration **8,18**
(*l-w-n*)
lawn - *mar'e* - colour **4,3**
(*m-th-l*)
mathal - *dimyon* - like **7,28; 8,24**²; **19,14**
mithl - *dome* - like **8,2** - the same **10,4**
(*m-d-d*)
mudda - *midda* - time period **19,16.19**
bi-lā mudda - *be-lo' shi'ur* - immeasurable **28,7**
mādda - *ḥomer* - matter **14,24; 25,16**
(*m-d-n*)
madīna - *medina* - city **1,7; 18,8**
ahl al-madīna - *anshei ha-medina* - people of the city **17,29**
siyāsat al-mudun - *hadrakhat ha-medinot* - political administration **17,29**
(*m-r-r*)
marra... wa-marra - *pa'am...u-fa'am* - sometimes ... and sometimes *passim*
(*m-s-s*)
tamāssa - *mishshesh* - to touch **1,6**
(*m-'-n*)
am'ana - *heṭiv le'ayen*^ - to continue **2,23**
(*m-k-n*)
yumkin (*amkana*) - *efshar* (*haya efshar*) - to be possible, can *passim*
imkān - *efsharut* - possibility **18,24; 19,8**
(*m-l-k*)
mālik - *molekh* - ruler **29,25**²
(*m-n-'*)
mana'a - *mana'* - to hinder, obstruct, prevent **2,24; 12,24; 19,19; 20,4**
imtana'a - *nimna'* - to be impossible **3,6**
māni' - *mone'a* - hinderer, preventer **2,24; 12,24.28.29; 19,20**
mumtani' - *nimna* - impossible **3,6; 4,11**
(*m-n-y*)
minān - *zera'* -semen **8,4**² - *shikhvat zera'* -semen **8,2**
(*m-w-t*)
amāta - *hemit* - to kill **26,31**
mayt - *met* - dead **7,29.30**
bi-mā'it - *met* - dead **22,6**
(*m-w-h*)
mā' - *mayyim* - water **2,19.21; 4,8**²
(*m-y-l*)
al-falak al-mā'il - *ha-galgal ha-noṭe* - the inclined sphere **8,20; 11,1**
(*n-b-'*)
anba'a - *nibba* - to foretell **8,22**
(*n-b-t*)
anbata - *hitzmiaḥ* - to grow [something] **14,26**
nabāt - *tzemaḥ* - plant **2,30; 3,3; 8,2.3.4**²**.5; 14,27**- *tzomeaḥ* - plant **1,6**
(*n-b-'*)
yanbū' - *mabu'a* - fountainhead **26,32**
(*n-t-j*)
antaja - *holid* - to conclude **29,8**
natīja - *tolada* - conclusion **29,8**
(*n-j-m*)
'ilm al-nujūm - *ḥokhmat ha-kokhavim* - astronomy **23,15**
(*n-ḥ-w*)
naḥw - *derekh* - way **1,9**
'alā naḥw - *'al derekh* - in a way **1,3.8**
(*n-z-l*)
bi-manzila - *be-derekh* / *ke-derekh* - as, like, the same as, etc. **17,15.16; 18,17; 20,23; 21,8; 22,15.19.22** - *'al derekh* - in a manner **11,31**
(*n-s-b*)
nasib - *yaḥas* - *logos* **8,3.5.6.11.14.15.18.23**
nisba - *yaḥas* - relation **19,29**
munāsaba - *yaḥas* - analogy **9,24.31**
(*n-sh-'*)
ansha'a - *bara'* - to originate **8,1**
nushū' - *gidul* - growth **3,26**
(*n-sh-r*)
intashara - *hitpashsheṭ* - to expand **2,34**
(*n-ṭ-q*)
al-riyāḍa bi-l-manṭiq - *ḥokhmat ha-higayon* - logical exercise **2,14**^
(*n-ẓ-r*)
naẓara - *'iyyen* - to theorize **26,23** - *ḥaqar* - to enquire **11,29**^
naẓar - *'iyyun* - theorizing **2,21; 8,9**

naẓīr – *ke-neged* – as **9,26².27².28²** – *dome* – like **4,3** – *dimyon* – counterpart **8,5**
(*n-ẓ-m*)
niẓām – *yosher* – order **17,25.28; 18,11; 21,12; 30,21** – rectitude **18,16**; organization **1,8**
(*n-ʿ-t*)
naʿata – *teʾer* – to describe
nuʿita – *toʾar* – to be described **1,13.14**
(*n-f-s*)
nafs – *nefesh* – soul **10,15; 22,14; 23,11** – essence **28,18; 28,19**
al-nafs allatī fī al-arḍ – *ha-nefesh asher ba-aretz* – the soul that is in the earth **8,19**
nafsuhu – *nafsho* – in itself **28,18**
fī nafsuhu – *be-nefesh* – in itself **10,22**
mutanaffas – *baʿal nefesh* – ensouled **21,14**
(*n-f-ʿ*)
intafaʿa – *hayta toʿelet* – to benefit **13,28**
(*n-f-y*)
nafā – *shalal* – to deny **1,20**
nufiya – *sullaq* – to be removed **27,22**
(*n-q-ṣ*)
naqaṣa – *qatzar* – to fall short **17,30**
nāqiṣ – *ḥaser* – lacking **28,4**
nuqṣān – *ḥissaron* – decrease **4,10**
tanaqquṣ – *ḥissaron* – decline **3,26**
(*n-q-ḍ*)
nāqaḍa – *satar* – to contradict **12,15**
(*n-q-l*)
intaqala – *neʿetaq* – to be transposed **20,23**
naqla – *heʿtteq* – transition **4,10**
muntaqil – *neʿetaq* – transposable **19,5**
intiqāl – *heʿtteq* – transposition **20,27**
(*n-k-r*)
ankara – *hikhḥish* – to deny **29,6**
(*n-m-s*)
nāmūs – *nimus* – law **17,18.21.25; 21,12.13².19; 25,25**
(*n-m-w*)
numuww – *gidul* – increase **4,10**
(*n-h-y*)
nihāya – *takhlit* – periphery **8,15**
bi-ghayr nihāya – *beli takhlit* – unlimited **22,7**
bi-lā nihāya – *be-loʾ takhlit* – unlimited **22,24**
lā nihāya lahu – *ein takhlit lo* – infinite **19,24**; unlimited **22,6.12.13.15.21.26.27; 25,10**
mutanāhan – *baʿal takhlit* – limited **22,7.11.17.28**
(*n-w-r*)
nār – *esh* –fire **2,19².21.32**
(*n-w-ʿ*)
nawʿ – *min* – species **7,30; 8,6²; 13,2**
(*n-w-m*)
nawm – *shena* – sleep **19,23; 26,29**
ghariqa fī al-nawm – *shaquʿa be-shena* – to be sound asleep **26,28**
(*h-r-b*)
haraba – *baraḥ* – to escape **27,28**
(*h-w-y*)
hawāʾ – *avir* – air **2,19.21; 4,8; 10,25**
hāwiyya – *avir* – abyss **14,19^**
(*h-y-ʾ*)
tahayyaʾa – *tukkan* – can **19,20**
mutahayyiʾ – *mukhan* – ready **8,6**
(*h-y-b*)
tahayyub – *ʿatzla* – apprehensiveness **10,13**
(*h-y-l*)
hayūlā – *hiyuli* – matter **14,23.28** – *ḥomer* – matter **25,18**
(lā) tashūbuhu al-hayūlā – *(loʾ) yitʿarev bo ha-hiyuli* – (im)material **20,20; 22,31**
(lā) yashūbuhu shayʾ min al-hayūlā – *(loʾ) yitʿarev bo davar min ha-hiyuli* – (im)material **14,7; 16,14**
(*w-j-b*)
wajaba – *hitḥayyev* – to have to, to follow [logically] *passim*
yajibu – *raʾuy* – must, ought, should *passim*
yajibu ḍurūratan – *yitḥayyev be-hekhreaḥ* – follows necessarily **15,21; 16,14;** must necessarily **23,8.10** – *raʾuy be-hekhreaḥ* – should necessarily **2,25; 15,23**; must necessarily **4,3**; follows necessarily **13,25**
awjaba – *ḥiyyev* – to necessitate **12,27²; 23,11** – *himtziʾ* – to necessitate **23,7^**
bi-l-wājib – *be-hekhreaḥ* – necessarily **15,27**

min al-wājib an – *min ha-meḥuyyav she-* – necessarily **27,15**
(*w-j-d*)
wajada – *matzaʾ* – to find *passim*
wujida – *nimtzaʾ* – to exist, to be *passim*; to be found **17,29**; **27,17**
mawjūd – *nimtzaʾ* – existent, existing [thing] *passim*
wujūd – *metziʾut* – existence **1,12**^{2}**.13.15.16.17.19**; **2,18.23**; **12,4**^{2}; **20,3**
(*w-j-h*)
wajh – *panim* – respect **3,14**; **4,12**
jiha – *tzad* – [signifying adverbial language] **4,13**; **16,16**; **19,4**; **20,27**; **22,28**
(*w-ḥ-d*)
wāḥid – *eḥad* – one *passim*
aḥad – *eḥad* – one *passim*
muttaḥidān – *mitʾaḥed* – united **1,5**
ittiḥād – *hitʾaḥdut* – union **1,5**
(*w-d-ʿ*)
wadaʿa – *ʿazav* – to leave **28,21**
(*w-s-ʿ*)
ittisāʿ – *hitraḥvut* – extension **29,6**
(*w-ṣ-f*)
waṣafa – *hetziʿa* – to suppose **9,24** – *sipper* – to state **4,6**
(*w-ṣ-l*)
muttaṣil – *mitdabbeq* – continuous **13,19.20.21**; **21,26**
muttaṣil al-baqāʾ – *daveq ha-hishaʾarut* – continuously everlasting **17,22**
ittiṣāl – *devequt* – continuity **13,15.17**; **27,15**
(*w-ḍ-ʿ*)
waḍaʿa – *hiniaḥ* – to suppose, to assume, to posit *passim*
mawḍūʿ – *noseʾ* – substratum **4,4**
mawḍiʿ – *makom* – place *passim*
(*w-f-q*)
ittafaqa – *hiskim* – to agree **2,27**
muwāfiq fī al-ṣūra – *naʾot ba-tzura* – to have the same form **10,31**; **11,3**
(*w-q-t*)
waqt – *ʿet* – moment, time *passim*
(*w-q-ʿ*)
awqaʿa – *hipil* – to apply **1,17.19.20.21.23.24**
tawaqqaʿa – *qivva* – to expect **19,26**
wāqiʿ – *nofel* – falling **2,28**
(*w-q-f*)
wuqūf – *ʿamida* – determination **23,14**
(*w-q-y*)
tawaqqā – *nizhar* – to be cautious **10,16**
(*w-l-d*)
walada – *holid* – to beget **10,5.8**; **21,11** – to birth **14,19**
tawallada – *hityalled* – to be begotten **7,29**^{2}**.30**; **8,1.3**^{2}**.5.12.24**^{2}; **10,21.23**
muwālid – *molid* – begetting **8,27**
tawallud – *huledet* – to be begotten **8,24**
(*w-h-m*)
tawahhama – *dimma* – to consider **3,13** – *ḥashav* – to think **3,18.19** – to consider **3,15**; **20,31**
tuwuhhima – *dumma* – to be imagined **12,24**; to be thought **22,22**
wahm – *maḥshava* – thought **1,25**; **2,12**
qāma fī wahm – *ʿamad ba-maḥshava* – to keep in mind **10,31**
wahmī – *maḥshavi* – according to thought **10,5**
(*y-s-r*)
yasīr – *qaṭan* – brief **19,19**

Subject Index

References are to page numbers in this volume. Readers are referred to the other indexes for an expansive list of terms and their specific occurrences in Themistius' text.

'Abd al-Laṭīf al-Baghdādī 10, 20n39, 95n165, 98n202, 104n267, 105n271, 105n275, 108n319, 111n357, 112n378, 112n379, 113n380
Abū Bishr Mattā 18n33, 89n103
accident, accidental 26, 28–9, 39, 42–4, 56, 58–9, 70; *see also* modification
Achard, Martin 15n15
action 26, 38
actuality, actualization 7, 30–1, 36–7, 40, 45–51, 53–4, 56–8, 65–6, 74, 76–7, 91n113, 98n200, 98n201, 100n220, 101n236, 103n251, 104n267, 110n337, 112n372
administration, governance 50–2, 56, 62–3, 70–1, 77, 96n170, 101n234, 107n292, 107n302; *see also* cosmos, political metaphor
affection 26, 38
Al-'Āmirī *see* Pseudo-Al-'Āmirī
Alexander of Aphrodisias 1, 89n103
Alexandru, Stefan 100n220
Al-Fārābī 18n32
alteration 28, 30, 33, 41, 43–5, 53, 57, 65, 95n163
Anaxagoras 31–2, 74, 85n74, 86n75, 86n76, 99n215, 116n424
  on intellect 9, 47, 72–3, 115n413, 116n418
animals 25, 27–8, 32, 35–6, 49, 51, 57, 63, 65, 70–1, 76–7, 106n286
Aristotle *passim*
art, artisan 32–6, 46, 61, 69, 71, 73, 76, 89n100, 89n101, 89n103, 91n116, 93n138, 115n415
Asclepius of Tralles 14n5
Asia Minor 1
Averroes 10, 19n37, 79n6, 84n58, 86n79, 89n103, 90n108, 90n109, 91n112, 91n113, 99n216, 107n291
Avicenna 20n40
Badawī, 'Abd al-Raḥman, 10–1, 19n34, 19n35, 79n1, 80n9, 81n25, 107n292
Baghdad 10
begetting 31, 35–7, 39–40, 73, 89n84, 90n107
body 6, 9, 25, 27–8, 30–6, 38–40, 42, 44, 47–8, 53–4, 57–9, 61–4, 67–70, 73–7, 81n23, 85n70, 87n89, 97n186, 97n187, 106n290, 109n326, 116n422, 117n438; *see also* celestial bodies; incorporeality
Brague, Rémi 11, 81n26, 82n29, 83n46, 84n61, 85n67, 86n81, 87n84, 87n87, 87n90, 88n94, 88n95, 90n109, 96n170, 96n175, 98n199, 98n202, 98n205, 102n238, 104n267, 106n283, 106n286, 107n292, 109n324, 113n384, 115n412

Callippus 59–61
Capone Ciollaro, Maria 16n16
categories 38, 92n129; *see also* entries for specific categories
cause 6–7, 17n24, 18n27, 26, 33, 36, 39–42, 44–5, 47–8, 51, 56–7, 64–5, 68–71, 73, 92n124, 94n153, 95n156, 97n196, 98n197, 99n206, 99n211, 103n257, 110n339, 110n340, 113n379, 114n400, 115n417, 116n421; *see also* first cause
  efficient (moving) cause 7–8, 39–40, 44–8, 61–2, 73–4, 76, 93n133, 97n194, 97n195, 98n203, 108n309, 108n311, 114n395, 115n413
  final cause 50, 72–3, 114n395, 115n413, 115n417, 117n430
  formal cause 7, 40, 76, 91n113
  material cause 40
  moving cause *see* efficient (moving) cause
celestial bodies 6, 9, 17n26, 27–8, 30, 47, 52, 59, 62–3, 70, 73–5, 82n35, 103n253, 107n299

fixed stars 52, 57–61, 70, 73, 99n211, 102n241, 108n307, 108n309
inclined sphere 36, 40, 60, 94n153
planets 48, 52, 59–61, 73, 99n211, 107n301, 108n309, 108n313
spheres 36, 40, 47–8, 52, 59–62, 68, 94n153, 99n211, 102n241, 107n306, 108n307, 108n309, 108n313
see also moon; sun
change, changeability 6, 28–32, 44–5, 52–3, 65, 74, 77, 84n53, 84n55, 84n60, 84n62, 94n153, 95n163, 97n192, 98n203, 103n245, 103n249, 103n252, 103n253, 103n255, 110n347; *see also* unchangeability
Code, Alan 94n143
coming-to-be 9, 29–38, 40, 42–4, 46–8, 50, 52–3, 57, 61–2, 65, 70, 72–6, 85n66, 85n67, 85n68, 86n81, 87n84, 89n101, 95n153, 96n176, 114n406, 116n421, 116n427; *see also* begetting; creation; perishing
Constantinople 1
contrary, contrariety 29–30, 43, 47–8, 51, 71–3, 75–6, 84n50, 84n65, 96n178, 103n252, 114n404, 116n419, 116n420, 116n428, 117n431; *see also* opposite
corruption *see* perishing
cosmos, political metaphor 9, 18n30, 18n31, 101n231, 106n283
creation, creator 8, 9, 29, 31–8, 40, 43–5, 48, 71–2, 76, 97n187,105n280; *see also* artisan; demiurge

demiurge 9, 86n77; *see also* artisan; creation
Democritus 85n74, 116n424
desire 33, 49–52, 62–4, 67, 71, 74, 92n120, 100n221, 100n223, 101n235, 102n238, 109n333

earth 9, 27–8, 46, 70, 73–4, 81n22, 81n26, 94n153, 98n203
Elders, Leo 89n103
element 26–7, 32, 37–40, 46, 50, 73–4, 81n23, 82n29, 82n33, 92n125, 93n132, 93n135, 94n149
relationship with matter 87n89, 108n316, 116n422
Empedocles 47, 72, 74, 85n74, 115n409
essence, essential 38, 45, 49, 51–2, 54, 56, 58–9, 66–9, 72, 87n90, 98n200, 102n238, 111n365, 112n378, 113n379, 115n411; *see also* accident
eternity 8, 18n27, 41–5, 47–9, 53, 56, 58–9, 76–7, 96n198, 97n180, 97n181, 99n206, 114n397
Eudoxus 59–60
Eugenius 2
evil 72–3, 116n418

Falaquera, Shem Tov 96n172
Farhat, M. Taïeb 19n38
Finzi, Moses 10, 20n42
first cause 40, 42, 49, 51–2, 55–8, 62–4, 74–5, 99n211, 101n235, 101n237, 102n238, 102n239, 102n242; *see also* first intellect; first principle; first mover; God
first intellect 55, 64, 66–7, 69, 105n275, 111n358, 112n378, 113n379; *see also* first cause; first principle; first mover; God; intellect, divine
first mover 7, 39, 45, 50, 53, 62–3, 103n257, 112n378; *see also* first cause; first intellect; first principle; God; mover
first principle 5–7, 37, 39, 42–3, 45, 49, 58, 64, 68, 72, 75, 77, 95n167, 98n199, 100n222, 104n258, 107n298, 111n365, 114n402, 114n404, 115n417, 116n418; *see also* first cause; first intellect, first mover; God; principle
fixed stars *see* celestial bodies
form 6–7, 9, 32–41, 46, 55, 62–3, 65, 69, 72–3, 75–7, 86n78, 86n80, 86n81, 87n84, 87n85, 88n94, 88n95, 89n100, 89n101, 91n115, 92n122, 94n148, 94n149, 94n151, 114n406; *see also* cause, formal; *logos*; Ideas (Platonic)
Fraenkel, Carlos 8
Frank, Richard M. 10–1, 19n36, 20n42, 81n20, 81n26, 83n41, 83n44, 83n46, 83n48, 95n167, 98n200, 106n283

Genequand, Charles 90n109, 91n112, 91n113, 92n121, 92n122
generation *see* coming-to-be; spontaneous generation
genus 25–6, 37–8; *see also* species
Geoffroy, Marc 19n38
God 1, 5–9, 18n31, 47, 51, 56, 67–71, 74, 99n211, 104n267, 111n351, 113n380, 114n392, 114n393, 114n404; *see also* first cause; first intellect; first principle; first mover
secondary gods 36

Golitsis, Pantelis 14n5
good, goodness 49, 61, 65, 70, 72–3, 77, 113n381
governance *see* administration
Guldentops, Guy 18n30, 101n231, 113n384
Gutas, Dimitri 12, 19n39

Hadot, Ilsetraut 117n435
Heath, Malcolm 15n7
Henry, Devin 90n108
Hesiod 46
Homer 117n441

Ibn Taymiyya 10, 19n38, 92n123, 93n130, 95n154
Ideas (Platonic) 5, 7, 28, 34–5, 45, 58, 75–6, 83n47, 85n67, 89n103, 90n106, 91n112, 98n197, 107n297
immateriality 7, 46, 49–50, 55, 58, 62, 68–9, 75, 99n219
immovability 30, 42, 49, 51, 53, 56, 58–9, 63, 96n168, 104n257, 108n311, 109n333
inclined sphere *see* celestial bodies
incorporeality 7, 28, 58, 62, 74, 82n36
inspiration 36
intellect 8, 33–5, 39, 47–9, 51–2, 54–6, 63–9, 70, 73, 88n95, 100n221, 100n222, 101n232, 101n236, 101n237, 102n239, 105n270, 110n340, 110n342, 110n345, 111n350, 111n361, 111n365, 112n374, 112n376, 112n377
  divine 53–5, 67–8, 111n356, 113n381
  human 53–6, 59, 67–9, 105n275
  self-intelligizing 51, 53–5, 64, 66–7, 102n238, 105n276, 106n283, 112n378, 113n379
  see also Anaxogoras, on intellect; first intellect
intelligible 64–9, 75, 83n46, 83n47, 110n340, 111n350, 112n376, 112n377
Isḥāq ibn Ḥunayn 10, 12–3, 18n33, 19n34, 83n45, 84n63, 91n112, 92n121, 94n145, 117n438

Kakavelaki, Antonia 14n7
knowledge, knowing 16n15, 29, 33, 36–7, 43–4, 47, 51, 53, 55–6, 59, 64, 67–9, 72, 74–5, 84n54, 92n122, 99n206, 104n262, 106n283, 112n372, 116n423

Laks, André 102n240
Landauer, Samuel 10–2, 20n42, 20n44, 109n323, 113n383, 114n408
Leucippus 47, 116n424
life, living things 7, 9, 51, 56, 61–4, 82n27, 106n283, 106n286
locomotion *see* motion, in place
logos (as formative principle) 7, 31, 36–7, 85n72, 91n111, 91n113, 91n115, 91n118
love 42, 47, 51–2, 62, 66–7, 72, 74, 111n352, 115n409
Lycurgus 56, 106n283, 106n284

Martin, Aubert 90n109, 91n112
matter 6–7, 9, 33–4, 36, 38, 40–1, 46, 54–5, 62, 69, 72–6, 85n67, 85n72, 86n78, 86n81, 87n89, 88n92, 88n95, 88n98, 91n111, 94n148, 94n149, 98n203, 103n245, 110n345, 114n392, 114n404, 114n406, 115n409, 116n418, 116n421, 116n422
  prime matter 88n98
  relationship with element 87n89, 108n316, 116n422
  topical matter 6
  see also immateriality
Meno's paradox 16n15
Michael of Ephesus (Pseudo-Alexander) 14n5
modification 8, 39, 42–3, 56, 65, 94n103, 97n180, 105n277; *see also* accident
moon 60–1, 73
Moses ibn Tibbon 10–3, 90n105, 92n121, 96n172, 100n220
motion 8, 17n26, 18n27, 25, 29–30, 37, 39, 42–5, 47–9, 52–3, 57–63, 65, 67–9, 73–5, 77, 96n172, 97n180, 97n181, 97n187, 97n189, 97n192, 97n194, 97n195, 98n197, 99n206, 99n208, 103n245, 103n246, 103n249, 103n254, 103n255, 103n257, 107n293, 107n301, 108n309, 108n310, 108n311, 108n313, 109n333, 110n347,115n413, 115n414
  circular 9, 44–5, 47–8
  confused 47, 98n204, 99n209
  rectilinear 44
  in place 6, 30–1, 44, 47, 52–3, 58, 103n246, 103n257
  see also celestial bodies; change; rest
mover 7–8, 34, 39–41, 43–6, 48–9, 52, 58–61, 63–4, 72–3, 87n83, 93n136, 93n137, 93n140, 95n157, 98n203,

108n311, 115n409, 115n413; *see also* cause, efficient (moving); first mover; unmoved mover(s)

nature 6–7, 18n27, 18n31, 28–37, 39, 41–2, 45–7, 49–57, 59, 61–6, 69–76, 82n35, 83n47, 87n84, 88n92, 88n94, 91n118, 93n137, 93n138, 96n172, 98n199, 98n203, 99n219, 103n245, 103n252, 104n267, 105n270, 109n326, 111n356, 113n389
Neuwirth, Angelika 104n267
number 25–6, 38, 58, 62, 76–7, 87n84, 107n297, 117n430; *see also* Ideas (Platonic); one, oneness

one, oneness 25–6, 31, 38, 50, 58, 62–3, 71, 74, 76–7, 87n84, 92n129, 100n228, 100n229, 117n435; *see also* Plotinus; simplicity; unity
opposite, opposition 30–1, 45, 48, 75, 84n50, 84n51, 99n213

Paphlagonia 1
paraphrasis 2–4
perishing 28–32, 34–5, 40, 42–3, 47–8, 52–3, 58, 70, 72–5, 77, 89n101, 95n153, 96n176, 115n412, 116n421; *see also* coming-to-be
Phidias 90n105
Pines, Shlomo 8, 104n264, 109n330, 112n378
place 6, 25–6, 28–30, 52, 57, 60, 67, 74, 82n37, 103n250, 103n252; *see also* motion, in place
planets *see* celestial bodies
plants 25, 27–8, 32, 36, 46, 57, 70–1, 76
Plato 5, 7, 27, 35–6, 47, 62, 81n19, 81n21, 88n95, 89n103, 91n112, 91n115, 97n180, 98n204, 99n209
pleasure 49, 53–6, 104n267
Plotinus 100n229, 117n435
Polycleitus 90n105
potential, potentiality 30–1, 38–40, 45–6, 48, 50, 52–5, 57–8, 64–6, 75–6, 84n65, 88n92, 98n199, 98n201, 103n251, 105n274, 117n341
power 43, 46, 57–9, 63, 67
prime mover *see* first mover
principle 5–7, 9, 17n24, 25–9, 33, 37–43, 45–6, 48, 50–1, 53, 61–2, 68–70, 72–7, 81n20, 85n72, 86n78, 91n111, 92n124, 92n125, 93n132, 93n133, 93n135, 94n149, 95n156, 97n188, 98n203, 108n311, 113n379, 113n389, 115n409, 115n411, 115n412, 116n419, 116n420, 116n425, 116n428; *see also* first principle
privation 31, 33, 38–40, 53, 72–3, 85n67, 86n78, 113n392
Provence 10
Pseudo-Al-ʿĀmirī 20n40
Pseudo-Alexander *see* Michael of Ephesus
Pythagoreans 56

quality 6, 13, 25–6, 29, 37–8, 84n62, 103n248, 103n253
quantity 6, 13, 25–6, 30, 37–8, 41–3, 50, 57, 59, 67, 69, 84n62, 96n180

reason, reasoning 38, 56, 58, 96n177, 107n298
  'bastard' reasoning 33, 88n95
recipient 9, 32, 74, 87n89; *see also* body; matter
Reeve, C.D.C. 81n19
relation 26, 37–8, 45–6, 70, 104n266
rest 44, 48, 57, 68, 85n67; *see also* motion

Shahrastānī 20n40
Shamlī 18n33
Schramm, Michael 18n31, 101n235
science 27, 59, 69, 75, 81n19, 109n328
  natural science 27, 30, 46, 57, 75, 82n35
senses, sense-perception 27, 29, 33, 45, 47–8, 53–8, 68, 75, 88, 104n267, 105n268, 105n270, 107n298, 112n371
Sharples, Robert 14n5, 111n356
simple, simplicity 38, 50, 56, 75, 82n32, 100n228, 101n229, 112n378; *see also* one, oneness; unity
Socrates 27, 30, 34–5, 62
soul 34–5, 39, 47, 56–7, 59, 67, 69, 76, 106n290, 107n299
  soul that is in the earth 7, 36, 92n119
species 35–6, 44, 62–3; *see also* genus
Speusippus 56, 106n287
spheres *see* celestial bodies
spontaneous generation 5, 7, 36
Stoics 85n72
strife 47, 72, 115n412
substance *passim*
sun 36, 40, 46, 57, 60–1, 73, 94n153, 98n203

Thābit ibn Qurra 18n33
Terah 34, 90n15
Themistius *passim*

Theon, Aelius 14n7
Theophrastus 12
time 8, 26, 29, 41–5, 57–8, 67–8, 96n173, 97n180, 97n181, 104n261
Todd, Robert 13n1, 15n10, 15n13, 16n16, 16n17, 17n20
tode ti ('this-something') 33–4, 87n90, 88n91
Twetten, David 18n30, 100n229, 101n231

unchangeability 28–30, 33, 41, 53–4, 57–8, 65, 82n36
unity 74, 117n437; *see also* one, oneness; simplicity
unmoved mover(s) 8, 49, 100n229, 102n238, 103n257

Volpe Cacciatore, Paola 16n15

Wakelnig, Elvira 112n368
Watt, John 18n32

zodiac 60, 108n307

www.ingramcontent.com/pod-product-compliance
Lightning Source LLC
Chambersburg PA
CBHW070640300426
44111CB00013B/2181